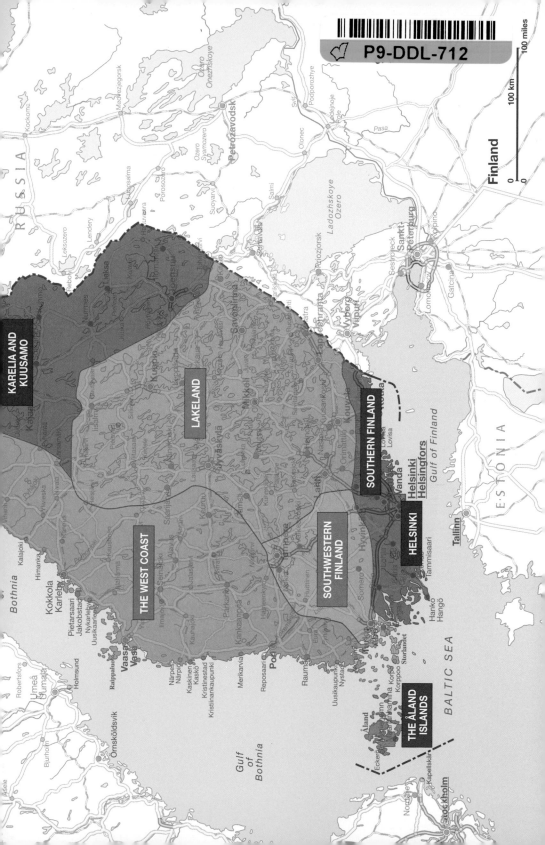

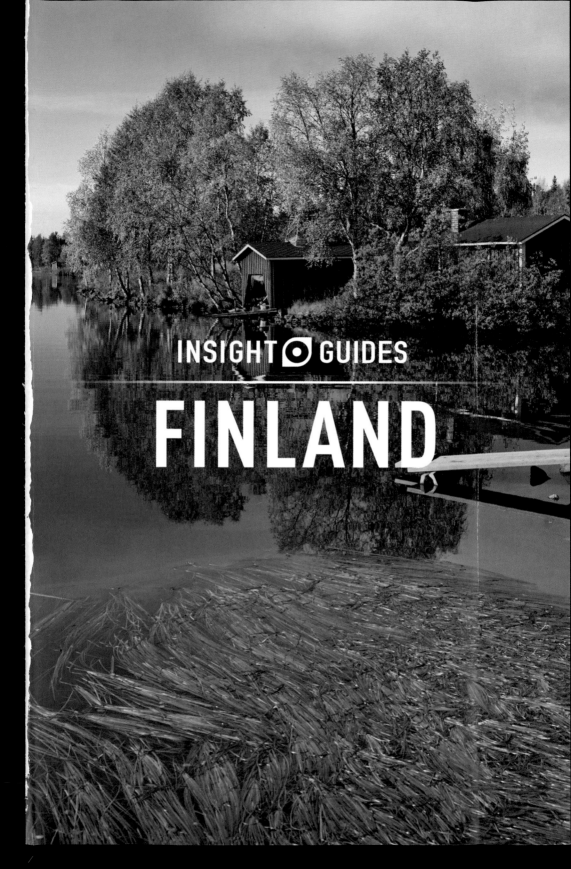

INSIGHT ⊙ GUIDES

FINLAND

PLAN & BOOK
YOUR TAILOR-MADE TRIP

BRAZIL **CHILE** **ECUADOR**

TAILOR-MADE TRIPS & UNIQUE EXPERIENCES CREATED BY LOCAL TRAVEL EXPERTS AT INSIGHTGUIDES.COM/HOLIDAYS

Insight Guides has been inspiring travellers with high-quality travel content for over 45 years. As well as our popular guidebooks, we now offer the opportunity to book tailor-made private trips completely personalised to your needs and interests. By connecting with one of our local experts, you will directly benefit from their expertise and local know-how, helping you create memories that will last a lifetime.

HOW INSIGHTGUIDES.COM/HOLIDAYS WORKS

STEP 1

Pick your dream destination and submit an enquiry, or modify an existing itinerary if you prefer.

STEP 2

Fill in a short form, sharing details of your travel plans and preferences with a local expert.

STEP 3

Your local expert will create your personalised itinerary, which you can amend until you are completely satisfied.

STEP 4

Book securely online. Pack your bags and enjoy your holiday! Your local expert will be available to answer questions during your trip.

BENEFITS OF PLANNING & BOOKING AT
INSIGHTGUIDES.COM/HOLIDAYS

PLANNED BY LOCAL EXPERTS

The Insight Guides local experts are hand-picked, based on their experience in the travel industry and their impeccable standards of customer service.

SAVE TIME & MONEY

When a local expert plans your trip, you save time and money when you book, even during high season. You won't be charged for using a credit card either.

TAILOR-MADE TRIPS

Book with Insight Guides, and you will be in complete control of the planning process, from the initial selections to amending your final itinerary.

BOOK & TRAVEL STRESS-FREE

Enjoy stress-free travel when you use the Insight Guides secure online booking platform. All bookings come with a money-back guarantee.

WHAT OTHER TRAVELLERS THINK ABOUT TRIPS BOOKED AT
INSIGHTGUIDES.COM/HOLIDAYS

Trip to Portugal

Every step of the planning process and the trip itself was effortless and exceptional. Our special interests, preferences and requests were accommodated resulting in a trip that exceeded our expectations.

Corinne, USA   ★★★★★

Trip to Vietnam

The organization was superb, the drivers professional, and accommodation quite comfortable. I was well taken care of! My thanks to your colleagues who helped make my trip to Vietnam such a great experience. My only regret is that I couldn't spend more time in the country.

Heather   ★★★★★

DON'T MISS OUT
BOOK NOW AT
INSIGHTGUIDES.COM/HOLIDAYS

CONTENTS

Travel tips

Maps

LEGEND
○ Insight on
◎ Photo story

THE BEST OF FINLAND: TOP ATTRACTIONS

▽ **Karelia and Russian Orthodox history.** Much of present-day Finnish Karelia was once a part of Russia, and the churches, monasteries, museums and frontier-running bunkers evoke a strong sense of history, beauty and – for Finnish people, at least – immense nostalgia. See page 243.

△ **Exploring Lakeland by kayak.** Finland is famous for its lakes, and one of the best ways to enjoy them is by renting a kayak. See page 225.

◁ **Snowmobiling along the Russian border.** Lapland is known for three things: Father Christmas, the Sami people, and its amazing, immense wilderness. Get to know the region's furthest reaches by hopping on a diesel-powered skidoo and taking to roads, trails and frozen lakes. See pages 255 and 273.

▷ **Taking a sauna.** Spending time broiling in a sauna and then cooling off by jumping into a nearby lake or the sea is a Finnish national pastime and favoured tradition. An invitation from a Finn to his or her sauna is not one to turn down – it means you have made headway to a close and lasting friendship. See page 166.

△ **Kiasma, Helsinki.** The cutting-edge art at this excellent museum gives a strong sense of what modern-day Finland is all about. See page 157.

▷ **Jugend architecture in Helsinki.** On the headland of the Helsinki peninsula is Katajanokka, the best-known historical part of town, with sights including the Russian Orthodox Uspenski Cathedral and architect Alvar Aalto's most controversial construction. See pages 144 and 149.

△ **Exploring the Baltic states.** From Helsinki it's easy to take a ferry to Estonia; Tallinn has a fine medieval Old Town, a lively nightlife and the lure of cheap alcohol. See page 164.

△ **Biking around the Åland archipelago.** This lush collection of islands off the western coast is one of the most enigmatic and handsome in all of Europe, and is great for exploration by bike. See page 205.

△ **Sibelius Hall in Lahti.** Only one concert hall in Finland is named after the country's greatest composer, and Lahti's world-renowned symphony orchestra is based here. See page 236.

▷ **Gold panning in the far reaches of Lapland.** Lapland once experienced a small but frenzied gold rush along the Ivalojoki river valley in the 1860s, and locals and visitors alike still come to sift for whatever might have been left behind. There's even a Gold Prospectors' Museum. See page 259.

THE BEST OF FINLAND: EDITOR'S CHOICE

Sailing round the islands.

ONLY IN FINLAND

Saimaa ringed seals. There are only about 390 of this endangered freshwater species in the world and all of them live in Finland's Lake Saimaa. See page 225.
Sapas. These Finnish tapas are some of the most unusual dishes you'll ever try in Finland. Noteworthy nibbles include black pudding with lingonberry, smoked reindeer heart and smoked bream with potato mousse and fried rye dough. See page 111.
Iittala glassware. Founded in 1881, the glassworks' ethos is to design beautiful things that last a lifetime, producing objects combining high quality, aesthetics and functionality. See page 81.
Northern Lights. Finland is probably the best place to see the Northern Lights: the *Aurora borealis* can be seen in Lapland more than 200 nights a year. See page 23.

Sauna bliss.

BEST OUTDOOR ADVENTURE ACTIVITIES

Huskies. Lapland is the place for outdoor adventure experiences – none as thrilling as driving a pack of sledge dogs through the snow and out towards the middle of, well, nowhere. See page 260.
Kayaking. Kayaking in Finland is great, whether you are experienced or a novice. Hiring a kayak or canoe is the best way to see some of the most remote, and otherwise inaccessible, parts of the country. See page 241.
Taking a sauna. No trip to Finland is complete without experiencing this most Finnish of activities, an invigorating and restorative way to get to know nature – and the locals. See page 166.
Cycling. Quiet, flattish roads and courteous car drivers make cycling in Finland a pleasure – particularly in the charming Åland islands, which even have two bicycle-only ferry services.
Snowmobiling. The Sami people have been relying on snowmobiles since the 1970s, so there are umpteen trails running through forests, across empty tundra and over frozen lakes. See page 273.

Huskies.

BEST MUSEUMS

Lenin Museum.

take in the compelling exhibitions. See page 157.

Lenin Museum. The world's only museum on the revolutionary covers his life both during and after he lived in Finland. See page 198.

Mannerheim Museum. An immensely engaging museum, with free guided tours filled with historical gems and fascinating anecdotes. See page 160.

SIIDA, Inari. An excellently curated museum on Sami history and society – virtually a reason in itself to visit Lapland. See page 261.

Aboa Vetus Ars Nova. This striking museum in Turku combines city history and modern art and is set right on the Aura River. See page 185.

Kiasma, Helsinki. The gorgeous architecture of Finland's premier modern art museum is a top attraction in itself, but venture inside to

Plush interior of the bar at Haven.

BEST BOUTIQUE/UNIQUE HOTELS

Hotel Haven. A luxurious choice, with designer linens, leather sofas and an extensive honesty bar attached to the sumptuous lobby. Helsinki's honeymoon haven is definitely Haven (www.hotelhaven.fi).

Kakslauttanen Arctic Resort. There could be no better place to sleep under the stars and see the Northern Lights than this collection of glass igloos tucked away in a far corner of Lapland (www.kakslauttanen.fi).

Klaus K. One of Finland's best hotels, with a refined designer ethos that is both ultramodern and enduringly classic. Service is top-notch, and

they also have two great restaurants and a hip bar. In the very centre of the capital (www.klauskhotel.com).

Omena Hotelli. These reception-free hotels have sprouted up in cities all around the country, offering minimal service, low prices and a very good standard of design-friendly accommodation (www.omenahotels.com).

Villa Lanca. This charming collection of rooms set right in the heart of one of Lapland's most fetching towns is run by a lovely Sami couple who also sell traditional handicrafts (www.villalanca.com).

BEST FOR FAMILIES

Moominworld. The gentlest-ever theme park will delight young Moomin fans, who can wander the island, exploring the homes of beloved characters from Tove Jansson's Moomin books. See page 190.

Santa Park. No trip to Lapland with the kids would be complete without a visit to this small theme park inside Santa's home. See page 258.

Särkänniemi. Tampere's beloved amusement park also holds a compelling aquarium, planetarium and a zoo observation tower with a lovely revolving restaurant. See page 196.

Tietomaa. Oulu's science museum teaches children about technology, physics and the natural world through a series of absorbing exhibits that can easily hold the interest of adults too. See page 221.

Festive Finnish baking.

Winter scenery in Lapland.

The Northern Lights, Lapland.

Finns love being outdoors.

A NATURAL BEAUTY

The Finns are among Europe's least understood but most direct people, fully confident in their unique position in the world between East and West.

A Finnish feast.

Flying over Finland's coastline on the way to Helsinki reveals scattered islands, glassy lakes, rushing rivers and pine-green forests, with small villages, summerhouses and tiny towns dotted in among the vast watery landscape. Surrounded by so much natural beauty, and separated from their neighbours by so much space, it is no wonder that Finns have grown to enjoy their own company.

You'll often hear it said that Finns are incapable of small talk. In reality, what you'll find are people with a healthy respect for others' space, a relaxed attitude to conversational gaps, and perfect directness when there is something important to say. It's utterly refreshing – and fits perfectly with the personality of the land itself. Whether you're rushing through snowy wastes on a husky ride, paddling on a mirror-like lake, or picking wild strawberries in a rustling forest, Finland's beauty will cast a profound peace over you, too.

Once you've nourished your soul with silence, head to Finland's capital, Helsinki, a vibrant metropolis with a clear identity of its own. Its restaurant scene has exploded, its bars are fresh, fun and full of Finns happily defying the 'silent' stereotype. Its history gives the city a unique feel, part Scandinavian, part Moscow-lite, with Jugend architectural delights and startling new buildings that have transformed its silhouette. Finnish confidence remains high to this day, even following the Great Recession.

Iittala glassware on sale in Tampere.

The local character is also shaped by climatic extremes – endless summer days and the blackest of winter nights – and its moods swing accordingly. From the rocky archipelago of the southwestern coast to the majestic sweep of the lakeland labyrinth and the sweeping fells of Lapland, Finland's natural environment is one of Europe's wildest. And Finns, modern as they are, still love to retire en masse to their lakeside cabins and saunas in the summer, and glide on skis through the snow-smothered woods in winter. The urban scene may have changed, but the unparalleled remoteness and tranquillity of Finland's lakes and forests make them uniquely timeless.

Total calm at Puruvesi Lake, Karelia.

A UNIQUE EXPERIENCE

From bear-watching to canoeing across silent lakes, Finland's natural attractions are a major draw. Throw in a thriving capital, unusual architecture, some weird festivals and Santa himself for the perfect offbeat holiday destination.

Finland, often neglected and sometimes even ignored, is one of the best-kept secrets in Europe. It's a country with few world-renowned attractions: no superlative fjords, no medieval monasteries and few spectacular old towns. Yet Finland offers an indigenous culture with much regional variety, thousands of lakes, rivers and islands, and unlimited possibilities for a wide range of outdoor – and indoor – activities.

NATURE AND HISTORY

Slowly, the world is taking notice. Finland, a member of the EU and the only Nordic country to use the euro, offers unspoilt wilderness, quaint historical attractions, tranquillity and free access to practically anywhere – all forests are potentially yours for trekking, berry-picking or short-term camping.

Finland has its share of great European legacy – about 70 medieval stone churches, several imposing castles and plenty of collections of old and new art. Its traditions are preserved in the hundreds of museums around the country, the vast majority of which are run by enthusiastic volunteers.

DISCOVERING FINLAND

Compared to the other Nordic countries, Finland has always been a quiet place when it comes to tourism. But over the past decade, many people have discovered Finland for the first time – and have come back for more. In 2017, almost 8.3 million foreign visitors enjoyed this subtle, unspoiled country.

And Finland challenges the idea of the traditional holiday. While there are plenty of hotels – even a number of five-star boutique places in the capital – Finland also offers thousands

Spend the night in a comfy, warm, glass-roofed igloo.

of campsites, lakeside holiday villages, guesthouses, youth hostels and even the ability to camp privately in the wild.

AN UNUSUAL DESTINATION

Over the past decades, the Finnish state has invested in the development of hundreds of museums, churches, parks, installations and traditional buildings into some of the most interesting and culturally rich places to see in Europe. Add to that literally hundreds of arts, music and culture festivals – plus dozens of off-the-wall festivals such as wife-carrying, high-heel relay and air guitar – and you quickly see that Finland is a unique destination that has turned upside down the idea of what it means to be a tourist. No wonder, then, that traditional tourists are confused.

TOP ATTRACTIONS

World-class attractions in the Finnish Tourist Board's top sites to see include Kiasma, the Museum of Contemporary Art (see page 157) in Helsinki, Rauma's Old Town (see page 213), Ateneum Art Museum (see page 143) and Suomenlinna, the 18th-century sea fortress sometimes called 'Gibraltar of the North', outside Helsinki (see page 161).

FINNS AND TOURISTS

Despite an increase in the number of visitors to their country, you'll still find that Finns – especially outside of Helsinki – can maintain a quirky, almost incredulous attitude towards tourists, as if they can't understand why anyone would come to their country for a visit. They may not always smile at you when you'd expect them to, and do when you wouldn't. They remain silent when you want to hear an explanation, or they speak (in Finnish) when you'd rather enjoy the serenity. Still, in many cases, tourists will experience unconditional

Tour guides take groups into the wild.

⚙ KAKSLAUTTANEN IGLOO

There is nothing more memorable than sleeping under the stars, but this is simply not possible in the freezing Finnish winter. The solution is to spend the night in your own personal glass-roofed igloo. The compound at the Kakslauttanen Hotel and Igloo Village (www.kakslauttanen.fi) features its famous two person glass igloos, perfect for marvelling at the majesty of the firmament and the Northern Lights in comfort. The grounds, near the Urho Kekkonen National Park, feature a gallery of ice sculptures, an ice bar and an ice chapel. Reindeer and husky safaris are also available. The igloos are open from late August to April.

warmth and hospitality typical of the Finnish people when invited into a local home, especially in rural towns and in farming communities.

If Finns are eccentrics, so are some of their attractions. The wife-carrying championships are an international media event, as is the mobile-phone throwing competition, the air guitar festival in Oulu and the swamp-soccer world cup, held every year in a Finnish bog. There are plenty of other weird festivals, offbeat art exhibitions and crazy habits.

Savonlinna, the annual opera festival held in a medieval castle (see page 230), is one of the most renowned in Europe. In Seinäjokki, the sultry sounds of South America attract more than 100,000 visitors to the annual Tango Festival.

Modern architecture shaped Lusto – the Finnish Forest Museum into an interesting exhibition on everything wooden – now the region is one of the top destinations in all the Nordic countries.

NATURE CALLS

As Finnish nature is so varied and so accessible, the only limit is imagination. Activity holidays are increasing. Several birdwatching towers have been built near major lakes and bays – one important wetland centre is Liminganlahti near Oulu, where the is also a

In the far northeast, the Ranua Wildlife Park is a managed wilderness area containing some 50 species including lynx, elk, brown bear and polar bear (although there are no wild polar bears in Finland).

interesting accommodation in isolated wilderness cottages, often well-equipped and of relatively high quality.

An invigorating post-sauna dip.

Bears roam in the northeast of Finland.

visitor centre, hotel and restaurant. Tourists have about 180,000 lakes to choose from for canoeing, swimming or skating in winter, when ice covers nearly every body of water. Fishing is possible in lakes, rivers and along the seashore, though a permit is required. Moving from one place to another in winter tends to be on skis, dog sleds or snowmobiles; and in summer by bicycle or trekking on foot.

Many tourists seek nature experiences in unspoiled areas of Finnish countryside. Finland's unique natural heritage is administered by the state-owned forestry service Metsähallitus, which controls 40 national parks, 19 nature reserves and nearly 400 other protected areas. The organisation (www.nationalparks.fi) rents

⊘ SOMETHING FOR EVERYONE

As Finland lacks mass tourism, most visitors have an individual approach to the country. At times, certain cities – such as Rovaniemi or possibly Jyväskylä – may be filled with a group of architecture buffs ogling buildings designed by Alvar Aalto; architecture fans may choose Functionalism, Art Nouveau, modern or neoclassical 'tours'. Music-lovers may choose from hundreds of small or large festivals, or follow Sibelius's footsteps from Hotel Kämp in Helsinki to Ainola to north Karelia. Visitors into design can tour various glass factories, pottery studios and cutting-edge shops. Santa Claus can be visited in Rovaniemi.

National parks are just the tip of the iceberg. Local municipalities often finance recreational hiking routes for local needs. Many of these can be combined, and thus was born the Karelian Circuit, Finland's longest trekking route, with approximately 1,000km (620 miles) of marked trails. This circuit offers genuine wilderness routes, variety in four different national parks, and a possibility to combine walking with mountain biking, canoeing and fishing.

Accommodation is possible in bed and breakfasts, free wilderness huts (or ones that have to

FARM HOLIDAYS

As Finnish farmers increasingly find it harder to earn money from agriculture alone, many families are now turning their estates (mostly in the south of the country) into guesthouses. Bed and breakfast may be the official term, but most farms provide visitors with a full range of options. It's an experience that will be unforgettable – bathing in a lakeside sauna, with a dip in the shallow, lukewarm water, riding horses across dirt tracks, paddling in the lake, then savouring an enormous buffet with fresh farm

Husky dogs in Lapland.

be reserved in advance) or lean-to structures. Pitching a tent is legal (and free) almost everywhere along this route.

ORGANISED TOURS

Small service companies are now popping up around Finland. An interesting one is Archtours (tel: 010-235 0560; www.archtours.fi), which runs trips based on architecture, design and culture. They offer several interesting tours in and around Helsinki. Up north in Rovaniemi, try Wild Nordic (tel: 050-059 9999; www.wildnordic.fi), an excellent adventure tour company, offering fishing, hunting, husky and reindeer tours, as well as skiing holidays and trips to see the Northern Lights.

produce, game, fish and wonderful cakes. The opportunity for individual freedom is an experience in itself, with mirror-like lakes and miles of forest tracks to enjoy all for yourself.

LAKELAND LEISURE

Increased tourism along Finland's lake system is bringing the lake steamers back into business. There are now regular passenger routes on several of the lake systems, but the oldest and probably the most romantic are those across Saimaa's vast expanses (see page 226). Steam first came to Saimaa, wheezing and belching its thick black smoke, in the 1830s. It revolutionised the timber business, until then reliant on sailing vessels – and, in turn, their dependence on the vagaries of the wind – enabling easier transport of Finland's 'green gold' from forest to factory during the short summer months.

The heyday of passenger steamers was in the early years of the 20th century, when the well-to-do of St Petersburg arrived by the night train at Lappeenranta for a leisurely nine-hour steamer trip to Savonlinna, then a new and fashionable spa. In due course the steamers covered the four points of the Saimaa compass, picking up and dropping off the lakeland's scattered inhabitants, along with livestock and every imaginable

there year-round to chat to his guests; his home straddles the Arctic Circle, so you can cross the line into the far north; and in winter there are reindeer rides through the snowy forest.

For the outdoor adventurer, Finland is ideal. Activities may include husky tours or snowshoe treks into the wilderness in winter, canoeing, rafting or trekking in summer.

The Northern Lights.

form of cargo, at communities of all sizes or no size at all. One of the great sights of Savonlinna each morning and evening was the Saimaa fleet of wooden double-deckers. Several still survive. Today, many Finns and foreigners alike come to this region to spend a relaxing time in waterfront cabins, steaming themselves in the sauna and then jumping into the cooling waters.

SANTA CLAUS AT HOME

Visitors eager to give their present requests directly to Santa Claus should head for Rovaniemi (see page 257), Santa's home. He lives in an ever-growing tourist village called Napapiiri – the biggest tourist trap in the country, but still great fun for kids (and kids-at-heart). Santa is

⊘ NORTHERN LIGHTS

The aurora borealis, or Northern Lights, is one of the most fascinating phenomena to see in Finland. It occurs all year round but autumn and winter are best. It is a magical experience: a flicker of fire will shine across the sky, for a few minutes at the longest. These iridescent ribbons of orange and green are created by solar particles crashing against the earth's atmosphere and magnetic field. Auroral activity depends on the amount of solar particles hitting the atmosphere, which is variable – but possible to forecast. The Finnish Meteorological Institute monitors disturbance levels: see http://aurorasnow.fmi.fi/public_service.

The Battle of Poltava ends Swedish domination.

DECISIVE DATES

EARLY HISTORY: 8000 BC–AD 400

8000–7000 BC
Tribes from Eastern Europe (ancestors of present-day Sami) settle the Finnish Arctic coast.

1800–1600 BC
The Central European 'Boat Axe' culture arrives from the east. Trade with Sweden begins.

c. AD 100
The historian Tacitus describes the Fenni in his *Germania*, probably referring to the Sami.

c. AD 400
The 'Baltic Finns', or Suomalaiset, cross the Baltic and settle in Finland. Sweden's influence over its 'eastern province' begins.

SWEDISH RULE: C.1157–1809

c.1157
Legends tell of King Erik of Sweden launching a crusade into Finland; further Swedish invasions subjugate large areas of the country.

1323
The Peace of Pähkinäsaari establishes the border between Sweden and Russia; western and southern Finland become Swedish, while eastern Finland is now Russian.

1523
Gustav Vasa ascends the Swedish throne. Lutheranism is introduced from Germany.

1595
The 25-year war with Russia is concluded by the Treaty of Täyssinä; the eastern border extends to the Arctic coast.

1640
Finland's first university is established in Turku.

1696–7
One-third of the Finnish population dies of famine.

1710–21
The 'Great Northern War'. Russia attacks Sweden and occupies Finland. Under the Treaty of Nystad (present-day Uusikaupunki) in 1721, the tsar returns much of Finland but keeps eastern Karelia.

1741
The 'Lesser Wrath'. Following Sweden's declaration of war, Russia reoccupies Finland until the Treaty of Turku in 1743.

1773
Finnish attempts to gain independence fail. A peasant uprising results in several reforms.

THE RUSSIAN YEARS: 1808–1917

1808
Tsar Alexander I attacks and occupies Finland.

1809
The Treaty of Hamina cedes all of the country to Russia. Finland becomes an autonomous Russian Grand Duchy.

1812
Because of Turku's proximity to Sweden, Tsar Alexander shifts Finland's capital to Helsinki.

1863
Differences of opinion between the Swedish-speaking ruling class and the Finnish nationalists are resolved, giving Finnish-speakers equal status.

1899
Tsar Nicholas II draws up the 'February Manifesto' as part of the Russification process. Jean Sibelius composes Finlandia but is forced to publish it as 'Opus 26, No. 7'.

1905
Russia is defeated by Japan and the general strike in Moscow spreads to Finland. Finland regains some autonomy.

1906
Finnish women are the first in Europe to get the vote.

1907–14
Tsar Nicholas II reinstates Russification and removes the new parliament's powers.

EARLY INDEPENDENCE: 1917–39

1917
The October Revolution in Russia. Finland declares its

A woman votes in 1906.

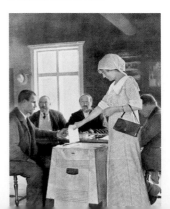

Sauli Niinistö.

independence from the new Soviet Union.

1918
A Russian-style revolution plunges Finland into civil war. The 'White Guard', right-wing government troops with German military support, finally defeat the 'Red Guard'.

1919
On 17 July 1919 the Republic of Finland comes into being, under its first president, K.J. Ståhlberg (1919–25).

1921
The Åland Islands are ceded to Finland and granted autonomy.

FINLAND AT WAR: 1939–47

1939–40
Soviet territorial demands spark off the 'Winter War' between Finland and the Soviet Union. Stalin is victorious and Finland is forced to surrender 11 percent of its territory to the Soviet Union.

1941
Finland clings to its neutrality, but in fear of Soviet invasion is drawn closer to Germany. Hitler begins his Russian campaign. The 'Continuation War' breaks out between Finland and the Soviet Union. Britain, allied with Russia, declares war on Finland.

1944
A peace treaty is signed between Finland and the Soviet Union. Finland is forced to give up the Petsamo region. The retreating German army destroys many towns in Lapland.

FINLAND IN EUROPE: 1948–2013

1948
The Treaty of Friendship, Co-operation and Mutual Assistance (FCMA) is signed, laying the foundations for good relations with the Soviet Union.

1952
Helsinki hosts the Olympic Summer Games.

1955
Finland joins in the formation of the Nordic Council and is admitted to the United Nations.

1969
The Strategic Arms Limitation Talks (SALT) begin in Helsinki.

1995
Finland joins the European Union.

2000
Helsinki celebrates its 450th anniversary. Tarja Halonen becomes the first female president of Finland.

2003
Anneli Jäätteenmäki becomes Finland's first female prime minister, but is forced to resign two months later.

2006
Rovaniemi-based heavy metal band Lordi wins the Eurovision Song Contest, Finland's first ever victory in the competition.

2008
Former president Martti Ahtisaari is awarded the Nobel Peace Prize.

2012
Sauli Niinistö is elected as Finland's first conservative president since 1956.

2013
Nokia's mobile phone business is sold to Microsoft.

2015
Juha Sipilä of the Centre Party becomes prime minister.

2016
Thousands of Iraqis, who arrived in Finland in 2015, cancel their applications for asylum, disillusioned with the harsh weather conditions and Nordic way of life.

2017
In May, Finland celebrates the centenary of its independence.

2018
Sauli Niinistö is re-elected president, winning 62.7 percent of votes in the presidential election.

2019
The Centre Party loses 18 seats in the parliamentary election with the Social Democratic Party winning the most seats (+6). With no overall majority Antti Rinne of SDP forms a coalition with the Centre Party, Green League, Left Alliance and Swedish People's Party.

2020
Men's World Floorball Championships are set to be held in Helsinki, expecting to attract around 100,000 spectators.

A 16th-century map of the Nordic countries and Lapland.

THE FINNS ARRIVE

The life of the early Finns is one of the least understood of all European cultures, but by the 12th century Sweden had dominated its eastern neighbour.

The study of race was an infant science in 1844 when M.A. Castrén pronounced: 'I have decided to prove to the people of Finland that we are not a ... nation isolated from the world and world history, but that we are related to at least one-seventh of the people of the globe.' Castrén had persuaded himself that language equalled race and had concluded that the Finns were kith and kin with every single tribe that had originated in the Altai Mountains of Siberia and Outer Mongolia.

A RACE APART

That the Finnish tongue is a branch of the Finno-Ugric language tree is undeniable and, to those who maintain, like Castrén, that language kinship equals racial relationships, the matter ends there. 'The Finns speak a Mongoloid tongue. Ipso facto they are a Mongoloid people.' To a scientist-patriot such as Castrén, this Far Eastern theory had the added attraction of establishing a relationship between his own people and a large part of the global population.

The conjectures of Castrén and others arose because of the exceptional isolation of Finnish as a language. Hungarian was, and still is, often mentioned as a language akin to Finnish, but the connection is actually remote. Finnish and Hungarian are about as similar to one another as English and Persian, and only Estonian is close enough to be even remotely mutually intelligible with Finnish.

Castrén's followers – and many millions who may never have heard his name – adhered to his theory. This led to the long-held belief that the Finns were a race apart from the mainstream of Europe, their language firmly classifying them as being of Asiatic extraction.

M.A. Castrén, creator of race theories.

THEORY REJECTED

This rather neat little slot in the huge and ever complex question of the origins of peoples is still accepted by the world at large. Many Finns, however, have for some time rejected this theory – most notably those in academic circles.

Recent archaeological research points to a Baltic people moving gradually into Finland from around 1800 BC to about AD 400, but there are no empirical signs of a migration from further east. All cultural contacts point to Western Europe and Scandinavia, even from the earliest times. Such theories lend credence to the notion that Finns and Europeans are intimately related, and discredit ideas of the Great Siberian Migration. The anthropological verdict now accepted by most people is that the forebears of today's Finns were 'purely European'. In common with Swedes, Norwegians, Danes and Germans, Finns are generally tall and blond, although there are slight height differences and there is a variant type known as the East Baltic.

The migrants from the Baltic who took up residence in the land of lakes and forests to the north were destined to live an age-long existence isolated from the mainstream of Europe. The longships left from the lands just over the Gulf of Bothnia or the other side of

An illustration from the epic poem Kalevala, which details ancient folk stories.

the Danish Sounds, and the trading, raiding and general sea roving of the Vikings involved little, if any, Finnish participation. Instead, the Finns were hunters and gatherers, surviving largely on the abundance of fish in the country's lakes.

SECRET PAST

Cut off in their sub-Arctic homeland from these early days, little light has been shed on the life and times of the early Finns. No single chronicler emerges from the forest mists to give later generations a glimpse of primeval life. There may well have been an oral tradition of poetry, song and story, a collection of folk memories

passed down from generation to generation. The *Kalevala*, Finland's national epic, points in this direction, but it was compiled and published in the 19th century and cannot itself therefore claim immemorial antiquity.

> *While Western Finns adopted Catholicism from Sweden, the Karelians followed the Orthodox faith, influenced by Russia to the east.*

When Finland finally emerged into the history books through the flickering candles of Roman Catholic crusading, around the year 1157, we find the Finns living in clans. They had apparently never developed statehood; the clans were descendants of common ancestors, often warring with one another and submitting to priests who led them in the worship of nature and natural forces.

TAMING PAGAN WARRIORS

Just as Finnish scholars had established a theory of race and language, a parallel movement in academic circles was arising on the subject of the arrival of Christianity. According to prevailing wisdom, the Finns had become a nuisance and a danger while raiding the Christian people of southern Sweden. Furthermore, they were pagans. It is thought that in 1157, King Erik of Sweden lost patience and set off on a 'crusade' to Finland. Taming the Finns was key to securing trading routes to the east, particularly to Russia. Sweden was to control Finland for almost the next 700 years.

Once subdued, the Finns were submitted to baptism by an English-born bishop, Henry of Uppsala. Swedish secular dominance and, with it, Roman Catholicism, were thus introduced into Finland.

Yet once again this theory, much like the language theory, has been discredited. Rome has no record of these events and Church documents make no reference to Erik or Henry. Many archaeologists have helped Finnish integrity with the assertion that the Finns practised Christianity years before 1157. The Swedes may have brought Romanism to Finland, but they didn't bring a new faith.

The Russian Orthodox Uspenski Cathedral in Helsinki.

A stained-glass window in Turku Cathedral shows Gustav II Adolf of Sweden.

ANNO 1615.

BIRTH OF A NATION

Finland's relationship with Sweden was peaceful in the early days, but by the 16th century Russia wanted control of its western neighbour.

The Finns lived under the rule of Sweden for nearly seven centuries (c.1157–1809), but there was never a Swedish 'conquest' of Finland. Instead, a race had developed between Sweden and the Novgorod Republic (which became part of the Tsardom of Russia in 1547) to capture power over the land of the Finns. Sweden won the race – and did so without resorting to conquest or dynastic union or treaty. Remarkably, the future relationship between Sweden and Finland was largely free of the stresses and strains that normally accompany such often-hostile takeovers.

A HAPPY UNION

Although there is no official documentation, it is quite likely that Swedes had hunted, traded and settled in Finnish lands for centuries. On both sides of the Gulf of Bothnia the land had sparse resources and gave little cause for friction. In effect, Sweden and Finland merged as constituent parts of a larger whole. No distinctions in law or property were made, and the history of these two people under one crown has been described as 'a seamless garment'.

Finns took part in the election of the king, although they were not involved in the choice of candidates. In areas of mixed population, language was the only real difference. Castles functioned as administrative centres, not as garrisons to subdue the people. The influences of the one people on the other were neutral largely because the cultures were identical. Sweden exerted a dominating influence on only one aspect, and that was religion.

SPREADING THE FAITH

Various monastic orders launched a slow but steady penetration of Finland during the 14th and

Relief sculpture of martyr St Henry on his empty sarcophagus in the church of Nousiainen.

15th centuries. Dominicans, Franciscans and the Order of St Bridget installed themselves alongside the clergy, greatly strengthening the power and influence of the Roman Catholic Church in the region. This activity gave impetus to church-building, worship, renovation and adornment. Life became more settled in the relatively densely populated areas of western Finland. Further east, people's lives were more mobile, less settled, and depended on hunting across the sub-Arctic tundra, a region rich in animals and game birds, but largely unsuitable for crop cultivation.

The most important centres from which the new influences spread were Turku (Åbo in Swedish, see page 179), with a bishop's seat and cathedral, and

Vyborg (Viipuri in Finnish). Both towns had close links with Tallinn (Estonia), Danzig (now Gdansk, in Poland), Lübeck (Germany) and Stockholm.

In these Finnish towns, artisans and professions flourished alongside the clergy and a civilised urban culture was spawned, markedly different from the coarser, more basic ways of life further east.

STIRRINGS OF NATIONHOOD

Sweden was now powerful and independent. The Middle Ages were over; the Reformation challenged Rome. Here was a mélange of influences, almost modern in their impact. Sweden and Finland were both slipping away from the old moorings. Slowly, the relationship was changing, and the first stirrings of nationhood date from this time.

Many more Swedes and Finns fell under the influence of Martin Luther in Wittenberg. The Reformation also attracted Gustav Vasa, because the Swedish crown needed more revenue and the Church could provide it. In fact, the Reformation was so irresistible that Sweden was the first state in Western Christendom to break with Rome. The

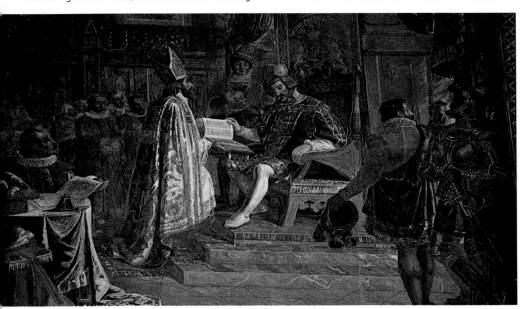

Mikael Agricola's 16th-century Bible translated into Finnish (Turku Cathedral).

Ⓞ DANISH AMBITION

At the end of the 14th century there was an attempt to unite Denmark, Norway, Sweden and, by implication, Finland as a result of the Kalmar Union of 1397. All the devices that had not been employed when Sweden united with Finland were invoked in this fated union, the dream of the Danish queen, Margrethe I.

In 1509, Finland became violently involved when the Danes burnt and sacked Turku (Åbo), the 'capital' of the country. It was just one incident in more than 100 years of conflict over the treaty, which was finally broken in 1523 in a rebellion by Gustav Vasa, who became king of Sweden.

split took place in May 1527. All over Sweden and Finland the Church suddenly lost property, authority, ceremonies and rites. Holy water, customary baptism and extreme acts of piety were banned, as were colourful processions and the worship of relics. But transforming Finns from a Catholic to a Protestant people was not painless – the early Lutheran pastors were a motley rabble. Yet Finns took a leading part in the transformation, and Pietari Särkilahti, Mikael Agricola and Paavali Juusten aided their Swedish brethren in severing links with Rome.

PEASANT SOLDIERS

During the three centuries before 1809, when Finland finally broke with Sweden, the Swedish crown was at war for more than 80 years. Involvement in the Thirty Years War and wars with both Poland and Russia raised taxes and took Finnish men away from the land – the burden of providing levies always fell heavily on the farmers. Finns were a vital part of the Swedish army, comprising a third of the foot soldiers and cavalry. In the wars with Russia, Finland bore the brunt of the suffering. Development of towns and cities became sluggish and many frequently went up in smoke. Turku (Åbo) suffered 15 major fires between 1524 and 1624; the worst reduced

Sweden no longer dominated the land and conflicts with the Russians kept recurring. The innumerable wars were destructive to Finland: 1554–7; a 25-year war (interrupted by truces) which started in 1570; two wars in the 17th century

> *Military service was compulsory except for the cavalry, in which volunteers enlisted eagerly in order to escape the harder life of an infantryman.*

Häme Castle at the end of the 1650s.

the city to ashes. Pori and Viipuri also suffered a similar fate several times, though fires were not the only dangers that beset the cities.

THE DUTCH INFLUENCE

In Turku, Helsinki, Porvoo and Viipuri, as well as the other Baltic trading cities, many leading merchants who controlled much of the foreign trade were of German or Dutch descent. 'The general area of our economic history during the 17th century and part of the 18th century bears a marked Dutch stamp,' remarks V. Voionmaa, a prominent Finnish historian. The Dutch were well established, and foreign ways of doing business gained ground in Finland. Foreign as well as Finnish capital fuelled industry and trade.

⊘ LINGUISTIC REFORMS

'You are instructing your charges in a manner that is both nasty and lazy,' wrote the bishop of Turku, Mikael Agricola, to his clergy in 1548.

Agricola (1510–57) sent out this admonition with a translation of the New Testament in Finnish, a work he had undertaken to make sure 'that not a single preacher or teacher could cover up his laziness by claiming that he did not know Latin or Swedish'. Agricola devised the first Finnish alphabet and created a sizeable body of Finnish writing on a religious theme. The whole Bible was published in 1642, the first official document of the Finnish language in print, formalising the language.

and the Great Northern War from 1710–21; war again 20 years later; and yet again from 1788–90. Sweden regained partial confidence and began to improve Finnish defences with the construction of fortresses such as Suomenlinna (see page 161), but when Peter the Great founded St Petersburg in 1703, Russian power was again on the rise.

CARROT AND STICK

The Swedish crown demonstrated an inability to hold Finland against Russian assault. It lost Finland on two occasions (1710 and 1741),

state whose head, the Tsar-Grand Duke, was an absolute ruler: Tsar of all the Russias. Yet in Finland he agreed to rule in partnership with the Finnish Diet. This made the tsar a constitutional monarch in the newly acquired territory. It was an experiment in kingship, and one which was an unqualified success for 60 years.

The Grand Duchy was declared before the end of the 1808–9 war with Sweden at the Diet of Porvoo. As a Grand Duchy, Finland benefited from Russia's precedent of allowing the countries annexed into its empire to retain

Swedish and Russian fleets fought at the Battle of Skärgård in 1790.

regaining it in 1721 and 1743, respectively. In 1808, Great Britain became a Swedish ally. The Russians now saw a dire threat to St Petersburg and to Russian naval access to the Baltic. Yet again Russia and Sweden fought. This time Russia held on to Finland and offered Finns a large say in the running of their land, while retaining Russian overall rule.

A NATION IS BORN

Sweden formally ceded Finland to Russia by the Treaty of Hamina on 17 September 1809. Along with Finland proper it gave up the Åland Islands, between Sweden and Finland, which had long been an administrative part of the Finnish half of the kingdom. Finland became a separate

social systems such as the legislature. The Baltic States, and later Poland, were granted the same rights. The enlightened policies of Alexander I could be seen as a step towards wider, progressive changes planned in other parts of the empire.

For most ordinary Finns, however, very little changed. No pressure was put on the people to switch from the Lutheran Church to the Orthodox, and Swedish continued as the language of government. Yet the formation of a Finnish Diet, as well as an administrative, senate-led body, allowed for the gradual rise in influence of the Finnish language and, over time, the general spread of the idea of Finnish nationalism and independence.

A WINTER JOURNEY

The early adventurer Joseph Acerbi left an interesting account of his travels across the ice from Sweden to Finland.

At the end of the 18th century, Joseph Acerbi embarked on what was then the only practical way of crossing from Sweden to Finland in winter, by sledge across the frozen Gulf of Bothnia. The distance was 70km (43 miles) but, using the Åland Islands as stepping stones, that left 50km (30 miles) 'which you travel on the ice without touching on land'.

Acerbi was advised that his party of three, plus two servants, would need to double their number of horses and hire no fewer than eight sledges for the crossing. He suspected he was being swindled by the Swedish peasants but, as things turned out, it was a sensible precaution.

Acerbi published the details of the difficult and at times terrifying journey in his work *Travels through Sweden, Finland and Lapland to the North Cape, 1802*, as follows:

'I expected to travel 43 miles without sight of land over a vast and uniform plain, and that every successive mile would be in exact unison and monotonous correspondence with those I had already travelled; but my astonishment was greatly increased in proportion as we advanced from our starting-post. At length we met with masses of ice heaped one upon the other, and some of them seeming as if they were suspended in the air, while others were raised in the form of pyramids. On the whole they exhibited a picture of the wildest and most savage confusion... It was an immense chaos of icy ruins, presented to view under every possible form, and embellished by superb stalactites of a blue-green colour.

HAZARDS ON THE ICE

'Amidst this chaos, it was not without difficulty and trouble that our horses and sledges were able to find and pursue their way. It was necessary to make frequent windings, in order to avoid a collection of icy mountains that lay before us. The inconvenience and the danger of our journey were still farther *encreased* [sic] by the following circumstance. Our horses were made wild and furious, both by the sight and the smell of our great pelices, manufactured of the skins of Russian wolves or bears. When any of the sledges was overturned, the horses belonging to it, or to that next to it, frighted at the sight of what they supposed to be a wolf or bear rolling on the ice, would set off at full gallop, to the terror of both passengers and driver. The peasant, apprehensive of losing his horse in the midst of this desert, kept firm hold of the bridle, and suffered the horse to drag his body through masses of ice, of which some sharp points threatened to cut him in pieces. The animal... continually opposed to his flight, would stop; then we were enabled to get again into our

Joseph Acerbi's travelogue details the trials, tribulations and triumphs of a winter's trip in Finland.

sledges, but not till the driver had blindfolded the animal's eyes: but one time, one of the wildest and most spirited of all the horses in our train, having taken fright, completely made his escape...

'During the whole of this journey we did not meet with, on the ice, so much as one man, beast, bird, or any living creature. Those vast solitudes present a desert abandoned as it were by nature. The dead silence that reigns is interrupted only by the whistling of the winds against the prominent points of ice, and sometimes by the loud crackings occasioned by their being irresistibly torn from this frozen expanse; pieces thus forcibly broken off are frequently blown to a considerable distance.'

Der Friedensengel

Caricature of Nicholas II and the russification of Finland.

Ein finnländisches Märchen

LIVING WITH RUSSIA

For 90 years Russia ruled Finland in relative peace but at the beginning of the 20th century the union dissolved into revolt and war.

Annexation by Russia defied all gloomy prophecies, at least at the outset. Tsar Alexander I seemed open to suggestions, and a group of leading Finns suggested that Finland should hold elections. Alexander agreed, and the first Finnish Diet met at Porvoo in 1809. The tsar had styled himself 'the Emperor and Autocrat of all the Russias and the Grand Duke of Finland'. Invested with this new title, the prototype of future constitutional monarchs, Tsar Alexander formally opened the Diet. In return, he promised to respect and maintain the laws, religion and constitution of Finland.

A DIPLOMATIC SUCCESS

The constitution's main pillar was a unique device in nation-building of those days: Finland was to be in personal union with the tsar. This meant that the Finns dealt directly with their head of state, bypassing the Russian government. Ultimately this became the cause of much jealousy, but the arrangement lasted for 90 years and was the basis of the relationship between Russia and Finland. When Nicholas I succeeded Alexander in 1825 a strong bond of mutual trust had developed. The change of overlord had brought advantages: the fear of attack from the east had gone; Finns could conduct their internal affairs but, if they felt restricted, opportunities existed in the armed forces and civil service of Russia. The Finnish army was disbanded, though its officers received generous pensions. Russian troops garrisoned Finland but never in large numbers. Taxation was raised for domestic needs only.

Behind all this liberality lay firm policy: to pacify Finland and woo it away from Sweden. To keep Sweden sweet, Alexander signed an

Tsar Nicholas I.

agreement, in 1812, in support of moves to unite Norway with Sweden. This became Sweden's new ambition.

THE NEW CAPITAL

The Grand Duchy chose a small, rocky fishing port as its capital, and within two generations, Helsinki had become a city of major importance. One visitor in 1830 remarked that the Finns were 'converting a heap of rocks into a beautiful city'. The urban centre was conceived and planned on an imperial scale, with neoclassical buildings designed by German architect C.L. Engel. The University of Turku moved to Helsinki in 1828, one year after Turku suffered yet another disastrous fire, making its eclipse inevitable.

The university became a tug of war between languages. There was no discrimination against Finns as a separate linguistic group within the Russian Empire, and the idea of introducing

> *Many of the signatures on the petitions to Tsar Alexander were collected by nationalistic students who travelled by ski from remote farm to distant cottage across the country.*

Statue of Alexander II in front of Helsinki Cathedral.

Russian in schools was canvassed, but little was put into place. Finns wishing to serve the tsar abroad had to learn Russian, but to serve the Grand Duke of Finland the requirement, until 1870, was to speak and write Swedish.

PEASANT POWER

The all-important vernacular being promoted by nationalist Henrik Porthan already resided in the countryside, on the farms and in the forests. But the farmers and peasants of the country were slow to awaken to the power they possessed. In part, the peasants distrusted notions of independence. The rural poor, workers, smallholders and the landless were on the periphery of political life and thought. In contrast to the elite, they were indifferent to ideas of liberty and national independence. When autonomy was in jeopardy under a changed Russian attitude at the end of the 19th century, some pamphleteers got to work to raise national consciousness. Grumpy peasants tossed back at them remarks such as, 'Now the gentry are in a sweat,' and, 'These new laws don't concern us peasants, they're only taking the power off the gentry.'

Yet, all the time, opportunities in higher education were increasing among the working class. Vernacular Finnish was introduced into secondary education, university and the new polytechnics, gradually supplanting Swedish. In spite of harvest failures and famine in 1862 and 1868, freehold peasant farmers with timber land grew richer as the demand for timber increased and prices rose. Their wives could now afford tables, sideboards and chairs in place of rustic benches and chests. Life for some was becoming more genteel and less rough-hewn. Since 1864 peasants had been able to buy land on the open market. Now their sons were taking advantage of higher education – reason for interest in the Finnish language to flourish.

RUTHLESS GOVERNOR

Tsar Alexander III, who freed the Russian serfs, knew his Grand Duchy. His son, the ill-starred Nicholas II (1894–1917), did not. The conception of a docile and contented satellite country acting as a buffer on Russia's northwest flank, the cornerstone of policy for 90 years, was cast aside. A new governor, General Bobrikov, fresh from a ruthless administration in the Baltics, was installed in Helsinki.

Finland lost its autonomy. Laws, soldiering and taxation, those pivotal issues which previous Grand Dukes had treated so delicately, were henceforth to be Russian concerns. It was too much for the Finns: 522,931 signatures on a petition were collected in just two weeks.

Abroad, another petition was launched in support of the Finns, signed by many eminent people. They addressed Tsar Nicholas: 'Having read and being deeply moved by the petition of 5 March of over half a million Finnish men and women in which they made a solemn appeal to Your Majesty in support of the maintenance of their full Rights and Privileges first confirmed by... Alexander I in 1809... and subsequently re-affirmed in the most solemn manner by all his illustrious successors, we venture to express our hope that Your Imperial Majesty will take into due consideration the prayer of the said Petition of Your Majesty's Finnish subjects.'

The tsar was unmoved. *The Times* of London thundered a declaration that 'the Finnish Diet can, legally, only be modified or restricted with its own consent'. This too fell on deaf Russian ears. They imposed strict censorship on the Finnish press. Conscription into the Russian army was the last straw.

THE FINNS REVOLT

Resistance began to escalate. Half the conscripts ordered to report for military service in the spring of 1902 did not turn up. In 1904 the governor general was assassinated by a patriotic student, Eugen Schauman, who then turned the gun on himself. Schauman became a national hero and is buried at Porvoo.

The Russian Revolution of 1905 and the Russo-Japanese War brought a respite. The Finns took the opportunity to put forward a bold measure. The franchise was outmoded;

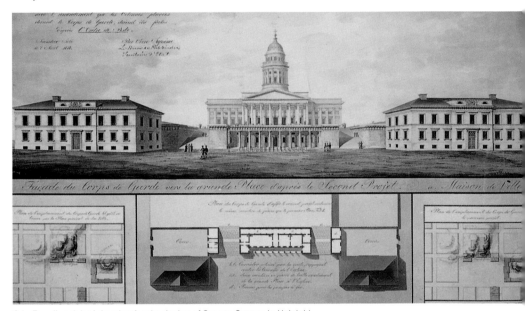

C.L. Engel's original drawing for the design of Senate Square in Helsinki.

⊘ THE FATHER OF FINNISH HISTORY

Bold ideas of Finnish independence had been nurtured by educated Finns ever since the days when Sweden had started to lose its grip during the struggles with Russia through the 16th century. Henrik Porthan (1739–1804), known as the 'father of Finnish history', awakened intellectual leaders. 'We must pray', he said, 'that Russia will succeed in situating its capital in Constantinople... But now that its capital city (St Petersburg) is located so near, I am afraid that Finland will... fall under the power of Russia.'

Nevertheless, the Finnish people, he advocated, should use this as an opportunity, and not be despondent. They must think of themselves above all as Finns.

History, language and tradition all suggested a Finland that was ultimately free. But barbarous, Byzantine and Eastern Russia – not Western, democratic Sweden – was the stepping stone to this end.

Porthan's long-term, pragmatic philosophy took hold and became the prevailing wisdom of his own and succeeding generations of Finnish nationalists. Their patience was finally rewarded in 1906, when Finland got its own national parliament. His disciples realised very quickly that if the Finnish language could replace Swedish, the battle for independence, at least in the hearts and minds of Finns themselves, would be won.

industrial workers had no representation; women no vote. This was par for the times in Europe, although New Zealand had just granted women the vote. Finland proposed no less than a universal franchise and a unicameral parliament. The tsar, doubtless distracted by the stirrings of revolt in Russia – a chain of events that would eventually bring him down – agreed to the changes. The Finns got their modern parliament. The electoral role was increased tenfold. The Social Democrats won the subsequent election.

aid played a significant part in the Red revolt. Finnish Red Guards were supplied with arms by the Russians. Russian officers and NCOs provided leadership; in the case of the artillery, they provided the entire command.

> 'We are no longer Swedes, we will not become Russians, so let us be Finns,' had been the cry for some decades by nationalists.

Eugen Schauman assassinates General Bobrikov in 1904.

CIVIL WAR

Now the country was united as never before in a determination to be free and Finnish. The decisive moment came during World War I, when the Russian army collapsed and Lenin seized power. The Bolsheviks allowed Finland to go free. Independence had finally arrived, but the event was to be marred by a bitter civil war between the 'Whites' and the 'Reds'.

The cause, in short, was the spilling over of the Russian October Revolution into Finland, where there remained contingents of Russian soldiers who sided with the Soviets. Thus Finland had a Red Army in its midst. Luckily, the Soviet government did not participate officially in the civil war in Finland, but Russian

The civil war's major contributory cause was labour unrest. After the Bolsheviks seized power in Russia, radical Finnish socialists became determined to overcome their minority position in parliament by increasing their extra-parliamentary activity.

A strike was the first step, accompanied by widespread lawlessness on a grand scale. After a week the strike was called off, but events escalated and a Central Revolutionary Council formed the Red Guards. They struck at the end of January 1918, in the hope that Russian aid would be enough to secure a quick victory. The civil war saw atrocities committed by both sides, with General Carl Gustaf Emil Mannerheim, for example, being condemned by the international left as a war criminal. The psychological wounds of this period of Finnish history are only recently being brought out into the open.

MILITARY GENIUS

The government lacked adequate forces to meet this situation. It did, however, appoint a commander-in-chief to a non-existent army. General Carl Gustaf Emil Mannerheim was an inspired military leader on a par with Turkey's Kemal Ataturk and the British General Montgomery. Mannerheim had been persuaded by

war against the enemy in the south. Tampere, Helsinki and Viipuri were retaken by the spring. After a last stand on the Karelian Isthmus, the Reds capitulated on 15 May. On 16 May, Mannerheim's 'people's army' held a victory parade in Helsinki to celebrate the end of the 'Red' threat.

The Finns flirted briefly with the idea of a monarch, with both Svinhufvud and Mannerheim acting as regents, before settling on a republic. They elected K.J. Ståhlberg, one of the main legislators of the new Finnish constitution, as the republic's first president.

White and Red troops at war in 1918.

Premier Svinhufvud to organise a government force to uphold law and order. On 18 January, he went to Vaasa on the west coast of Finland, to plan for and organise a 'White' army. Vaasa became the seat of government when war broke out. Four cabinet members escaped there from Helsinki hours before the Reds seized control of the capital on 27 January.

RED DEFEAT

The Reds, without full Russian support and up against the strategic ability of General Mannerheim, found their hopes short-lived. Mannerheim disarmed Russian garrisons in central and northern Finland, and then turned them into bases from which government forces waged

⊘ PREMIER LEADERSHIP

Although different in character from Mannerheim, the civilian leader Pehr Evind Svinhufvud was very much his equal. He was an experienced political leader and had been a member of the Turku Court of Appeal, which was dismissed early in the 20th century for indicting the Russian governor of Helsinki for his brutal suppression of a peaceful demonstration. In 1917, Svinhufvud travelled to St Petersburg to gain the recognition of the Council of People's Commissars for Finland's independence. When the Red Army seized Helsinki, Svinhufvud was still there and was forced to hide, eventually escaping to Vaasa via wartime Germany.

AN INSECURE START

In 1920 the conflicts between Finland and the Soviet Union were dealt with by the Treaty of Tartu, which recognised Finland as an independent republic and ceded it the Arctic port of Petsamo. Some small adjustments were made to the geography of the border, while Finland neutralised its islands close to Leningrad. However, the Soviets seemed unable to forgive the Finns for their bourgeois defeat of revolution; in turn, there arose an almost fanatical distrust of the Soviet Union in Fin-

was ably put down but which caused a severe shock to the body politic. The second problem was emigration.

LAND HUNGER

Once Russian overlordship had taken a nasty turn, the resulting insecurity had already started a trend towards emigration. But there were other causes, and land hunger was the foremost. 'No land, no fatherland,' was the cry. There was a landless proletariat of 200,000 in the 19th century, plus a host of peasants with

Civil war bomb damage in Tampere, 1918.

land. Fear of Russia, civil war and the political polarisation that had caused it deeply affected the national psyche. Sandwiched between Communist Russia and neutral Sweden, and with a militaristic Germany to the south, independent Finland was born, one historian has noted, 'not with a silver spoon, but with a dagger in its mouth'. Finland had to learn the trick of 'sword-swallowing'.

One matter that needed no adjustment in the constitution of independence was the Parliament Act of 1906, far ahead of its time in granting votes to both men and women. But social and economic disparities were not mitigated by legalities. Two symptoms were manifest. One had been the upsurge of Red rebellion, which

> *Finland was the first European country to give women the vote and an equal political voice when it adopted universal suffrage in 1906.*

meagre plots. These people looked to the New World for opportunities.

Before and after the civil war there had been times of famine in the countryside. 'Nature seems to cry out to our people "Emigrate or die",' one university lecturer told his students in 1867. By the 1920s, 380,000 Finns had left for other lands, the majority to the US. The Great Depression hit Finland in 1929, and by 1930 the figure for emigration had reached 400,000.

DIVIDED POLITICS

In the 1920s the two branches of the labour movement (the bulk of the 'Reds') grew further apart. For election purposes, the outlawed Communist Party metamorphosed into the Socialist Workers' and Smallholders' Election Organisation, while the Social Democrats began to co-operate with the bourgeois parties, culminating in a Social Democrat

Finland grew closer to the Scandinavian countries, where democracy was advancing, with a long period of cooperation between the Agrarian Party and the Social Democrats, the aptly named 'red-green' coalition.

CULTURAL ADVANCES

Though the initial priority of the infant nation had to be survival and the strengthening of its democracy, life was not all gloom. In the 1920s, sport, travel and the cinema all came into their own, with a profound effect on social habits. It was a

King Gustav V of Sweden on a state visit to Finland in 1925, with President Lauri Kristian.

government in 1926, led by their moderate leader, Väinö Tanner.

Anti-Communist feeling continued, nevertheless, and led to the Lapua movement, which resorted to violent methods, such as capturing and driving suspected Communist leaders over the Soviet border. Even the respected former president Ståhlberg did not escape one attempt and was driven close to the border. In 1930, the Lapua movement inspired a peasants' march to Helsinki, and led to armed rebellion in 1932.

The formidable duo of the Liberation period, Svinhufvud and Mannerheim, returned and, after anti-Communist laws were passed, it was left to Svinhufvud to persuade the rebels to disband peacefully. Despite these strains,

time of strong cultural expression, particularly in architecture and design. Up until 1939, a degree of cultural and commercial harmony had existed between Russians and Finns. Communism kept a low profile, while Fascists failed to gather significant support. By the time of the war, Finland's agriculture had developed and the forest industry took the lead, supporting progress in other industries; forest product exports boosted national earnings. Optimism was widespread and infectious. Still, despite a growing threat in Europe (particularly from Germany) and Mannerheim's warnings, little was done to build up the country's armaments. When parliament eventually approved 3 billion marks for military procurement in 1938, it was already too late.

THE TWO WARS

The bravery and prowess of Finland's soldiers on their treacherous, ice-bound terrain became legendary during the Winter and Continuation wars.

By the spring of 1938 Moscow was making demands on the Finnish government to give guarantees that, in the event of hostile acts by Germany, Finland would accept Soviet military aid. The railway line between Leningrad and Murmansk was vital to Soviet security: hence Moscow's fear of German invasion through the Gulf of Finland.

PERILOUS TIMES

The Finnish government was reluctant to enter into discussions, fearing that doing so would compromise neutrality. The Munich Agreement of September 1938 prompted Finland to build up its defences, and Mannerheim advised the government to carry out partial mobilisation. The Soviet Union again made representations to Finland, this time suggesting that the Finns lease the islands of the Gulf of Finland to them for 30 years. Soviet pleas to Britain and France for collective security had fallen on deaf ears and Leningrad was vulnerable from the sea.

War memorial to the dead of the 1939 war.

> By April 1939, Hitler had managed to drive a wedge through Finland's policy of joint Nordic security. Estonia, Latvia and Denmark accepted a German plan of non-aggression, while Sweden, Norway and Finland refused.

Unsurprisingly, Finland was still suspicious of Soviet ambitions. After Sweden withdrew, and Germany and the Soviet Union had signed a non-aggression pact (which included a secret protocol on spheres of influence), Finland, placed within Moscow's sphere, was in a very dangerous position. After the German invasion of Poland, the Soviet Union began to press the small countries within its sphere to make pacts of 'mutual assistance'. Delegates from Helsinki travelled to Moscow for discussions. Mannerheim now pressed for full mobilisation of Finnish forces, and the Soviet Union moved swiftly onto a war footing.

WINTER WARRIORS

The first Soviet demand was to move troops from the Karelian Isthmus. When Mannerheim refused, the Kremlin broke off diplomatic relations and launched an attack on Finland on 30 November 1939. What became known as the Winter War had begun.

While Soviet forces had almost overwhelming superiority, they were untrained and ill-equipped to fight a war in severe winter conditions. Finnish soldiers, though they were short of heavy armaments, had already been training for just this sort of warfare. They were used to moving in dense forests through snow and ice, and the Finnish army's tactical mobility was at a high level. The Finns were also accustomed to the climate and dressed sensibly when winter set in and the temperature dropped several degrees below zero. Soldiers were issued with white 'overalls' – now standard in 1939, Finland had about half a million horses in the country. The army used around 20 per cent of them and, as half the reservists called up to fight were farmers or lumberjacks, there were plenty of skilled horsemen. During the summer of 1939, the Finns had also built dams in the small rivers on the Karelian Isthmus and elsewhere, which raised the water level to form an obstruction against the enemy advance. When the Finnish army opened the gates in the Saimaa canal in March 1940, the Russians found operations in the flooded areas difficult.

A female cook working in a military field kitchen in 1939.

for winter warfare – to cover their uniforms so that they blended invisibly with the snow.

By copying the methods used by farmers and lumberjacks to haul logs from the forest, the Finnish army solved a second key problem: how to operate in the forests flanking the roads. They would open a trail in the woods using skis, avoiding gorges, cliffs and steep rises. When a few horses and sleighs had moved over this trail, a winter road would form along which a horse could pull up to a 1-tonne load.

WAR PREPARATIONS

Anticipating what might happen, the army had already perfected these techniques in its prewar winter manoeuvres and, when war started

> To compensate for the lack of anti-tank guns, the Finns used gasoline-filled bottles and TNT charges and destroyed a large number of tanks in this way.

Attempts to raise the water level were less successful during the coldest winter period; but equally, as the ice covered the uneven features of the terrain, the enemy had less shelter and was not concealed from air reconnaissance. Later, the Finns opened lanes by blowing up the ice and developed special ice mines which detonated when the Soviets approached.

SURPRISE TACTICS

Finns and Russians fought the Winter War during the darkest period of the year. In the area of Viipuri, daylight lasted from 8am to 5pm. On the level of Kajaani the day was a couple of hours shorter while, at the turn of the year, Petsamo in the north had hardly any hours of daylight at all. Finnish soldiers made use of the darkness for the loading and unloading of trains, transports and supply traffic. This prevented the enemy (with its command of the air) from noticing and disturbing operations. Furthermore, the troops

For these attacks, the Finns either carried their ammunition, mines and explosives or pulled them along on sledges, which they also used to evacuate the wounded, often along the specially prepared winter roads through the wilderness. At night, for longer distances, they ploughed a road over ice to bring in troops and equipment. In any attack, surprise was the essence. Strike force commanders and their troops, all on skis, moved stealthily forward to block the road so that the sappers had time to destroy the bridges and lay mines to catch the tanks before any counterattack.

Finnish refugees flee from advancing Soviet troops, 1939–40.

carried out all their tactical movements in the forests, which offered even better protection.

As the Soviet army moved west, the Finns had insufficient forces and equipment for classic air, tank, artillery and similar operations, and their aim had to be to force the enemy to attack under the worst possible conditions. But the Finns, bred on the land, knew the terrain. The Soviet divisions, in contrast, had no choice but to stick to the roads, advancing in a tight column, strung out over some 100km (60 miles). On either side lay a strip around 110–220km (70–140 miles) wide of uninhabited, forest-covered wilderness, with numerous lakes and marshes, where the Finnish troops had all the advantages of surprise and manoeuvrability.

⊙ SURVIVING THE LANDSCAPE

One of the most difficult problems for winter warfare had already been solved by Finland in the 1930s: how to camp and make shelter in a winter wilderness. Finland had developed a tent for the use of half a platoon (20 men), which could be folded into a small, easily handled bundle. A portable box-stove was enough to keep the tent warm even if the temperature fell to –40°C/F. It was also relatively easy to prepare coffee and basic warm food on top of the stove. The Finns also had the valuable know-how to operate for several weeks in uninhabited regions without tents by building shelters out of snow and evergreens.

The Finns fought against great odds during this Winter War (and partly during the Continuation War that followed). Their number of anti-tank guns was so limited that the troops could use them only against an armoured attack on an open road, and gasoline bottles and TNT charges were more likely to destroy an enemy tank. Despite that, the advantages were not always on the side of the invading army. The ill-informed and often ill-clad Soviet troops could not move from or manoeuvre outside the roads, and they, too, often lacked supplies when insufficient air drops left

to the end. This guaranteed pre-conditions for an honourable peace and, in 1940, the two sides concluded an armistice. The Soviet Union's original aim – a base in Hanko, in the southwest, and the moving of the border further from Leningrad – were its only gains.

Nevertheless, Finland had to surrender 11 percent of its territory, with a proportionate shift of population, and, in this respect, suffered a heavy defeat. On the other hand it was obvious that Stalin's real intention had been to annex the whole of Finland, and their defeat in the Winter

Danish volunteers fighting for Finland, on the march with skis and white camouflage, January 1940.

them short of ammunition and food. Throughout the war's skirmishes and more formal encounters, the 'ski troops' inflicted hard blows on this badly deployed Red Army. (It was partly this poor performance that persuaded Hitler later to launch an attack on Russia.)

HONOURABLE PEACE

Though Marshal Mannerheim's resourceful troops had taken full advantage of territory and climate to achieve several victories, Finland could not last long against such an incredibly powerful enemy. The Finnish army was forced to surrender at Viipuri, and the Soviet Union set up and then abandoned a puppet government on the Karelian Isthmus. But the long front held out

British leader Winston Churchill was unstinting in his praise of Finnish resistance during the Winter War. He wrote: 'Finland shows what free men can do.'

War was mitigated for the Finns by the maintenance of national sovereignty.

The Winter War lasted exactly 100 days. But the European powers were still fighting and the inevitable result for Finland was to be swept up in yet another conflict. On 22 June 1941, Operation Barbarossa went ahead. Hitler attacked the Soviet Union, achieving complete surprise.

Russian commanders signalled to Stalin: 'We are being fired on – what shall we do?' Stalin didn't believe them and instead scolded them for sending unencrypted messages. There had been

> During the Winter War, some units had been short of potatoes. This led to a few veterans reporting for duty in World War II carrying a sack or two of potatoes as well as their kit.

Russian High Command retaliated against the Finns. Russian bombs fell on Finland even before any were dropped on German targets.

The Finnish army was larger, war-hardened and better equipped than at the start of the Winter War. Even so, Marshal Voroshilov, who was in charge of the Russian Northwest Army Group, had a formidable number of troops under his command.

Many in Finland expected the army to make an advance towards Leningrad. The idea of capturing this city had at one time attracted Mannerheim, but now he informed the Finnish

Aerial view of Tampere in winter.

some collusion between the German and Finnish military authorities and the Finns had had to allow the west of Finland to be used for transit traffic. Partial Finnish mobilisation was ordered, and 60,000 civilians moved from front-line areas.

ALONGSIDE GERMANY

On the day preceding Barbarossa, Hitler had announced that 'Finnish and German troops stand side by side on the Arctic coast for the defence of Finnish soil.' Marshal Mannerheim was convinced that his statement was intended as an announcement of a *fait accompli.* 'This will lead to a Russian attack,' he said, 'though, on the other hand, I am convinced that in any case such an attack would have occurred.' The

government that 'under no circumstances will I lead an offensive against the great city on the Neva'. He feared that the Russians, faced with an advance on Leningrad, might summon insurmountable forces and inflict a heavy defeat on the Finnish army.

The campaign aimed to reconquer Ladoga-Karelia, followed by the Isthmus, and finally penetrate Karelia. All these objectives were achieved. Mannerheim had some German units placed at his disposal, but he kept them at arm's length. The Finns were co-belligerents, not allies of the Germans. When the Finns had regained all of their old frontiers, Mannerheim commented: 'Here we could have stood as neutral neighbours instead of as bitter enemies.'

ADMIRING ALLIES

The fact that Great Britain and Russia were allies led to a tricky diplomatic situation between Mannerheim and Churchill, as is illustrated in the following exchange of letters. At this point, the outcome of the war was far from clear.

Churchill wrote asking Mannerheim to halt the advance of his troops. 'It would be most painful to the many friends of your country in England if Finland found herself in the dock with the guilty and defeated Nazis. My recollections of our pleasant talks... about the last war

Field Marshal Mannerheim with officers near Helsinki in 1939, prior to the Russian invasion.

lead me to send you this purely personal and private message for your consideration before it is too late.'

Following this request, Field Marshal Mannerheim replied to Prime Minister Churchill: 'I am sure you will realise it is impossible for me to halt the military operations at present being carried out before the troops have reached the positions which in my opinion will provide us with necessary security.

'It would be deplorable if these measures, undertaken for the security of Finland, should bring my country into conflict with England, and it would deeply sadden me if England felt herself forced to declare war on Finland. It

was very good of you to send me a... message in these critical days, and I appreciate it fully.' Nevertheless, a few days later, in order to satisfy his ally Josef Stalin, Churchill did declare war on the Finns.

PAYMENT IN FULL

The 1941–4 war is known in Finland as the 'Continuation War' because it was understood as an extension of the Winter War and as an attempt to compensate for losses suffered in that war. In the Continuation War Finland's number of dead was 65,000 and wounded 158,000. Homes had to be found for more than 423,000 Karelians. After 1945 the Soviets insisted on staging show trials in Finland of the politicians who had given the orders to fight. These men received prison sentences, but served less than a full term and, in some cases, returned to public life with little or no damage to their reputation.

> *Winston Churchill wrote to Mannerheim on 29 November 1941: 'I am deeply grieved at what I see coming, namely, that we shall be forced within a few days, out of loyalty to our ally Russia, to declare war upon Finland.'*

Finland also had to pay reparations to the Soviet Union, mostly in the form of metal products. The Soviets insisted on calculating their value according to the exchange rates of 1938, thus Finland paid almost exactly twice the price stated in the agreement. The reparations to the Soviet Union were paid in full. This was a point of honour to the Finns.

The years of struggle and of suffering were over at long last, and a war-weary Finland set about the difficult and lengthy business of national reconstruction. More poignantly, the dead soldiers, who had been removed from the battlefields to their home parishes, were buried with full honours in cemeteries alongside memorials attesting to their courage and sacrifice. Unassuming, dignified and patriotic, the spirit of these graveyards and memorials is a fitting tribute to the memory of a people who had persevered and conquered.

THE GREAT GENERAL

Commander-in-Chief of the Finnish army, Mannerheim was one of the country's most influential figures from the civil war to World War II.

Carl Gustaf Emil Mannerheim was born at his family's country house at Louhisaari on 4 June 1867. The Mannerheim estate was in Swedish Villnäs, in the Turku district. The family was Swedish-speaking and of Dutch origin.

Furthermore, this great son of Finland, to whom the modern nation state probably owes its very existence, was a Russian officer for 28 years before he ever served Finland's cause. Yet Gustaf (he used his second Christian name) was not following any family tradition when he enlisted as a cavalry officer cadet in 1882. He was even expelled from the cadet school, and considered for a brief moment becoming a sailor. Fortunately for Finland he was given a second chance and went to St Petersburg for cavalry training; in 1889 he was commissioned into the tsarist army, passing out in the top six out of a total of 100.

INTERNATIONAL EXPERIENCE

While waiting for a Guard's commission he was posted to Poland as a subaltern in the 15th Alexandriski Dragoons. The Poles were far more restive under Russian rule than the Finns and had nothing like the same freedoms as the Grand Duchy. But Mannerheim later recalled: 'The better I got to know the Poles, the more I liked them and felt at home with them.' Transferred to the Chevalier Guards, he returned to St Petersburg to train recruits, and in 1892 married Anastasia Arapov, a relative of Pushkin. They had two daughters, and a son who died at birth. The marriage lasted seven years, although they did not divorce until 1919.

Mannerheim served as a colonel in the Russo-Japanese War, journeyed for two years through Siberia, Mongolia, China and Japan, and then came back to Poland to command a cavalry regiment in 1909. In World War I, he served in the Eastern European theatre, fighting against the Germans and Austrians. By 1917 he was a lieutenant-general.

The Russian Revolution cut short his career in the Emperor's Army, and after the tsar was murdered and Russia seething with revolutionary activity, Mannerheim considered himself released from his Oath of Allegiance.

After Finnish independence, the senate named Mannerheim commander-in-chief of the armed forces in Finland. Quickly, he had to raise and mobilise an army against the Red Guards and Russian troops. When the war was over and won, the senate appointed Mannerheim regent of Finland but he lost the presidential election.

Carl Gustaf Emil Mannerheim.

His finest military hour came during the Winter War in 1940, when Finland fought against Soviet Russia for three-and-a-half months under fierce winter conditions. It came through the war with its independence intact, due largely to the deployment of mobile 'ski troops'.

Mannerheim was briefly president of Finland after the war, but retired due to ill health in March 1946. His final years were spent quietly, mainly in Switzerland, where he died in 1951, aged 83. His home in Helsinki is now a museum, and holds trophies and mementoes from the five wars in which he fought. On the library wall is a painting of military personnel on skis and in white overalls. The sense of urgency portrayed in the human figures contrasts with the peace of the Finnish forest. Most curiously, the painting is dated 1890 – the year the oppressive Russian rule began in Finland.

Parliament Building, Helsinki.

A SHIFT IN BALANCE

In breaking free from Russia and moving towards a higher profile in Europe, Finland has endured economic hardship. But its efforts have clearly borne fruit.

Finnish statesman Max Jacobson once stated that, 'until the disintegration of the USSR, [Finns] were subjected to a kind of character assassination through use of the term 'Finlandisation' to denote supine submission to Soviet domination'. Although in the past, Finland has often been strongly associated with a backward, Cold War Russia – due to its tangled and tumultuous political history with the country – this conflation has all but disappeared since the opening of the Iron Curtain. Finland has discarded its dual identity, in which it was seen on the one hand as an enlightened, peace-loving Nordic nation, clean and unspoilt and heroic and healthy, and on the other hand as dictated by its position – both physical and political – in relation to Russia.

Night view of the capital.

By committing itself to active membership of the EU, which it joined in 1995, and by participating in the first wave of the euro, Finland has made it clear that it is a long way from the Russian sphere of influence.

BALTIC ATTITUDES

In 1991, President Mauno Koivisto referred to the crisis in the Baltics as 'an internal Soviet affair', causing dismay to some Western and Baltic leaders. Most betrayed of all, perhaps, were the Finns themselves, among whom pro-independence sentiment for the Baltics, especially Finland's ethnic cousin Estonia, ran high. One newspaper editorial remarked: 'Public opinion is finding it difficult to accept the realism of this country's foreign policy leadership and its appeal to Finland's own national interest.'

Defenders of the government line explained their belief that interference from the outside would only increase tensions. (A week after the Koivisto statement, Russian Interior Ministry troops attacked the Lithuanian TV station and more than a dozen ended up dead.) Some also reasoned that other countries could take stronger stances because they did not share a border with the Russians, and that this border has always made things different for Finland.

In addition, Finnish Communists played a big role in organising the labour force that powered early post-war industry. At one stage they held 50 out of 200 seats in the *Eduskunta* (parliament or national assembly). The Russians used them as a vessel through which to channel influence. This method was most effective when the Communists were most powerful. Twice, the Russians were able to wield enough influence to lead the government to resign.

There was a flip side as well. Until 1947, Finland was observed by the Allied Control Commission, which included many Russian officers. (The Commission, among other tasks, observed war crimes trials; the longest

MOVING RIGHT

The Social Democrats' gradual move towards the centre was emblematic of the political picture as a whole. Since the war, the sympathies of the majority have moved steadily towards more traditional, 'bourgeois' European values. After the 1991 parliamentary vote, Finland was ruled by a centre-right alliance that was the most politically conservative in the republic's history.

The move right kept step with the economic growth of Finland, a phenomenon causing

The Finnish parliament, with one of the world's highest quotas of women, in session.

sentence given was 10 years, served on ex-president Risto Ryti for his dealings with the Germans.) The officers' presence was often frightening to the anti-Communist Finns. The fear that Finland would go the way of Czechoslovakia in 1948 so rattled even the brave Marshal Mannerheim (who was regent briefly after the war; see page 53) that he made personal provisions to flee the country, just in case.

The Communist left eventually lost its grip on the country, and in time the Social Democrats (SDP) became the dominant political party in Finland. The SDP held that position until 1987, when it found itself in a so-called 'red-blue' coalition with the leading rightist party, the conservative Kokoomus.

rapid change. Divested in 1917 of the lucrative 19th-century trade links it had enjoyed as a trading post of Imperial Russia, Finland had to start from scratch. Until World War II, Finland had a stagnant subsistence agricultural economy. Post-war industrialisation pulled it out of this quagmire, and Finland became, eventually, relatively wealthy, even if some of the richest individual Finns often lived abroad in order to avoid the otherwise huge tax bills. This accomplishment was of crucial importance to Finns, and also somewhat calmed Western worries that the country was too close to the USSR.

But Finland had to carve out its political place in the post-war world, a world that rapidly began to militarise along East–West lines. Finland chose neutrality. Instituted by J.K. Paasikivi, as prime minister (1944–6), then president (1946–6) of the Finnish republic, and Urho Kekkonen, president from 1956 to 1981, the doctrine of neutrality was one that shunned commitment in favour of 'peace-oriented policy'. Non-alignment remains the official government foreign policy line, reconfirmed in a 2012 Finnish Ministry of Defence report on Finnish security. A poll conducted on 5–23 November 2015 by the Advisory Board for Defence Information (ABDI) showed that 54 percent of Finns support their country's military non-alignment.

But newspapers no longer temper their criticisms of their eastern neighbour, as was the case under Kekkonen's code of 'self-censorship'. Finland also allows itself the option of participation in United Nations or NATO crisis management, a policy that saw Finnish forces in Lebanon and Kosovo.

Neutrality has meant many different things in many different situations. In post-war Finland, the neutral Paasikivi-Kekkonen line seemed to reassure Finns that their country would not become a battleground for the Soviet Union and its considerable enemies. To gain such reassurance, Finland had to walk a narrow line. The tense mistrust that ruled East–West relations during the Cold War caused a foreign policy challenge that would have been formidable even to a nation far older and more powerful than this one.

Finland, which had not been independent for even three decades by the war's end, resolved that it wanted 'out' of the conflict, and bargained for post-war agreements along this line. The Soviet Union pushed hard for certain concessions, and a much-depleted Finland had little bargaining power. Compromises were inevitable.

SOVIET LEASE

The most controversial compromise was in the 1944 peace treaty with Moscow. In it, the Finns agreed to lease the Porkkala Peninsula (near Helsinki) to the Soviets for 50 years for use as a military base (see page 173). The situation was defused in 1955 when the two parties agreed to the lease's cancellation.

Porkkala's return seemed to signal good things to the West, as Finland joined the United Nations; in the 1950s, the country also joined the International Monetary Fund.

When Paasikivi began formulating his foreign policy line he stressed 'correct and irreproachable neighbourly relations' with the Soviet Union. The phrase may have sounded like grovelling to Western ears but made sense to the majority of Finns, who needed to believe that the Soviet Union could be moulded into a benign neighbour.

Finland was among the first countries to adopt the euro in 2002.

In 1948, Finland and the Soviet Union signed the Treaty of Friendship, Cooperation and Mutual Assistance (FCMA), which was originally to have expired in 2003. This complex agreement was not a military alliance per se. Drawn up in clear reference to the Germans having used Finland to attack the Russians, it demanded mutual protection; both pledged to prevent outside forces from using their territory to attack the other; and Finland promised not to join any alliances hostile to the Soviet Union.

This last measure was perceived by the Finns to be in line with the policy of neutrality they had already decided on. Other Western nations, however, beginning to labour under sharp Cold War polarities, felt that if Finland was not for them, it could easily be against them. In this way began the declamations that Finland was teetering on the edge of becoming part of the Eastern Bloc.

THE NATO QUESTION

All the other nations liberated by the Western Allies in World War II eventually became NATO members. It was only Finland, the one country with a border with the Soviet Union to emerge outside the Eastern Bloc after World War II, and Yugoslavia who did not become allies of either East or West.

When Finland joined the Nordic Council in 1955, the Soviet editorials became hysterical:

> *In 1955 Finland was admitted into the United Nations; in 1994 it became a member of the NATO Partnership for Peace programme.*

Floating logs down lakes and rivers to Finland's wood and paper factories.

⊘ SUPPORT FOR THE UNITED NATIONS

Finland has been deeply committed to the United Nations since joining in 1955.

Finland strongly supports UN peacekeeping functions, in which more than 35,000 Finnish military personnel have participated in the last 60-odd years. A maximum of 2,000 Finnish military personnel can be deployed at any one time to situations around the world, with Finns recently engaged in UN operations in Liberia, Lebanon, Syria, India and Pakistan. Involvement ranges from armed military units to unarmed military observers. Involvement began during the Suez Canal crisis in 1956. There has since been a strong Finnish presence in peacekeeping operations in Lebanon, the Golan Heights,

Gaza and the Sinai. But the most outstanding efforts were made on behalf of Namibia. On a Finnish initiative, in 1970 the UN set up a Namibia Fund, and Finland also pursued the 1971 International Court of Justice ruling that South Africa's presence in Namibia was illegal. When Namibia gained independence in 1990, Martti Ahtisaari directed the transition.

Finland contributes generously to refugee aid programmes; the total contribution from Nordic governments equals 13 percent of the UN High Committee on Refugees fund. Ahtisaari was awarded the Nobel Prize for Peace in 2008 to acknowledge his long-lasting contribution to global peace.

'Surely this means Finland will be joining NATO?' read one Russian headline. The fact that the Summer Olympics were set to be held in Helsinki also in 1952 added fuel to the fire. The Soviets interpreted preparations for the event, such as the building of a south coast highway, as proof of more plans to include Finland in a general military threat – perhaps even war – against the USSR.

Whatever else is true of the immediate post-war period, the fact that Finland decided not to enter into the Western fold but rather chose to go it alone did not endear it to the non-Communist world: a lone wolf is always suspect. Finland even refused to join the Marshall Plan.

ECONOMIC PROGRESS

Nonetheless, economic progress began in earnest. The Finnish-Soviet 1944 peace agreement had included demands for war reparations of more than US$600 million. Ironically, this demand for money helped build the new economy. Post-war Finland was low on cash but met payments by negotiating the payment of some of its debt in manufactured engineering products such as farming and forestry machinery, and ships.

These items became staple sources of export income in Finland's post-war years as a growth economy. Before that economy got off the ground, however, most Finns lived in poverty. To this day, older Finns enthusiastically buy chocolate when they travel abroad because of post-war memories of chocolate being impossible to obtain.

Finland had to stretch its meagre resources yet further to deal with one of the largest resettlements of a civilian population in the world. Nearly 400,000 dispossessed Karelians (and a handful of Skolt Sami) were given free land and donations of whatever the others could afford to give, which was not very much. Most Karelians, already poor in their homeland, arrived only with what they and their horses could carry.

In 1950, a barter agreement was signed between the Finns and the Soviets. It was in force until 1990, when the Soviets abruptly announced they would not sign the next five-year extension. The reason given was that continuing it would hinder Soviet pursuit of survival on a free market economy basis.

The true Soviet aim was to sell its oil for hard cash. While in force, the barter agreement was worth a fortune. It provided Finland with a completely protected market for tonnes of consumer goods each year. The heavy equipment and cheap clothes and shoes sent over were traded for Soviet oil, enough to cover as much as 90 percent of Finnish needs.

The Finnish trade balance suffered due to the treaty's cancellation by a disputed but significant amount as the USSR was Finland's fifth-largest trading partner. Soviet-orientated

President Kekkonen arriving in Moscow, 1961.

Finnish producers foundered or went bankrupt. The Finns had to pay cash for oil and wait for the Soviets to pay them a US$2 billion debt.

CONTINUING CRISIS

While Finland was quickly able to shine in the United Nations arena, crises at home went on. In 1961, the USSR sent Finland a note suggesting 'military consultations' regarding the 1948 FCMA. That note was probably sent because of Soviet fear of escalating (West) German militarism in the Baltic. The harm the note caused to Finland derived from the term 'military consultations'. Both sides had maintained the Treaty of Friendship, Cooperation and Mutual Assistance, which was not a military alliance, but an emblem of cooperation between two neighbours who were not allied.

Nikita Khrushchev and Urho Kekkonen conferred privately and the consultations were announced 'deferred'. What the Soviets had been worried about, though, was clear: that Finland was not equipped to stop the West from using it as an attack flank. The Kekkonen-Khrushchev exchange was never made wholly public, but after the 'Note Crisis', Finland began shoring up its military forces. Finland sought, and got, from the British a reinterpretation of the Paris Peace Treaty of 1947, allowing it to purchase missiles, forbidden by the original treaty.

Throughout the 1970s the Soviets tried to make life difficult for the Finns several more times. When one Soviet ambassador decided to meddle in an internal wrangle of the Finnish Communist Party, President Kekkonen swiftly demanded his deportation back to the USSR. With the fibre of Finnish society now more firmly established, such left-wing elements were mere ragged ends.

Industry plays a key role in modern Finland.

⊘ TECHNOLOGY TODAY

In terms of being linked up to the rest of the world, Finland wins hands down. Helsinki maintains a technological infrastructure among the most sophisticated in the world, with free, city-wide Wi-Fi on all trams and buses and in all parks and thoroughfares. In 2010, the government became the first in the world to guarantee its citizens a broadband internet connection. Finnish firms such as Kone, F-Secure and Rocla now vie for office space in the city with large foreign subsidiaries and research units. There are more experts in science and technology per capita in Helsinki than in any other world capital city.

A more prosperous Finland was much harder to strong-arm, and by this time West Germany, Sweden and the United Kingdom had become Finland's major trading partners – no longer the USSR. Trees had become the country's 'green gold', and it looked as though the pulp and paper industry's economic success meant no end to prosperity.

HIGH LIVING

In the 1970s and 1980s, Finland enjoyed one of the highest gross national product figures in the world and pulled up its standard of living and social services to be in line with those of Sweden. It was then one of the most expensive countries in the world – even outstripping Japan.

Fantastically high agricultural subsidies and industrial cartels that set artificially high prices were the main culprits for the high cost of living.

A lot of Finns, however, made a lot of money and spent it with abandon. By the end of the 1980s, prices were still very high, especially on imports. It was not until EU membership in the latter half of the 1990s that prices levelled and began to resemble those in other Western European countries. Although Helsinki was once the world's most expensive city, it has since been overtaken by European rivals such

such circumstances, however, the Finnish economy was not very likely to make rapid improvements.

Those attitudes changed rapidly in the 1990s. The collapse of the former Soviet Union, which had accounted for a fifth of Finland's trade, combined with the global slide into recession to produce the worst slump suffered by any European state since the 1930s. Between 1991 and 1993, the economy lost 14 percent of its gross domestic product and unemployment soared from 3 percent to

Enjoying that much-rated Finnish lifestyle.

as Copenhagen, Oslo, Reykjavik and Vienna (in 2018, it was ranked 18th out of 133 cities in the Economist Intelligence Unit's annual worldwide cost-of-living ranking).

ECONOMIC AGONY

The economic growth of the 1970s and '80s was not set to continue. Beginning in the late 1980s, Finland entered economic recession. At the same time, the challenges of the 'new' Europe were growing. While the rest of Europe was drawing together like a large mutual aid society, Finland seemed to repel the trend, being committed to the European Free Trade Association but strongly opposed to joining the European Community. Under

around 20 percent. Pragmatists saw the need to shift from a commodity-based economy looking towards Russia to a manufacturing and service economy looking towards the West. Nokia, the country's leading electronics company, paved the way when its sales of mobile phones doubled its profits, and by the end of the 1990s the company had established itself as the world leader in the communications sector. The changed circumstances also convinced many people that it would be worth seeking safety within the parameters of the European Union, and 57 percent of the country's 4 million voters opted in a consultative referendum in October 1994 to become part of the EU from January 1995.

RELUCTANT MEMBERS

Objections to EU membership were still vociferous. Many argued that joining the European Union would not improve things since the EU had an unproven agricultural policy. However, in the first year of membership, food prices fell by 8 percent, and the feeling of being part of a massive trading group created a sense of security that promised well for the future. The five-party 'Rainbow Coalition' that came to power in 1995 promised little except austerity, but the new mood of realism enabled them

The Kiasma art complex, one reason Helsinki was named as European City of Culture in 2000.

to peg pay rises to 1.7 percent and 2 percent over two years, helping to keep inflation very low at around 1.5 percent.

Deeply rooted agrarian loyalties were also hard to shake in Finland, even if full-time farmers were a dying breed. Finally, Finns had an instinctive wish to keep foreigners from buying a slice of their wealth-producing forests. The idea of foreigners buying up forests brought fears of loss of privacy, something sacred to the national character. The forest industrialists had more pragmatic fears: namely, that introduction of foreign buyers would mean the break-up of the cartel-style domestic price-fixing mechanisms which

helped shield the industry from real competition. Prices in this and other industries were thus artificially high, and in some sectors competition was virtually impossible.

The objection to EU membership had always been the risk of compromising Finnish neutrality, although neutral countries like Ireland had flourished in the EU and neutral Sweden was keen to join (which it did, also in 1995). Not only was Sweden one of Finland's most important trade partners, it was also a beacon of political and socio-economic policy for Finland.

Ten years prior, the country could never have contemplated a move such as joining the EU without first seeking permission from Russia. But Finns were now beginning to enjoy the freedom of making their own decisions – even if Russia would eventually regain its economic strength. There was some immediate benefit, too: because of poor storage and transport facilities at Russian ports, Western exporters began shipping bulk goods to Finnish harbours and transporting them on by road to Russia.

PRUNING THE WELFARE STATE

Until the recession that hit Finland in the early 1990s, the welfare state was one of the great and sacrosanct untouchables of Finnish life. Using the model provided by its neighbour Sweden, Finland launched a programme to extend its state welfare facilities in the years following World War II.

Before the war these facilities had been relatively modest, with the first measure affecting the whole (still largely rural) population taking the form of a Pensions Act in 1937. A Child Allowance Act followed in 1948, giving state recognition to the need for child protection, and the Pensions Act was brought up to date in the late 1950s, along with the introduction of the private pensions option. The 1960s and 1970s also saw the establishment of laws that made provision for sickness insurance and health care.

Unemployment was in any case insignificant in European terms, and poverty was all but eradicated. Then came the economic turmoil of the early 1990s: suddenly, the percentage of unemployed was soaring into double figures and reaching unprecedented post-war peaks of about 20 percent, and Finnish banks found themselves in a crisis which had to be solved with the backing of state funds. Pressure mounted on the availability of funds for welfare state provision, and the agreements between

For decades, Finns were prepared to endure massive income tax rates in return for generous and comprehensive welfare benefits.

business, government and then influential trade unions no longer seemed written in stone. Charges for health care increased and taxation on pensions was introduced; at the same time, workers were encouraged by tax breaks to contribute to private pension schemes to supplement their less generous state pensions.

Finland's social structure has withstood considerable pressure from the increased poverty and unemployment that followed the recession. Still, the welfare state has held firm and continues to provide a sound, basic safety net.

Businesswomen in Helsinki.

⊘ BUSINESS IN FINLAND

With a population of 5.5 million, Finland maintains one of the wealthiest and healthiest economies in the world, boasting a 2018 GDP of €244 billion. Furthermore, according to the 2017–18 Global Competitiveness Report, the Finnish economy is the 10th most competitive in the world. Helsinki, home to a quarter of the country's population, generates around a third of the country's revenue production, serving as headquarters to thousands of businesses, the largest of which trade in paper manufacturing, shipbuilding (every fourth cruiseline ship in the world sails out of a Finnish port on its maiden voyage) and information technology

(make a phone call from Dublin to Delhi and you're likely to ring through Finnish networks, hubs and routers).

With its high proportion of specialists in the science and technology industries, Helsinki was well placed to ride the economic downturn. High levels of expertise, training and savvy are supported by a strong tradition of cooperation in research between technology companies and Finnish universities. And thanks to government assistance available to small- and medium-sized firms, many foreign entities doing business in Helsinki often grow at a quicker rate than native Finnish companies.

Finns have been prepared to see it trimmed and pruned as the aging population has increased pressure on the system, but most would baulk at the idea of removing it completely. In 2019, the Centre Party's failure to reform the healthcare system and successfully implement a guaranteed minimum income scheme led to Juha Sipilä's resignation.

ELECTING A NEW FUTURE

The lead up to the 21st century saw an element of stability in Finnish political life, with succes-

Woman in Lapland.

sive Social Democrat-led coalition governments under Paavo Lipponen ruling from 1995–2003, and Social Democrat presidents gaining victory in 1994 (Ahtisaari) and 2000 (Halonen).

But things changed in the March 2003 election, when Finns voted for change. The Centre Party became the largest group in parliament and Finland's first female prime minister, Anneli Jäätteenmäki, was elected, although she resigned two months later amid accusations of information leaks. The Centre Party retained its lead in 2007, but slipped to fourth place in the 2011 elections – the biggest loss in the party's history, and, in fact, for any party post-World War II. This election, however, was even more memorable for the surprise success

of the populist far-right party the True Finns, who more than quadrupled their support to win 39 (out of 200) parliamentary seats. The Centre Party was back in front in the 2015 parliamentary elections, winning 49 seats in parliament, while the True Finns retained their high support with 38 seats. The Centre Party's leader, Juha Sipilä, became prime minister and formed a centre-right coalition government. Following the government's resignation in 2019, a parlimentary election was held with the rival Social Democratic Party winning the most seats, however, no overall majority has led to coalition discussions.

A MODERN EUROPEAN STATE

There is now a feeling that Finland has evolved into a more outward-looking and cosmopolitan country. Finns, especially the younger, urbanised generations, have looked to Europe as their centre of political reference. And with the benefits and advantages of Europe come the responsibilities of a modern nation.

Finland had its chance to prove such responsibility in the second half of 1999 when it took on the EU presidency, hosting more than 70 special European meetings, including two major summits. Helsinki's European City of Culture role, shared with eight other European cities in 2000, and the celebration in the same year of the capital's 450th anniversary, gave the whole country a confident platform upon which to enter the new millennium.

But the global economic crisis did not spared Finland. In the face of increased competition from Apple's iPhone and smartphones using Google's Android technology, Nokia began to struggle from 2011 onwards and announced big job cuts. In 2013, Nokia's mobile phone business was sold to Microsoft for 5.4bn euros, a fraction of its former worth. However, it remains an important part of the Finnish economy.

The Finnish capital of Helsinki has developed to such a point that it is now a city where many languages – English, Russian, German, Swedish, French and Italian, among others – are routinely heard (see page 99), yet where the local language remains as strong as ever. It is the capital of a country that is newly certain of its place in the world and which is learning to relish and nurture that self-confidence.

LADIES FIRST

When it comes to gender equality and provision of childcare, Finland is streets ahead of most European countries.

There was never really a strong feminist movement in Finland, probably because its women have always been tough cookies: *sisu* is a word synonymous with the Finnish character, implying self-reliance, determination and tenacity, and it is applied to the country's men and women equally.

WOMEN IN GOVERNMENT

In 1906, Finnish women became the first in the world to gain unrestricted political rights to vote and to stand for election. They were quick to take up the challenge, forming 10 percent of the first Finnish government. By doing so, they were directly able to influence government policy from the nation's beginning. The tradition of women in politics continues: a law introduced in 1995 stipulates a 40 percent quota of women in leadership in national and local government.

Finland elected its first female president in 2000, when the Social Democrat Tarja Halonen beat the Centre Party's Esko Aho. Halonen had a long past in radical and social politics, and in spite of the reduced powers of the president, enjoyed high approval ratings over her 12 years in office.

'Power to the women' has spread through all levels of government, with Eva-Riitta Siitonen serving as Helsinki's mayor at the end of the 1990s, and Anneli Jäätteenmäki and Mari Kiviniemi both briefly in the prime minister's post in 2003 and 2010 respectively. Following the 2019 election, the 200 member Finnish parliament has 94 female MPs (47 percent). This is the highest proportion of female members in the Parliament's history.

CHURCH AND BUSINESS

Finland has been progressive in other areas of society, too, regarding gender equality. The country's Lutheran Church opened the priesthood to women as far back as 1986, and today there are around 1,000 women priests. Sirkka Hämäläinen became the first female governor of the Bank of Finland in the early 1990s. Female lawyers, editors-in-chief, doctors and other professionals abound, although there is still a glass ceiling in the higher echelons of business. Sari Baldauf, former Executive Vice President and General Manager of Nokia, was a rare exception to this boardroom gender rule.

President Tarja Halonen, Finland's president from 2000 to 2012.

Legislative support for women at work is very strong and very effective. The Finnish woman who does not work full-time has become a rarity and time off to raise a family is not a barrier to a successful career. All children up to the age of seven are guaranteed a daycare place. Both parents are entitled to childcare leave until their child turns three, during which time their jobs are secured and an allowance is granted. Standard parental leave of 158 days after the birth of a child, usually taken by the mother, is subsidised by an allowance equivalent to two-thirds of the parent's normal income. Finland is well ahead of many other countries in how it provides for the rearing, education and professional success of its men, women and children.

Skidoos have become popular.

A Helsinki café.

THE FINNISH SOUL

Blond, reserved, rustic – some of these stereotypes are not far off, but Finns are moving with the times, embracing a more international approach to modern living.

'The only constant is change,' many Finns will tell you. The vicissitudes of fortune are well known to this young nation, not yet 100 years old. Tussled over for centuries by Sweden and Russia, Finland's turbulent history seems to have given the country an old soul. Poverty and prosperity are viewed equally phlegmatically – everything might be different again tomorrow.

The Finns' own habitat reinforces the lesson. Seasons flip abruptly from freezing winter (with almost total darkness 24 hours a day) to balmy summer with 24 hours of daylight. Better to adapt and survive to ever-changing conditions than waste energy fighting the inevitable.

Perhaps it is because such seminal change is deep-rooted in the Finnish soul that the nation has no fear of the new. The Economist ranks Finland third in the world in its latest innovation index, and Finnish people accept new technology, cuisine and transport without blinking. National pride in high-tech industries is strong; but long-standing national traditions are never completely forgotten.

Fun in the snow.

COMBAT AND CONCORD

Finns entered the 21st century with style and class – it's incredible how quickly the country forged its own identity, after centuries of Swedish and Russian domination. But while Finns may have forgiven, they are less quick to forget: small details such as success against Sweden or Russia in sports are scrutinised carefully. For example, in ice hockey, a particular highpoint for Finland was trouncing Sweden 6–1 in the 2011 World Cup Final.

National policy is to remain outside foreign conflicts, searching instead for peaceful solutions. In the recent past, Finland has helped broker momentous peace deals in the Balkans and Northern Ireland, and its enthusiasm for UN humanitarianism contrasts with a scepticism about NATO operations. Yet Finland's own freedom was hard-won, and the country today has compulsory military service (of 165, 255 or 347 days' duration, depending on the conscript's allotted role) for all men over the age of 18. Creating its own legion of defenders is all the more important to the country as it does not belong to any military alliance.

GHOSTS FROM THE PAST

To what extent can a land be judged by its ancient heroes? In the case of many countries, only an enemy would wish to invoke the memory of certain inglorious characters. With Finland, however, the idea is appealing. The main characters in the Finnish epic the *Kalevala* are patriotic, with the heroes painted as noble warriors (see page 91). Yet these strong men are troubled hair-tearers in private, and experience great difficulty in waxing poetic when setting out to woo and win the girl. The women, in contrast, are strong-headed, matriarchal and very family-orientated.

The land itself is filled with nature and wood spirits. No one in the *Kalevala* would deny that the woods have sanctity, and that the lakes and

For every ranting drunk, there's a raving teeto-taller. For every patriotic Finn who is as attached to Finland as to his own soul, there's one who leaves to make it big abroad, seldom to return.

> *'We are forest people,' says Jarl Kohler, managing director of the Finnish Forest Industries Federation. 'The forests are our security and our livelihood.'*

Pike fishing.

rivers are pieces of heaven on earth. When one of the female heroes wants to escape her fate, for example, she simply turns into a nimble, stream-swimming fish.

One can only take the analogy so far, of course, but it's far better to start with a nation's self-made heroes, where at least some roots are tied to reality, than the stereotypical characters other nations, often invading armies in the case of Finland, have created for them.

CONTRASTING CHARACTERS

There are so many paradoxes in the Finnish character that it would be hard to convince the sceptical foreigner that there isn't more than a dash of schizophrenia in the national psyche.

Yet some national stereotypes are universally recognised as being more valid than others – the importance of the forest to the Finns, for example: more than 600,000 Finns own a plot of forest and by law every citizen has the right of access to the land.

NORDIC LINKS

It has been claimed that the 'typical Finn' is the result of a genetic combination that is 75 percent identical to that of Swedes or other Scandinavians, but 25 percent descended from tribes that wandered to Finland from east of the Ural Mountains – although some academics now dispute this (see page 29). This Western Asian strain may account for certain physical traits that set Finns apart from their Nordic neighbours – finely pronounced cheekbones and comparatively small eyes, often blue or slate-grey.

Karelians (Finns from the very east of the country), meanwhile, are stockier and tend to be slightly smaller in stature than people from the west coast. Until the end of World War II, the Karelians' diet was extremely poor and they experienced one of the highest incidences of heart disease in the West, which may in part account for some differences.

CITY VERSUS COUNTRY

For a traditionally rural country, Finland has become much more urbanised in recent years. Some 85 percent of Finns live in an urban area. Domestic emigration is accelerating – Finns are moving from small towns to bigger centres such as Greater Helsinki, Tampere, Turku and Oulu. While many Finns are early adopters of *etätyö* (telecommuting), an equal number of people still try to escape to the cities. This shift is often a result of unemployment and a reduction of services, as post offices, shops and bus links close in villages.

Enjoying a drink at a pavement café in Helsinki.

The remaining Finns are taller, usually fair-haired (though, overall, Finns are considered the 'darkest' of the Nords) and, much like any other nationality, vary greatly in most other ways.

PHYSIQUE AND PERSONALITY

Some of the most famous Finns are sportsmen and women, taking advantage of their generally strong and healthy physiques. As a nation, Finns are great lovers of the outdoors and of sport, and some young Finns seem to live for little else (see page 105).

The Finnish personality is harder to pin down. Often considered the most reserved people in Europe, this trait actually applies as much to other Nordic peoples as it does to Finns.

⊘ A RESERVED NATION

Finns are known for being quiet, laconic and reserved. An old joke goes, 'What's the difference between a Finnish introvert and a Finnish extrovert? An introvert looks at his shoes while talking to you; an extrovert looks at yours.' Finns value words: they think before they speak, and silences are part of the conversational flow. Finns also value privacy. The summer cabin *(kesämökki)* is usually set back from the lakeshore among the trees, and as far from other dwellings as possible. The idea of time spent here is to bask in the short summer sunlight, immerse yourself in a simpler life, and enjoy your own space on your own time.

But rural life has its attractions. People tend to live in large houses surrounded by gardens. Farmers are fewer but receive enough subsidies to continue a comfortable lifestyle. Farm holidays are common, although some wonder whether parts of rural Finland may be turning into a tourist reserve.

> *Honesty is another Finnish stereotype, and Finns regularly are considered to have the world's most honest business practices. In spite of high taxes, evasion is no higher than in any other European country.*

Old and young in Finland.

SOCIETY

Although Finns fought a bloody class war in 1918, modern Finland is less class-conscious than it has ever been. There is a faint jostling rivalry between town and country folk, but Finland tries to favour equality and discourage social divisiveness. Still, poverty does haunt certain suburbs in Helsinki and entire regions in the northern half of Finland. Whether this divide between rich and poor will grow remains to be seen. The 2008 economic crash hit Finland hardest of all the Nordic countries, putting its all-encompassing welfare system under the spotlight. Despite this, in 2018 Finland was ranked the top country in the World Happiness Report, winning the top spot two years in a row.

POPULAR CULTURE

Popular culture has exploded, along with commercial media – the switch to digital broadcasting means there are now five state-run TV channels and eight private channels. Finns have always had their fingers on the technological pulse. The worldwide success of Angry Birds, created by Finnish game developer Rovio Entertainment, has encouraged many a Finn into the app-creation and gaming industry. Many younger Finns, shedding their parents' unease, have also gone on to study, work and travel abroad, and now eagerly welcome all things foreign to Finland. While some older Finns may not have abandoned the dreary, grey outfits that once dominated the clothing racks, their grandchildren adopt the latest fashions as quickly as anyone in New York, Milan and Paris.

HOME AND DRESS

The home is still highly venerated, and Finns spend a considerable amount of time and money on their properties. Although Finns live like royalty, they can often dress somewhat crudely. One female minister raised eyebrows in an international meeting by wearing a violet jean jacket. Despite the move towards international lifestyles, you might find that sartorial style remains somewhat low on the Finnish agenda.

⊘ GYPSY ROOTS

One of the oldest groups in Finland who are not ethnic Finns are the Romany gypsies, whose womenfolk are instantly recognisable by their elaborate embroidered lace blouses and voluminous skirts. Although today most speak only Finnish, few have intermarried, so their Southern European looks stand out against fairer Finns.

Most gypsies are no longer nomadic and live fairly modern lives in one place, but some do still wander, especially in autumn, from one harvest festival to another. Little horse-trading is done these days, however, and the gypsies' appearance at these fairs is merely continuing an age-old tradition.

Mariehamn, Åland Islands.

ART, ARCHITECTURE AND DESIGN

Finland's struggle for national identity has led to an artistic heritage that spans ancient rural traditions all the way up to sparkling Modernism.

When Diaghilev, founder of the Russian Ballet, divided the Finnish painters of the 1890s into two camps – 'those with a nationalistic outlook and those who follow the West' – he described a tension which has been present in Finnish art ever since.

The art world of Western Europe and the artistic expression of Finnish nationalism have been persistently seen as opposing forces: artists either belonged to Europe or to Finland. Paradoxically, those who have achieved world renown were able, by creating something essentially Finnish and therefore unique, to leap over national boundaries. Today, Finnish design and architecture are among Finland's best-known products, partly because they combine a universal Modernism with something inherently Finnish.

Because Finland is still relatively young as an independent country, much of the art produced during the past 100 years has dealt with the creation of a national cultural identity. Until the 1880s, the nascent Finnish cultural scene was influenced by the country's political masters – first Sweden, then tsarist Russia. The few practising Finnish artists who were able to make a living from their work either trained or lived in Stockholm or St Petersburg.

SEARCHING FOR IDENTITY

The seeds of a specifically Finnish culture were sown when organised, professional art training began in Turku in 1830. In 1845, Finland held its first art exhibition, and in 1846, the Finnish Art Society was founded. But it wasn't until the 1880s and 1890s that a truly Finnish artistic idiom began to emerge, and Finnish artists were at long last granted some

Akseli Gallén-Kallela, Finland's 'national' artist.

recognition at home and, by the end of the 19th century, internationally as well.

European artistic influences were strong as painters such as Albert Edelfelt (1854–1905) utilised the style of French Naturalism. Yet, while his style was initially imported from abroad, the specific subjects of Edelfelt's paintings became increasingly Finnish in character.

In the 1880s, a motley group of painters took up the struggle for cultural identity, which paralleled the growth of Finnish nationalism and the desire for independence. Among those artists were Akseli Gallén-Kallela (1865–1931), Pekka Halonen (1865–1933), Eero Järnefelt (1863–1937), Juho Rissanen (1873–1950) and Helene Schjerfbeck (1862–1946). They looked to the Finnish landscape and to ordinary Finns for subjects that were quintessentially Finnish. Within that framework, artistic styles varied from powerful realism to pure romance.

NATIONAL ROMANTICISM

While some painters, like Hugo Simberg (1873–1917), followed idiosyncratic, transcendental, and Europe-based modes of Symbolism, a body of artists came to represent what was to be called Finnish National Romanticism. Their focus on Finnishness – a subject dear to the heart of every Finn – meant that these artists enjoyed, and continue to enjoy, considerable popular appeal in Finland. Several artists chose deliberately to move among people whose mother tongue was Finnish (at that time many urban intellectuals spoke Swedish) and whose traditional folk culture and rural living had, the artists believed, remained largely uncorrupted by either Swedish or Russian influences. They maintained that the Finnish peasant was the true Finn, and that a rural landscape was the only credible Finnish landscape – the country's

Karelian women, painted by Albert Edelfelt in 1887.

⊘ KARELIAN INFLUENCE

Gallén-Kallela, often acclaimed as one of the most original talents in Nordic art, followed in the footsteps of author Elias Lönnrot (see page 91) and in 1890 ventured into Karelia. So began the 'Karelia' movement, which sent droves of 19th-century artists and writers to the area, considered to be the cradle of 'true Finnishness'. The *Aino Myth (Aino-taru), The Defence of the Sampo (Sammon puolustus)* and *Joukahainen's Revenge (Joukahaisen kosto)* show his use of a stylised, allegorical idiom. A seminal figure in Finnish culture, Gallén-Kallela's enormous contribution laid the foundations for contemporary Finnish design.

cities had been planned and designed under the sway of foreign rulers.

BREAKING FREE FROM NATURE

In a general sense, the legacy of National Romanticism is large, often restricting later artists who wished to look at urban Finland, follow European movements or pursue abstract styles. Finnish popular taste in art continues to be dominated by both a nationalistic and a naturalistic preference.

Groups like the October Group, whose motto was 'in defence of Modernism, against isolationist nationalism', pushed hard against what is sometimes forbiddingly described as the 'Golden Age' of Finnish art. Sculptor

Sakari Tohka (1911–58) was a founding member of the October Group. Overthrowing the classicism of his Finnish forebears, he cast his sculptures in cement.

The October Group was not alone. Townscapes and urban Finland were the chosen subjects of another artistic backlash group, the Torch Bearers, which consisted of Väinö Kunnas (1896–1929), Sulho Sipilä (1895–1949) and Ragnar Ekelund (1892–1960).

Today, contemporary art in Finland is well supported by state and private grants, and the other art forms, especially crafts, architecture and design. Firmly turning their backs on the neoclassical designs of their predecessor C.L. Engel (1778–1840), whose buildings include Helsinki's Senate Square and the Cathedral, the architectural leaders of National Romanticism – the partnership of Herman Gesellius (1874–1916), Armas Lindgren (1874–1929) and Eliel Saarinen (1873–1950) – used peasant timber and granite architecture as their sources. Another leading exponent of the movement was Lars Sonck (1870–1956).

Kiasma, the striking Museum of Contemporary Art in Helsinki, designed by Stephen Holl.

work on show in the permanent and temporary exhibitions at Kiasma, Helsinki's museum of contemporary art, would hardly be recognised as art by the National Romantics. 'There are more opportunities to be experimental in Finland because of the support for the arts,' says Minna Heikinaho. Her three-screen video installation *Mun koti on katu ja se on näytelma (My Home is the Street and it's a Performance)* was one of Kiasma's early shows, and her work epitomises the bolder attitude of Finnish artists born in the early 1960s.

NATIONAL ARCHITECTURE

The pattern of Finnish fine art – ranging from nationalism to Modernism – is mimicked in

Decidedly Gothic in outline, and uneasy on the eye because of the clash of smooth timber or symmetrical roof tiles with rough-hewn granite, National Romantic buildings like Helsinki's National Museum (designed 1901) and Tampere's Cathedral (designed 1899) maintain something of a gawky ugliness. The partnership trio of architects did, however, begin to draw on more soothing, elongated Art Nouveau influences too. The plans for Helsinki Railway Station, originally designed by all three, were amended by Saarinen. The fetching building as it now stands is far more Art Nouveau than National Romantic.

After independence in 1917, the driving need for a national identity diminished in the face of the need to rebuild the country. Beyond the capital, there are abundant instances of original and well-considered municipal architecture: the public library in Tampere, for instance, completed in 1986, is named *Metso*, Finnish for wood grouse, the forest bird whose shape its plan resembles and one that cropped up in seminal works of Finnish painting. The forest reference is deliberate, but the attractive combination of copper and granite, both indigenous Finnish raw materials, transcends the gimmick. The library's design was the result of an architectural competition and was the work of the husband-and-wife team of Reima and Raili Pietilä.

STRUGGLING WITH MODERNISM

This relatively new nation, whose cities were also deeply scarred in World War II, has bravely embraced Modernism and tried to make a virtue of it. Not all efforts have been successful, however. The Merihaka estate of apartment blocks near Helsinki's Hakaniemi Square is bleak and heartless, while many

Finlandia Hall at Töölö Bay in Helsinki.

ⓞ ALVAR AALTO

One designer who became a household name in Finnish architecture was Alvar Aalto (1898–1976), who managed to fuse something Finnish with Modernism and revolutionised 20th-century architecture in the process. Aalto was the foundational mover in the struggle to get the principles of modern architecture, and Modernism as a whole, accepted in Finland. Once that was achieved, he then turned his attention to the rest of the world at the Paris Exhibition of 1937 and the New York World Fair of 1939. This was primarily to prove that Finland could contribute internationally to the world of architecture and design.

Aalto saw the building in its entirety as his architectural responsibility, applying his craftsmanship to the furniture and fittings within, as well as to the structure itself. He also practised 'organic' architecture, designing buildings to suit their environment as well as their purpose. Some of his designs (such as the Enso Gutzeit building in Helsinki) appear to be of the archetypal 'concrete block' variety, but, aesthetics aside, they are respected by most people because they were the first to employ nakedly modern materials. More highly regarded is Aalto's Finlandia Hall, the capital's concert and congress complex. Its crisp white profile seems to complement the contours of the park overlooking Töölö Bay, and it's hard to imagine Helsinki without it.

individual buildings in the Sörnäinen district make one wonder quite how Finland earned its reputation for fine architecture.

Nor is there a universal consensus about the virtues of various showpieces which have shot up in central Helsinki over the last few decades. Kiasma, the extraordinary museum of contemporary art designed by American Stephen Holl and opened in 1998 (see page 157), sprawls in metallic asymmetrical splendour behind the statue of the national hero, Field Marshal Mannerheim, and it was this bold contrast – and the choice of an American architect – that was condemned by older Finns. It does, however, provide an ingenious, striking counterpoint to the stolid, humourless Parliament House across the road.

The adjacent glass cube of the Sanoma media group head office is regarded as cold and transparent by some; the stately Finnish National Opera House (designed by Karhunen-Hyvämäki-Parkkinen, 1993), another landmark near Töölö Bay, is sometimes described as a characterless block (see page 155); and some Helsinki residents have sniffed at the striking Kamppi Chapel of Silence (K2S Architects, 2012) for its incongruous appearance and 'inappropriate' external colour. The latter was built during Helsinki's stint as the World Design Capital of 2012, a concept that both recognised the city's creative heritage and saw a proliferation of new projects during the city's tenure.

SUPERB DESIGNS

There is a boldness in the field of design, too. Whatever the object – a tap, a telephone, a bowl, a chair – if its lines are smooth, if it employs modern materials like chrome or plastic with confidence or reinvents glass or wood, and if it fits its purpose perfectly, it is likely to be Finnish. Encouraged, like architecture, by the financial and prestigious carrot of open competitions, everyday items are ceaselessly redesigned and reinvented.

It's an environment that has given rise to the creative spirit of the spiky inventions of internal and industrial designer Stefan Lindfors (born 1962) on the one hand, and the gentle paper jewellery of Janna Syvänoja (born 1960) on the other. Finland's giant names in the plastics (Neste), ceramics (Arabia), textiles (Finlayson, Marimekko), jewellery (Kalevala

Koru, Lapponia) and glass (Iittala, Nuutajärvi) industries periodically introduce pieces by new designers as well as those with established reputations such as Yrjö Kukkapuro, whose contemporary furniture is now displayed in New York's Museum of Modern Art.

Marimekko, specifically, is one of the country's most recognisable names, offering modern interpretations of kitschy, polka-dot styles that are some of the trendiest-looking items in the world today. In fashion, Hannah Sarén's must-have handbags have featured in *Sex and the City*;

Iittala glassware.

while Ivana Helsinki's one-off pieces of clothing, often made using traditional Finnish techniques, have graced the catwalks at the Paris and New York fashion weeks.

A legacy of Alvar Aalto is the Artek design and furniture company set up with his wife Aino, critic Nils-Gustav Hahl and arts patron Maire Gullichsen in the 1930s, which still has a showroom in central Helsinki. The company's designers, working with bold colours and geometric shapes, have created products which are as identifiably Finnish as the traditional handicrafts – woodcarving, rag-rug weaving and tapestry-making. The distinctive and popular Fiskars scissors (Fiskars being a small village in southern Finland and a once-thriving foundry) is one more example of how Finnish design has invaded international consciousness.

> The glass-and-copper Helsinki Music Centre (Musikkitalo; 2011), with its subtle green facade, was designed not to compete with its neighbours. Most of its auditoriums are underground: all the pizzazz is reserved for its concert halls.

Fiskars garden tools.

A TALENT FOR INVENTION

Just to the west of Helsinki, in the neighbouring city of Espoo close to the Helsinki University of Technology, is the Innopoli Building, housing the Foundation for Finnish Inventions. Started in 1971 with backing from the Finnish Ministry of Trade and Industry, the Foundation epitomises Finland's encouragement of the inventive spirit. But this is not a case of inventiveness for its own sake. The Foundation's function is to serve 'as a link between inventors, innovators, consumers, businesses and industry in Finland or other parts of the world'. The Foundation's activities are also a sign of how Finns have recognised the need to diversify their industry. The

staples of pulp and paper and related metals and engineering remain strong, but there is a need to continue looking elsewhere.

Communications and information technology are strong sectors in Finland. Finnish-born but Californian-based Linus Torvalds was the inspiration behind the wildly successful and geek-friendly Linux operating system in the late 1990s. One of the country's most conspicuous and commercially successful companies is Nokia, often mistakenly believed to be of Japanese origin, which takes its name from the small and uneventful town in central Finland where it was founded. Once the world's bestselling mobile phone company, Nokia struggled for a few years even having its mobile phone businessbeing sold to Microsoft. By 2018, Nokia was licensed through HMD Global, another Finnish company, and thriving once again becoming the world's third largest network equipment manufacturer.

And, of course, the *Angry Birds* game took the world by storm, with more than one billion downloads, and eventually becoming a major motion picture. Created by the Finnish mobile game developer Rovio Entertainment, it has given a boost to young Finnish app and game designers, bringing international attention – and money – to the industry.

A BETTER MARGARINE

But Finnish innovation is not confined to electronic technology. It spreads to Benecol, for instance, a margarine shown to decrease blood cholesterol levels. The only problem for the manufacturing company, Raisio, is how to bring the price of this product, a headline-grabber in the fanatically health-conscious USA, down to a level near that of other margarines. The sweetener Xylitol, pioneered in Finland in the late 1970s, is used to flavour chewing gum and confectionery, and has been shown to help prevent tooth decay.

Finns have exploited their maritime heritage to good effect as well: shipbuilding innovations include the Azipod propulsion unit. The Azipod was developed and installed in vessels made at the STX Finland shipbuilders, whose yards in Rauma and Turku have turned out the most advanced icebreakers and the biggest passenger ships in the world.

GLASS AND WOOD

Finland has long been at the cutting edge of modern design, and today's artists sculpting in glass and wood are no exception.

In view of the prominence of its modern glass design, it is surprising that Finland's glassmaking industry dates back only to the late 17th century, when the first glass factory, at Uusikaupunki on the west coast, enjoyed a brief life. Glassmaking was the first design industry to make attempts at breaking away from copies of standard European prototype designs. A turning point was a competition staged by the Riihimäki glass company (named after the southern Finnish town of the same name, today the home of the Finnish Glass Museum) for the design of cocktail glasses. Individual glass designers began to make names for themselves, not least Aino Aalto, who was upstaged by her husband Alvar in 1936 when he contributed his celebrated Savoy vase to the Milan Triennale.

Gunnel Nyman became well known in the following decade for his designs for Iittala, Riihimäki and Nuutajärvi, setting standards which were then equalled and later surpassed by designers such as Tapio Wirkkala (the frosty surface of the Finlandia vodka bottle is thanks to him), Kaj Franck and Timo Sarpaneva. Eero Aarnio and Yrjö Kukkapuro were other notable design innovators of the period.

Their traditions of style and a distinctively Finnish grace have been maintained more recently by the likes of Brita Flander, Vesa Varrela and Heikki Orvola. The Young Finnish Designer of the Year 2012 was the versatile Linda Bergroth, whose works encompass everything from garden sheds to an unusual gavel for the Finnish Parliament. Harri Koskinen, a former winner of the same prize, has done extensive work for Iittala, producing lamps, glass and industrial design work that has garnered international acclaim. Items from Iittala, Pentik and Nuutajärvi's frequently updated glassware ranges have become iconic in Finnish design and make popular and desirable gifts.

Finland has also been exceptionally good at taking its natural resources and utilising them for design purposes. Finland's forests have always been the country's most plentiful and sustainable natural resource, and the traditions of woodcraft were crucial to every aspect of Finnish agrarian life right into the early 20th century, providing shelter, tools and even clothing. The old quarters of Porvoo, 50km (30 miles) to the east of Helsinki (see page 176), and Rauma, on the west coast, preserved since the 17th century (see page 213), contain charming remnants of wooden house-building skills.

Traditional Finnish birch cups called kuksa.

These basic timber patterns used in rural buildings around the country are today preserved in the structure of the country's lakeside log cabins and saunas (see page 222). But wood has also been adapted with characteristic Finnish innovation to everyday functions, most notably with Alvar Aalto's 'bentwood' technique that skilfully moulds birch into laminated fluid curls and curves. Since Aalto's time, other architects have picked up the technique and run with it: Lahti's Sibelius Hall (2000), the Kamppi Chapel of Silence (2012) and the Finnish Nature Centre Haltia (2013) are just some of the most recent buildings to take advantage of its strength, flexibility and acoustic properties. In 2016, Helsinki saw the opening of Löyly, a striking wooden sauna-like building with a restaurant and a waterfront terrace.

The Aarikka gift shops are some of the best places to buy glass and wooden Finnish souvenirs, utensils and jewellery.

MUSIC AND FILM

On the international stage, Finland's artistic heritage has long been associated with Sibelius, but modern classical musicians, rock bands and film directors are keeping the country's arts alive.

When people think of Finnish music, they still think of Jean Sibelius. The great Finnish composer, after all, sprang from a little-known country to become one of the most famous composers of all time – and Finland's most famous export. But there is much more to modern Finnish music than simply Sibelius, and audiences everywhere are starting to recognise this.

CLASSICAL MUSIC

The Society of Finnish Composers today numbers more than 200 members. All have had works performed professionally, and many possess distinguished discographies. Playing their works in Finland are nearly 20 professional orchestras, and many other semi-professional, chamber and other orchestras. Helsinki is home to two symphony orchestras: the Finnish Radio Symphony and the Helsinki Philharmonic, the first permanent orchestra anywhere in the Nordic countries.

Karita Mattila, Finnish operatic soprano.

> Bearing in mind the country's population of just 5.5 million, a startling number of Finnish musicians and orchestras have won both domestic and international acclaim.

Finland takes its music seriously and has proved it through a generous policy of funding for musicians and musical institutes; talented graduates can audition for one of the 15 conservatories, which include the celebrated Sibelius Academy in Helsinki. Finland also sponsors scores of annual music festivals (see page 88) attracting both native and foreign artists.

Finnish instrumentalists have also been winning global attention. Cellists, of whom Finland has an especially strong tradition, have done particularly well. Arto Noras, second-prize winner at the 1966 Tchaikovsky Competition, and Erkki Rautio are renowned virtuosi, as are Anssi Karttunen and Martti Rousi. The brothers Pekka and Jaakko Kuusisto are acclaimed violinists; and both are enthusiastic promoters and directors within Finland's music-festival scene. Classical guitarist Timo Korhonen may be less high profile, but he is often compared to Andrés Segovia. Pianist Ralf Gothoni commands a confirmed place in Europe and further afield, as does pianist and composer Olli Mustonen – 'Finland's Mozart' – who performed his own concerto with the Radio Symphony Orchestra at the age of 12. Esa-Pekka Salonen is the most notable achiever, a principal conductor with an international reputation second only to Sibelius.

After Sibelius and Salonen, however, it is Finland's singers who have gained the most fame. Finland has bred some powerful baritones and basses: Matti Lehtinen in the 1950s, Martti Talvela before his premature death in 1989, and (Finland's equivalent of the Three Tenors) the 'Three Basses' Matti Salminen, Johann Tilli and Jaakko Ryhänen, who occasionally perform together to the delight of Finnish audiences. Nor have sopranos missed out; in the past, Ritva Auvinen, Anita Välkki and Taru Valjakka wooed international audiences. Today, Karita Mattila, is Finland's bestselling classical artist and one of the world's top sopranos (along with fellow Finn, Camila Nylund), and has spent much of her career performing abroad, including stints at the Royal Opera House in London and the Metropolitan Opera in New York.

Although its sopranos have sought fame overseas, the Finnish National Opera has always

Outdoor classical concert in Esplanade Park, Helsinki.

⊘ WANDERING MAESTROS

Talented Finns are often lured abroad, thereby spreading the musical word. Finnish conductors are particularly in demand. Every Nordic capital has had a symphony orchestra with a Finn as principal conductor. The country has many world-class maestros, including Okko Kamu, Esa-Pekka Salonen, the principal conductor of the Philharmonia Orchestra in London, and Sakari Oramo: the chief conductor of the BBC Symphony Orchestra since 2013. The well-loved Leif Segerstam was extremely prolific, both as a conductor and as composer of 327 symphonies. Another famed conductor was Helsinki-born Paavo Berglund, who died in 2012.

punched above its weight. It made operatic history in 1983 as the first foreign company to be invited to perform at New York's Met Opera.

Vocal works have always been the backbone of the Finnish musical tradition, which may, perhaps, explain why about three new Finnish operas are published every year. These operas offer additional proof that Finnish composition, too, lives on beyond Sibelius. Erik Bergman (1911–2006) was one of the modern geniuses of Finnish musical composition, who delighted in combining ancient texts and motifs with avant-garde techniques, and whose influence resonates through the work of younger composers. Magnus Lindberg, Kaija Saariaho, Aulis Sallinen and Einojuhani

Rautavaara (1928–2016) are also of special note. *Le Monde de la Musique* has called Lindberg 'one of the best composers in the world of his age', and he held the position of composer-in-residence at the New York Philharmonic for three seasons, until 2012. He has held the same role at the London Philharmonic Orchestra since 2014.

Even the most recalcitrant sopranos come home for the annual Savonlinna Opera Festival. Held in a 500-year-old castle in July, it is one of the most delightful opera festivals in the world.

POPULAR MUSIC

One of the refreshing aspects of Finnish art generally is its lack of elitism. In music, Finns are especially passionate about heavy rock and metal, the latter splintering into a kaleidoscope of ever more specific subgenres. Although the lines between classical and rock music are well drawn, as they tend to be in most countries, it's not uncommon to find Finland's classical musicians headbanging on an amped-up stage. The internationally recognised band Nightwish has combined heavy rock music with operatic singing, and 'cello metal' band Apocalyptica were originally formed by four classically trained cellists who loved Metallica.

Finnish rock thrives, but on its own terms. While neighbouring Sweden has achieved stellar pop success with bands such as ABBA, The Cardigans and more recently Avicii, Finns take quiet delight in seeing their darker musical exports succeed. These include indie players The Rasmus, who have sold four million albums worldwide; heavy rockers HIM; melodic death metallers Children of Bodom; and – joy of joys – Eurovision Song Contest winners Lordi.

Less well known outside Finland are rockers Eppu Normaali (one of the most popular bands in Finland) and the bluesy J.J. Karjalainen, whose language and style are sufficiently Finnish to restrict them to an exclusively homegrown audience.

Country and western, folk and tango also have their adherents. Kari Tapio was a singer of sentimental country ballads, and is still

Finland's bestselling solo artist years after his death. Nordic folk music tends to be punkier than milder British and US fare: try the sophisticated sound of Värttinä, a group of female singers who perform spine-tingling songs in the Karelian language.

One other aspect of the Finnish music scene which is a true regional phenomenon is the passion for the tango. Tango first arrived from Buenos Aires in the early 20th century, but became truly popular in Finland in the aftermath of World War II, providing the griev-

Tango festival in Seinäjoki, one of the biggest summer festivals in Finland.

ing nation with an outlet for its passion. Unto Munonen composed many of Finland's favourite tango tunes, before committing suicide at the age of 37. One that you'll hear wherever tango is danced in Finland is Satumaa, the quintessential Finnish tango tune. The Tango Festival (www.tangomarkkinat.fi) held in mid-July at Seinäjoki is one of Finland's best-attended summer gatherings, with dancing that continues through the night. Generally, the further north you travel, the louder the music gets. Windy and cold Oulu in northern Finland has the most intense core of rock fans, as well as the only male choir in the world that doesn't even try to sing: Huutajat (literally

'The Shouters'). Dozens of long-haired men in suits and gum ties shout their hearts out in perfect order: Arctic hysteria at its best.

> *Film directors Mika and Aki Kaurismäki have created a body of work that has been seen in 65 countries, won prizes at international festivals and brought the two widespread acclaim, veneration and fame.*

Lights in the Dusk.

FINNS ON FILM

It is the Kaurismäki brothers, Aki and Mika, who are largely to thank for wrenching the Finnish cinema industry to worldwide attention with their rough-edged individuality and prolific output. Contemporary Finnish cinema received little exposure until the advent of the brothers, most notably Aki, who was the youngest director ever to receive a retrospective at the Museum of Modern Art in New York.

Born in Helsinki in 1957, Aki toiled as a postman and film critic before working as a scriptwriter, assistant and actor on his elder brother's 1980 film *Valehtelija (The Liar)*. The following year, the two men formed a production company. They also own a distribution company,

a cinema in downtown Helsinki and were among the founders of the Midnight Sun Festival held each June in Sodankylä, Lapland.

Aki, the better known of the siblings, worked with Mika on the 1983 rock documentary *Saimaa—Ilmiö (The Saimaa Gesture)* before striking out with a freewheeling adaptation of *Crime and Punishment* (1983). A lugubrious figure himself, Aki's films revel in the deadpan humour of morose outsiders desperate to escape the confines of a gloom-ridden country. *Calamari Union* (1985) is an unscripted comedy in which the 17 characters are all called Frank, while *Hamlet Liikemaailmassa (Hamlet Goes Business*; 1987) is a modern-day version of Shakespeare set in a rubber duck factory. Aki then moved his settings from his native land with the Ealing-style comedy *I Hired a Contract Killer* (1990), filmed in London. He went back to his roots with his 'Finland' trilogy *Drifting Clouds, The Man Without a Past* (winner of the Grand Prix at Cannes) and *Lights in the Dusk*. His latest French-language film *Le Havre* (2011) was also acclaimed at Cannes.

Mika, two years older, studied film in Munich and has lived in Brazil since 1992, working in a variety of genres from the road movie *Helsinki Napoli* (1987) to comedies *Cha Cha Cha* (1988) and the *House of Branching Love* (2009). Many of his films, such as *Amazon* (1990), have Brazilian themes.

Flying the Finnish flag in quite a different way is Hollywood action specialist Renny Harlin, director of blockbusters like *Die Hard 2, Cliffhanger*, and *Deep Blue Sea*. Meanwhile, the new millennium has seen a number of cinematic successes, including A.J. Annila's *Sauna*, Kaisa Rastimo's *Myrsky (Stormheart)* and Dome Karukoski's *Tummien perhosten koti (The Home of Dark Butterflies)*, all of which won international awards in 2009. In 2013, Antti Jokinen's film *Purge*, based on the harrowing bestseller by Sofi Oksanen, was doing the film-festival rounds. Foreign directors have also looked to Finland as a setting: for example, the winter landscapes and silent forests give the thriller *Hanna* (2011) an eerie edge. However, one of the most beloved depictions of Finland in any film – foreign or domestic – is Jim Jarmusch's 1991 *Night on Earth*, in which famed actor Matti Pellonpää brings a winter Helsinki to life through his role as poker-faced, late-night taxi driver Mika.

JEAN SIBELIUS

Finland's most famous artist is Jean Sibelius, whose music played a significant role in the formation of the Finnish identity.

It cannot be easy for a man to find himself a figurehead in his country's search for an identity, yet it was this label rather than the simple genius of his music that many Finns tied to their most famous composer, Jean Sibelius (1865–1957), during the years before Finnish independence. His tone poem *Finlandia* in particular became an emblem of everything Finnish, and this aura of reverence must have, at times, irked the composer.

Yet Sibelius did embody many things Finnish; even his ancestry took in areas of Finland as far apart as the coastal town of Loviisa, towards the Russian border, the Swedish influence of Turku, the northwest Gulf of Bothnia and, nearer at hand, Häme province, where he was born.

Though Sibelius's family in Loviisa was wealthy, his father, a well-known doctor, was better known for his medical care than his skills in financial management. When his father died looking after his patients in the typhus epidemic that raged during Finland's last great famine, young Jean's mother, Maria, had little choice but to file for bankruptcy. The family remained in Hämeenlinna. All three children showed musical talent, displaying their concert skills on family visits to Loviisa.

Although it is simplistic to think of Sibelius as being solely influenced by the Finnish landscape, he was undoubtedly part of the late 19th-century movement of artists, writers and intellectuals who turned for inspiration to Finland's land, people and past. Yet, after the first performance of his early *Kullervo* symphony, based on Finnish folklore at the height of the National Romantic movement (see page 76), Sibelius withdrew the work and it was not played again until after his death.

The great Sibelius scholar Erik Tawaststjerna insists that Sibelius moved in the mainstream of European music and was heavily influenced by Beethoven, as well as by Bruckner and Tchaikovsky.

His relationship to Wagner's music could best be described as love-hate.

Sibelius travelled to Bayreuth and Munich in the 1890s and planned an opera, something he did not achieve, though some of its proposed music went into *The Swan of Tuonela*. He wrote his *First Symphony* just before the turn of the 20th century and followed it with the popular *Second* in 1902, at which time he began planning his *Violin Concerto*, now regarded by many as his greatest work. Its first performance in 1904, arranged hurriedly because Sibelius had financial problems, was not a success and it was revised.

Sibelius wrote seven symphonies and many other compositions, including Finlandia.

Not long after, the family moved to Ainola (see page 202), close to the retreat of his friend the artist Pekka Halonen. The site for Ainola (named after his wife Aino) was located by the painter Eero Järnefelt, Aino's brother. Another friend, architect Lars Sonck, designed the house, and Sibelius wrote some 150 works there, including the remaining symphonies. Sibelius lived for 53 years at Ainola until his death in 1957, and the small artistic colony spent much time in one another's houses. To compose, Sibelius needed silence: his children were sent away to friends, while the servants would creep around the house on tiptoe.

Sibelius wrote no music in his final years. Until his death, there were constant rumours of one more symphony, but nothing can have satisfied him. The *Seventh Symphony* was his last.

📷 FINLAND'S SUMMER FESTIVALS

In common with other Nordic countries, Finland has a long tradition of festivals, which make the most of summer nights with music, song and dance.

The soprano Aino Ackté founded Savonlinna Opera Festival in 1912, and its castle backdrop remains one of the most dramatic settings for any music festival. Then came Jyväskylä, an arts festival opened in 1956 by the composer Seppo Nummi – for many years the only one of its kind in the Nordic countries. Celebration of the country's music and culture continues apace. Finland's festivals reel in international audiences, even to remote revelries such as the Kuhmo Chamber Music Festival, which draws 39,000 people to some 70 concerts.

Other arts festivals include Tampere (theatre), Kuopio (dance), Pori (jazz), Lieksa (brass bands), Seinäjoki (tango) and Sodankylä (film).

FOLK FESTIVALS

One source of traditional festivals was the old-time fire brigades, who got together to play music and dance at annual festivals. Some festivals have more sinister roots: in 1643, the Ruovesi Witch Trials condemned Antti Lieronen as 'a witch most obvious and potent' and burnt her at the stake. Today's 'trials' include drama and concerts, but no one is burnt.

Kaustinen is the biggest and oldest folk-music bash in the Nordic countries. Fiddlers also flock to the small-scale Kihaus Folk, with its particular focus on Karelian music and dance.

Soaking up the atmosphere at Qstock, an annual two-day rock festival held at the end of July in Oulu.

On stage at a Finnish music festival.

Folk band at a festival in the Åland Islands.

Pori Jazz Festival.

Rock, jazz and blues festivals

Finland has a broad rock scene, highlighted by a number of summer festivals. Provinssirock, held in Seinäjoki in June, traditionally marks the opening of the rock festival season. As well as the best of the Finns, Provinssirock has attracted big names from abroad, such as the Foo Fighters, Nick Cave, Patti Smith, Tori Amos, Garbage, Nine Inch Nails, Tool and Calvin Harris.

The other huge summer rock festival is Ruisrock in Turku, the second oldest in Finland, which also hosts some of the biggest names; recent guests have included Morrissey, The Cardigans, Ozzy Osbourne, The National, Paramore and Pharrell Williams. Hot on its heels is Helsinki's Flow, with similarly interesting line-ups. For jazz, the best festival in all the Nordic countries is the huge Pori Jazz Festival. Another festival with a family atmosphere is Puisto Blues in Järvenpää, north of Helsinki, at the end of June.

onlinna provides a fabulous setting for its opera tival; in all, the fortress has seen the world premieres o fewer than five operas by Finnish composers.

Founded in 1970, Ruisrock is the oldest rock festival in Finland, and some of the ageing rockers may have been coming here since its inception.

ge bonfires, built up on esides and by the sea, common as part of the lsummer celebrations, erved on the nearest urday to Midsummer , between 20 and June.

Elias Lönnrot, creator of Finland's national epic poem, the Kalevala.

THE WRITER'S DILEMMA

Finnish literature emerged in the 19th century as an embodiment of national character. Today, Finnish writers continue to use writing to understand their world.

Eino Leino, poet, novelist and playwright, wrote of Finnish literature in 1910: 'Literature is the country's interpreter. Literature is the nation's mirror. Without literature the nation is like a blind man, like a deaf mute.'

The story of the past two centuries of Finnish literature is the story of a country struggling to find its voice and its identity. Mimicking Finland's political development, there have been peaks and troughs, high expectations and disappointments. Writers have expressed the fortunes of their country by veering from romanticism to cynicism and realism. The written portrait of the Finn has covered the spectrum from noble hero to drunken buffoon.

A BLANK CANVAS

Until the 19th century, Finland's literary tradition had been primarily an oral one. Because there was no written precedent, writers had a free hand to invent the Finn on paper, and many made him a hero.

Finland's epic poem from the 19th century, the Kalevala, is based on four pairs of syllables on each line, with two or more lines having a synonymous meaning – making it particularly easy to remember and recite.

Johan Ludvig Runeberg (1804–77), Finland's national poet, offered just such a romantic vision of his countrymen. In his three collections of Swedish-language poems, *Dikter I–III (Poems)*, and in his patriotic ballad series, *Fänrik Ståhl Sägner (The Tales of Ensign Ståhl)*, he created loyal, gracious and noble Finns, and they were readily embraced.

Gallén-Kallela's illustrations of the Kalevala.

In the 1820s, Elias Lönnrot (1802–84) began a project that was to generate yet more national pride, and inspire the National Romantic artists and architects who were to follow. Lönnrot travelled through Finland recording folk poetry. The result was the *Kalevala* of 1835 (now commonly called the *Old Kalevala*), a collection of 12,078 verses compiled by Lönnrot into a cohesive whole. After further collecting trips to the eastern border regions, a new, longer version was published in 1849.

The *Kalevala* itself is a heroic epic on the scale of the *Odyssey* or the *Iliad*. But it is also a ragbag of narratives and light interludes, existing to preserve old customs and songs. The narrative is interrupted by poetic 'charms', some of which belong to the realms of Shakespearean comedy. The *Kalevala* managed to include in its poetry a national fiction-cum-history which stretched back to the beginning of time and did not include the humiliating details of real life – such as foreign rule. In Lönnrot's mythical Finland, power lay with the good and the just. Lönnrot's Finn is a participator in the creation of the world.

At the same time as Lönnrot was compiling the *Kalevala*, other Finnish-language writers such as Aleksis Kivi (1834–72) were celebrating rural life, casting the ordinary people in the role of heroes: true Finns leading virtuous lives among the forests, harmonious with nature.

Veijo Meri (1928–2015).

TWENTIETH-CENTURY WORKS

By the early 20th century, real events cast doubts on this unimpeachable national character. Political achievements were quickly soured by subsequent crises. It became the job of writers to make sense of events such as the civil war, which lay heavy on the nation's conscience. Mainstream Finnish writing concerned itself with events in the world at large.

The best-known work of prolific author Mika Waltari (1908–79), *The Egyptian*, has been translated into more than 25 languages. Ostensibly set in ancient Egypt, it is a subtle allegory of World War II. Equally pessimistic, F.E. Sillanpää wrote about rural life and the social struggles of its peasantry, winning the Nobel Prize for literature in 1939 – his books include *Meek Heritage* and *The Maid Silja*.

During this time, Swedish-language writers drifted away from the main pulse of Finnish writing, becoming more isolated, and occasionally more daring. Some, like the poet Edith Södergran (1892–1923), nonetheless enjoyed considerable popularity. Christer Kihlman, author of *Den Blå Modern (The Blue Mother)* and *Dyre Prins (Sweet Prince)*, and Tove Jansson's Moomintroll books, show just how idiosyncratic Swedish-Finnish writing has become.

CONTEMPORARY VOICES

Today, Finnish heroes no longer have to act as vessels for the nation's pride. They are as troubled as the heroes of other literatures. Modern writers like Leena Krohn and Pentti Saarikoski reflect Finnish humanity. Veijo Meri (1928–2015) was seen as a reformer of Finnish prose with his *Manilla Rope*.

Other authors, meanwhile, draw on the new diversity of Finland and its people for inspiration. Prominent recent authors include Johanna Sinisalo, Kjell Westö, Ilkka Remes, Leena Lehtolainen, Leena Parkkinen, Hannu Raittila, Asko Sahlberg, as well as Ranya El Ramly, Johan Bargum, Margaretha Hupa and Rakel Liehu. While their interpretations may have diverged from the 'classic' notion of what it means to be Finnish, they are making the cultural heritage of Finland richer and more complex.

MODERN WORKS IN TRANSLATION

Although Finns are great readers, with the second-highest number of books published per capita in the world, many Finnish works remain in their original language, inaccessible to the outsider. However, the books of bestselling author Arto Paasilinna have been translated into 39 languages, the most famous of which is *The Year of the Hare* (1975), the surreal tale of a journalist who heads into the Finnish wilderness carrying a wounded young hare.

Those with a strong stomach could try *Purge* (2010), by Finnish-Estonian writer Sofi Oksanen, which won the European Book Prize and the Nordic Council Literature Prize. Another author who has won the latter prize is Kari Hotakainen: his winning title *(Juoksuhaudantie)* is not available in translation, but his later book, *The Human Part*, is an equally spiky and satirical work about Finnish manhood and the state of the modern world. Another noteworthy author is Laura Lindstedt, who won the prestigious Finlandia Prize in 2015 for her *Oneiron*, an engrossing novel about a group of women who meet to discuss their lives... after their deaths.

THE MOOMINS

Tove Jansson's eccentric Moomin family – with its quirky bohemian characters – struck a chord with readers all over the world.

At first sight Tove Jansson's Moomin books seem like storybooks to buy as gifts for children. But the mystical fairy-tale world of mighty nature and ever-changing seasons inspires even diehard realists.

TOVE JANSSON

Tove Jansson (1914–2001) was born to an artistic family – both her brothers were artists and writers. A diminutive Swedish-speaking woman, meek to the point of humility, Jansson lived much of her life in seclusion with her partner on a small island off Finland's southern coast. Here Jansson created another world, just as C.S. Lewis and J.R.R. Tolkien did in their books.

And like the works of Lewis and Tolkien, Moomin books appeal to both children and adults. Younger readers may be more attracted to the books' imaginary worlds and illustrations, while older readers enjoy Jansson's basic philosophy of acceptance, a quest for space and solitude.

MOOMIN CHARACTERS

The books are all led by the Moomin family characters. The bohemian Moominmamma takes care of everything, while Moominpappa is a philosopher, who writes his memoirs and becomes active only when it's time to explore the unknown. The Moomin house is always open to adopted children and any strange creature that appears on the doorstep. Love and tolerance reign; difference is always accepted. There are no wars, and nothing threatens the idyll except natural phenomena.

Each character is a sensitively illustrated personality, so every reader will identify with at least one of them. Moomintroll is perhaps Tove Jansson's own alter ego, along with tinges of Snufkin, a world traveller who prefers wandering alone. Little My is an adventurous girl, with no patience and not much

of a moral compass. Fillyjonk is a neurotic pedant, the Hemulen an absent-minded botanist, and the Snork Maiden just a little vain. The strange, worm-like electric creatures Hattifatteners represent foreigners, with whom communication is possible if not easy; and the monstrous Groke, who freezes the ground wherever she walks, is a personification of winter – or perhaps loneliness, depending on your perspective. The Moomin life pauses for hibernation when the winter comes, and is reborn at the thaw when Snufkin returns from his world travels, except when the magical winter is brought to life in *Moominland Midwinter*.

The Moominworld theme park near Turku recreates favourite Moomin characters.

These unpretentious little books have conquered the world, having been translated into 45 languages. The Japanese love the Moomin figures; Finnair has had Moomin figures painted on planes flying to Japan, and Finnair's flight attendants sell enormous quantities of Moomin paraphernalia to travellers. (Be aware that the commercialised Moomins are not always entirely faithful to the originals.)

MOOMINWORLD

Though Jansson's world was based around the village at Pellinki, south of Porvoo, a modern Moominworld theme park (www.muumimaailma.fi) recreates the stories at Naantali, near Turku, and a small museum celebrates the family and their creator in Tampere.

FINNS WHO SPEAK SWEDISH

Finland is officially bilingual, using both Finnish and Swedish, a tradition that goes back centuries between these two neighbouring countries.

'Why do so many Finns speak Swedish?' is a question that is often asked by visitors. The main reason is that for more than 600 years, Finland was a part of Sweden. In that time, the Finnish language had no official status: Swedish was the language used in government, education and for cultural works, and many Finns adopted the Swedish tongue to survive in society. The great-grandchildren of some of these early Finns still use Swedish, the language having been passed down the generations.

EARLY SWEDISH SETTLERS

The earliest inhabitants of the Åland Islands and many other coastal communities were Scandinavian settlers, adventurers and fishermen, who brought their language with them. Many who still live on these islands speak a unique Swedish dialect which may be difficult to understand, even by Swedish tourists.

As Finland was a lucrative territory, many Swedes also emigrated, mostly to Nyland ('New Land') and Osterbotten. Some came as industrialists and founded factories and sawmills. Many of these ancient communities remain, including the cardboard factory in Verla, now a Unesco World Heritage site.

THE MILITARY'S ROLE

The military also played a major role in the Swedish 'takeover'. In many cases, successful soldiers in the Royal Swedish Army were granted privileges in Finland, such as territory and tax-free status, which brought a Swedish upper class to many previously remote regions of Finland.

As Swedish became the *lingua franca* in large towns such as Turku, Helsinki and Vyborg, many German, Jewish and Russian burghers

Turku architecture.

living in these areas adopted Swedish, and this usage remains today.

A BILINGUAL NATION

Swedish-speaking Finns, or Finland-Swedes as they are described by the government, are not immigrants, nor are they Swedes. They may not even have any family connections with Sweden.

When Finland is described as a 'bilingual' nation, it means that the two languages are given an official status, very much the same as English and French in Canada – one may assume the right to use either Swedish or Finnish at offices or even in shops in 'bilingual' towns. However, this is not always successful – in some cases Finns have to resort to English in order to understand each other.

LINGUISTIC ROOTS

Swedish-speakers are a reminder of the 600-or-so years when Finland was the eastern part of the Kingdom of Sweden. At that time, and even during the time when Finland was a Grand Duchy of Russia, from 1809 to independence in 1917, Swedish was the official language, the language of the civil service, of the law, of higher education, at the University of Turku (Åbo in Swedish), and of the monied classes.

Fed by students from Turku University, Finnish cultural life was dominated by Swedish-speakers too. It was not until 1828 that the university established a Finnish language lectureship, and not until 1850 that a professorship of Finnish was introduced.

Because the Swedish language held sway in this way, it was the principal language of the nascent Finnish mid-19th-century cultural and political life. Early political activists like the Fennomen, who supported the Finnish language and campaigned for its recognition as an official language, often faced the paradox that they were Swedish-speakers whose love

The League of Nations meets to decide the fate of the Åland Islands' status in 1921.

⊘ SWEDISH-SPEAKING WRITERS

The compiler of the epic poem the *Kalevala*, Elias Lönnrot (1802–84), was born in Nyland in southwest Finland and has a Swedish name. Yet he was a great champion of the Finnish language and folklore and went on to become Professor of Finnish at Helsinki University. He also produced a Swedish–Finnish dictionary, which is credited with establishing a Finnish literary language. Johan Ludvig Runeberg (1804–77) taught at the Porvoo University for 20 years. The opening words of his Swedish-language *Fänrik Ståhl Sägner (Tales of Ensign Ståhl)* became Finland's national anthem (*Vårt Land, or Maamme in Finnish*).

of their country was paramount. A number of 19th-century cultural ambassadors, painters and writers, who searched determinedly for an artistic expression of Finnish nationalism, were also Swedish-speakers.

OFFICIAL STATUS

Thanks to the growing nationalist movement, the Finnish language achieved official status in 1863, and thereafter began to dominate in public life. When Finland gained its independence, the 1919 Constitution decreed that Finland should have two official national languages: Finnish and Swedish. At that time, Swedish-speakers accounted for 12 percent of the Finnish population (today, the figure has shrunk to 5.4 percent).

But political disputes over the two languages and their relative prominence flared up from time to time, especially in the 1920s and 1930s, when it became a central political issue. Accusations that Finland-Swedes were wealthier or disproportionately powerful have rumbled on over the decades.

WHERE DO SWEDISH-SPEAKERS LIVE?

Swedish-speakers are very much spread out around the country. About half of them live in purely Swedish regions in Nyland, around Turku,

Swedish spoken in Finland is not identical to that of Sweden. Many local dialect words which have their roots in Finnish are included in Finland's Swedish, and the language maintains a very distinct accent.

and by 2019, the number had decreased to 10. Finland-Swedes have a choice of papers from either Sweden or Finland. Daily papers from

Swedish Ålanders enjoying a summer's day.

on Åland and on the west coast. Regional centres, such as Ekenäs (Tammisaari in Finnish), Borgå (Porvoo) and Jakobstad (Pietarsaari) have their indigenous Swedish culture, and larger towns such as Åbo (Turku), Vasa (Vaasa) or the capital Helsinki (which Swedish-speakers call Helsingfors, actually the city's original name) are home to about half of the Swedish-speakers.

A DECREASING POPULATION

The population of Finland-Swedes is decreasing; as of 2017 it was around 286,700, or 5.2 percent of the country's total population. In 1960, there were 21 Swedish-language newspapers (compared to 182 Finnish publications); in 1988, the figure was 14 (with 374 Finnish publications),

large publishers in Stockholm are always available in Finland's Swedish-speaking centres, and Sweden's culture, politics and daily gossip is popular among Finland-Swedes.

MINORITY POLICY

In fact, Finland has been dubbed a model for minority policy. The government spends a significant amount of money per capita on Swedish radio and TV programmes, and the largest Swedish daily in Finland, *Hufvudstadsbladet*, manages a circulation of almost 37,000, which means one paper for every eight Swedish-speakers. As a comparison, Wales has no daily newspaper in the Welsh language – a language that is spoken by 19 percent of its population.

The situation does not please all Finnish-speaking Finns, however. Their Swedish-speaking countrymen have sometimes been accused of being the world's most pampered minority. Mandatory Swedish lessons in schools are a source of friction, particularly when election time swings around and the more right-wing parties take up cudgels. Some believe the lesson time would be better spent learning English or Russian; while others are happy to learn Swedish, viewing it as a gateway language for Finns who want to live, study and work in Sweden, Den-

The official language in the Åland Islands is Swedish.

mark, Norway and Iceland. It is a long-running debate, and one that will not be resolved soon.

It's not easy being a Swedish-speaker in a predominantly Finnish-speaking area either. Although the Language Act makes both languages equal in law, in practice, where there are few Swedish-speakers, services tend to be provided in Finnish only.

A UNIQUE SITUATION

This is not a problem in the case of the Åland Islands (see page 205), which lie off the southwest of Finland almost halfway to Sweden. Though this is Finnish territory, the roles are reversed. When Finland became independent in 1917, the Ålanders' background and culture

were (and are) more clearly Swedish and they voted overwhelmingly in a referendum to become part of Sweden. After much wrangling, the matter went to the infant League of Nations in the early 1920s, which managed to complicate matters by deciding that the Åland Islands would remain Finnish but that the islanders' use of the Swedish language would be safeguarded.

The official, legal language, therefore, is Swedish. However, the 29,500 residents consider themselves to be autonomous from the government of Finland, with their own flag and postage stamps. The Ålanders have their own parliament and government to run their internal affairs, using a proportion of the Finnish budget. They also send a member to the main parliament in Helsinki.

As part of Sweden, Ålanders would be 'normal' citizens; as part of Finland, however, they may retain their 'special' status. Åland became even more of a special case on 1 July 1999, when tax-free sales were banned within inter-EU travel. Åland is 'outside' the Union, however, and some ferries between Finland and Sweden stop briefly at the Långnäs pier to take advantage of the popular tax-free sales.

POLITICAL REPRESENTATION

The main political party representing mainland Finland-Swedes, the Swedish People's Party (SFP), was founded in 1906. The SFP got 4.9 percent of the vote in the 2015 elections, which translates to nine of the 200 parliamentary seats. In spite of its small size, the nature of Finnish politics (post-vote negotiations as to who should enter government) means that the SFP has frequently wielded cabinet-level power within coalition governments. In the 2019 elections the SFP received 4.53 percent of votes, retaining all their seats, and entered negotiations with Antti Rinne of the Social Democratic Party to join the coalition and form part of the government. .

THE FINLAND-SWEDE VIEW

Talk to Finland-Swedes about the problems of being a linguistic minority and you may end up in a fascinating conversation lasting several hours – both on the complications of being able to express oneself fully in two languages and on the advantages of hailing from a cultural background comprising three different societies: Sweden, Finnish Finland and Swedish Finland.

IMMIGRANTS

In Finland, immigration is less of a political hot potato than it is in other Nordic countries.

Increased industrialisation and a shortage of labour in the 1950s saw the first immigrants arrive in Sweden, Denmark and Norway. They initially received a warm welcome, but the tide has turned and today anti-immigrant rhetoric is increasingly finding willing ears, revealing a rather dark side to Scandinavian society.

The situation in Finland is somewhat different. In the 1950s, Finns themselves emigrated to Sweden as 'guest workers'. Few migrants came to Finland: the country, which only finished paying off its war reparations in 1952, was not an attractive prospect. Over the past 60 years, Finland's transformation from a primarily agriculture-based society into a competitive, technologically advanced information society has made the country a little more inviting. These days, 5 percent of the population were born abroad or speak a foreign language (other than Swedish); but this still does not compare to Sweden, where 19 percent are foreigners.

Immigrants may not receive the warmest welcome, but many Finns accept that foreign labour is required to keep the service sector ticking over and pay taxes, particularly bearing in mind Finland's ageing population. All other major European countries have a far-right, anti-immigration political party. In Finland, the Finns Party (formerly the True Finns), founded in 1995, inject nationalism into most of their policies and seek to restrict immigration, but stop short of the hate-filled hyperbole of many far-right groups.

ETHNIC MAKE-UP

The biggest influx of foreigners occurred soon after the Soviet downfall, when Russia's borders opened up, allowing freer movement in this region. Russians (69,000) and Estonians (46,000) now constitute the largest ethnic groups in Finland and many have taken Finnish citizenship. Among Asians, Chinese (10,000) and Thai (8,000) people form the largest ethnic groups.

A small proportion of Finland's foreigners arrive here as refugees. Government policy allows for a set 'quota' of refugees, based on UN guidelines, fixed in 2014 and 2015 at 1,050 per year. Forced migrants have included Vietnamese boat people, and refugees from Pinochet's Chile and from Iraq. Although the number of asylum-seekers arriving in Finland increased tenfold from 3,600 in 2014 to over 30,000 in 2015, the majority being Iraqis. By 2017, the number was back down to 2,476 and the country continues to have one of the lowest percentages of non-European immigrants in Europe.

Although racism in Finland is not prevalent, it flared up when the first Somali refugees arrived in 1990. The small town of Joensuu became notorious for a 'skinhead' gang who terrorised foreigners. Thankfully racism has cooled since then, with organisations like the Finnish Somali Association helping to forge understanding.

Teenagers of African origin walking in Vaasa.

Unemployment among refugees tends to be high, sometimes due to xenophobic attitudes, partly because most employers require employees to speak fluent Finnish. Loneliness and isolation are also factors: some refugees are settled in tiny towns where contact with locals is practically non-existent. Interestingly, in 2016, thousands of Iraqi immigrants who had arrived in Finland only the year before, cancelled their asylum applications and returned to Iraq.

All these issues notwithstanding, many immigrants still choose to live in Finland: some may fall in love with a Finn, others appreciate the country's generous social security schemes and high standard of living. There are now approximately 370,000 immigrants in Finland, and many more who have been granted Finnish citizenship.

Sami reindeer herder.

THE SAMI AND THEIR LAND

The Sami of north Finland have a distinct culture that remains an emblematic example of the struggle of traditional peoples as they move towards modernisation.

For the Sami (Lapps), who, generally speaking, prefer to mind their own business and hope other people will mind theirs, modernisation has brought mixed blessings, putting pressure on a fragile social structure and an ecosystem already under threat. However, the many recent changes in the Samis' world have also triggered a much greater awareness of their own identity.

EARLY DEVELOPMENT

Most academics agree that the Sami descend from a people who, following the retreating edge of the continental ice, reached Finland and East Karelia from the Ural Mountains in the last millennia BC.

The cornerstone of early Sami society was the *siida*, a community of several families and the territories in which they cooperatively hunted, trapped and fished. Place names in southern and central Finland suggest that Sami communities thrived here until the Middle Ages. But as the Finnish settlers moved in, so the Sami – those who were not assimilated – moved on, ever northwards. In Finland today there are about 9,000 Finnish Sami, concentrated in northern Lapland around Utsjoki, Karasjoki, Inari and Enontekiö (see page 260); this is roughly 12 percent of the total number of Sami, who live across the far northern parts of Norway, Sweden, Finland and the Kola Peninsula.

LAND OF THE MIDNIGHT SUN

The Sami home in Lapland (Lappi) is Finland's northernmost province and covers nearly a third of the country's total area, most of it north of the Arctic Circle. Away from the few towns and scattered communities, its extraordinary beauty is still predominantly primeval wilderness.

Sami handicrafts.

Extensive swamps and forests of conifer and birch rise in the far north to bareheaded fells, the highest topping 1,300 metres (4,270ft); all this is laced by swift rivers and streams and punctuated by lakes and pools.

You may think of it as the land of the midnight sun, which, depending on latitude (and cloud cover), is visible for up to 70 summer days. In winter there is an almost equivalent sunless period, tempered at times by the flickering veils of the Northern Lights or, around midday, by the lingering dawn effects from the invisible sun or the inescapable, all-pervading whiteness of the snow. Spring is a swift green renaissance in the wake of the big thaw. And autumn flares in colours so spectacular the Finns have a special term for it: *ruska*.

You may also think of it as the land of the Lapps. They, however, prefer their own name for themselves: Sami (pronounced 'Sah-mi'), a preference which is now respected, revered and very much protected.

SOCIETY AND SPIRIT

The nomadism associated with the Sami people of Norway and Sweden has never been so widely practised among the predominantly Forest Sami of Finland's Lapland and, gradually, an economy based on hunting and fishing evolved into one dominated by reindeer husbandry as the wild herds once vigorously hunted were semi-domesticated. Early on, many Sami adopted the more settled life of the Finns, keeping a few cattle and tilling scraps of soil to grow oats and potato, the only viable crops in these latitudes. In reverse, many Finns have opted for the reindeer economy.

Integral to early Sami culture were the shamanist beliefs rooted in the power of nature. Everything, it was believed, living or inanimate, had a soul and the spiritual world was as real

Reindeer round-up at Vuotso, Lapland.

⊘ SAMI WORDS AND MUSIC

The religious missions that came to Lapland to convert the Sami not only brought the influence of God, they also brought education. However, the Sami already had a rich oral tradition that ensured a wealth of tales and legends as well as centuries of acquired wisdom passed through the generations. There was also their simple brand of pictorial art. Very special to Sami culture is the *yoik*, a kind of yodelling chant, each a unique tribute to an event, landscape, emotion or person. Mari Boine Persen, a Sami based in Norway, is famous for having brought the *yoik* to the masses in a series of genre-breaking albums. Finland's most famous *yoiker* is Wimme Saari, with six solo albums

and two critically acclaimed collaborations with Swedish folk-rock trio Hedningarna.

Sami culture has always lacked early written sources, and the first books in Sami were all of a religious nature. Later, with education, came grammar books and diction-aries and, finally, though not until well into the 20th cen-tury, the beginnings of a Sami literature. Nils-Aslak Välkeapää (1943–2001) was one of the most fervent spokespersons for Sami art and culture and was himself a poet, composer, yoiker and painter. His epic poem *Beaivi, áhčážan* (The Sun, My Father) traces the history and culture of the Sami people, and won the Nordic Council's literature prize in 1991.

as the material one. The wise man *(noaide)* was skilled in crossing one world to the other, achieving a state of ecstasy with his magic drum and entering the spirit world.

CHRISTIAN INFLUENCE

Religious missions made every effort to discourage such goings-on. Shamanism survived well into the 19th century, but drum-burning and many other deterrents led to the old gods giving way to Christian worship. Today many of the brightest events on the Lapland calendar are associated with Church festivals – notably Lady Day and Easter: popular times for Sami weddings, lasso competitions, reindeer races and get-togethers for dispersed families.

MODERNISATION

The rebuilding programme following the devastation of World War II marked the beginning of changes that have altered Lapland for ever. Since 1945, Lapland's population has soared to 180,000 (predominantly Finns), though in an area of nearly 100,000 sq km (38,600 sq miles) this is hardly overcrowded: the population density is just 2 people per square kilometre.

The administrative capital of Rovaniemi has been virtually rebuilt and expanded to take in a satellite sprawl of light industry. A network of new and improved roads penetrates regions accessible a few decades ago only by foot or ski. Rivers, notably the Kemi, have been tamed for their hydroelectric power. And a trickle of visitors has grown into a steady stream, spawning a whole range of facilities. Perhaps most importantly, the introduction of snowmobiles and motorbikes into Sami culture has for ever altered Sami patterns of settlement and nomadism, as well as the day-to-day lives of families and individual herders.

SAMI ORGANISATION

Organisations dedicated to Sami interests go back to the turn of the 20th century, but their efforts were only officially coordinated in 1956, when the Nordic Sami Council was founded to 'promote cooperation on Sami issues between Finland, Norway and Sweden'. In 1973 Finland's Sami population acquired an assembly, which evolved in 1996 into the Sami Parliament (Sámediggi), based in Inari. It has

no legislative mandate, but its 21 representatives, elected every four years, are concerned with cultural self-government, with working groups focusing on the Sami language, education, social care and the erosion of age-old territory rights in northern Lapland. One may regret the adulteration of a culture under pressure, but people outside Finland have already begun to see the enriching potential emerging from the melding of the Sami's ancient culture with innovative modern ways of life.

A man wearing traditional Sami dress.

⊙ A VERSATILE BEAST

The docile reindeer means much more to the Sami than a meal on four legs: its skin has contributed to bedding and winter clothing, its antlers and bones have been the raw materials for tools and utensils. It has also provided a major means of transport, sledge-hauling across the winter snows, only recently ousted by the noisy, motorised skidoo. Even now, the annual cycle of the reindeer – rutting, herding, separating, slaughtering, calving, marking – moulds the north Lapland calendar. The winter round-ups are among Europe's most colourful events, resembling scenes from a Wild West film transposed to an Arctic setting.

Finns excel at the World Rally Championships.

FROM FLYING FINNS TO FORMULA ONE

A strong physique and a determined nature have combined to make Finns a force to be reckoned with in the world of national and international sports.

Later on in his life, when asked about the relationship between Finnish independence and the performance of Finnish athletes in the early part of the 20th century, the great Finnish runner Paavo Nurmi commented: 'The higher the standard of living in a country, the weaker the results often are in the events which call for work and effort. I would like to warn this new generation: do not let the comfortable life make you lazy!'

Despite their prosperity, Finns have managed to perform remarkably well in sport and achieve international reputations since Nurmi. In football, Finnish players such as FC Copenhagen's goalie Jesse Joronen and Werder Bremen centre-back Niklas Moisander follow the trail blazed by Sami Hyypiä and Jari Litmanen, widely considered to be Finland's all-time best. Ice hockey tops even football for popularity in Finland, and many Finns play professionally in the North American NHL, including Mikko Koivu, captain of the Minnesota Wild, Mikko Rantanen, Patrik Laine and living legend, Teemu Selänne.

Alpine skier Andreas Romar.

START THEM YOUNG

The Finnish sporting tradition is ingrained in every child from the moment he or she is put on skis at the age of two. In the centuries before motorised vehicles, Finns often invented athletic ways to get across their great distances and traverse their vast forests and lakes. The best known was the church boat race, a rowing competition between villagers to see who would arrive at church first.

Sport was associated with religion at other times of the year, too. At Easter, there were competitions in tug-of-war and high and long jumping, while Christmas was the time for shows of strength by weightlifters and plough-pullers. Finland has, by virtue of its landscape, always produced a healthy crop of cross-country skiers. Even now, cross-country skiing is as much a form of transport as it is an enjoyable winter pastime. Visit Finland and you will be both amazed and impressed by the number of skiers either Nordic walking or practising on roller skis throughout summer, keeping in trim for when the snow falls again.

A snow tunnel in Vuokatti sports centre, not far from Kajaani, enables skiers to practise in a realistic environment while other people enjoy the few hot summer days.

MOTOR RACING

Finns have won 14 World Rally Championships since the competition began, with Tommi

Mäkinen, Juha Kankkunen and Marcus Grönholm dominating the sport – at least, until the appearance of French driver Sébastien Loeb! Finns have also had some success in Formula One racing, with Mika Häkkinen crowned World Champion in 1998 and 1999. His prodigious compatriot Kimi Räikkönen became the highest-paid driver in motor sport, with an estimated salary of US$51 million per year, and secured his first Formula One World Drivers' Championship in 2007. After taking a couple of years' break from Formula One, Räikkönen returned in 2012 for a two-year stint with Lotus, then returned to Ferrari (2014 to 2018) before joining Alfa Romeo for the 2019 season. Valtteri Bottas is also prominent on the F1 scene driving for Mercedes.

No one has satisfactorily explained why Finns should excel in this particular field, but the answers perhaps apply to all successful Finnish athletes: the fact that Finns come from a quiet northerly country that feels a need to make its mark on the world must have something to do with it. Another reason is, of course, the landscape: anyone who can orientate himself or herself in

Finnish ice hockey fans.

⊘ FINLAND AND THE OLYMPICS

Outstanding performance in sport is a point of national pride which dates at least as far back as the Stockholm Olympics of 1912 (the last to be held before World War I), when Finland was still part of Russia. During those games, the Finnish medal winners far outstripped the Russian winners, gaining 23 medals against the Russians' three, although officially Finland and Russia were competing under the same flag. At the 1912 Games, the Finnish competitors dared to raise a Finnish flag at the medal ceremonies, the first sign that the yearning for Finnish independence was not to be taken lightly. Five years later, Finland had become an independent republic. On an understandable high, the Finns won 34 medals in 1920,

and an all-time best of 37 medals at the 1924 Paris Games.

With so many medals in the bag, Finland began to dream of hosting the Olympics. World War II meant the plans had to be put on hold. Finally, in 1952, the dream came true when the Games came to Helsinki, with Paavo Nurmi himself lighting the torch.

Since then, Finland's medal performance has dropped off disappointingly. The country fared best at Sydney 2000, taking two golds – with Arsi Harju (shot put) and Thomas Johansson and Jyrki Järvi (49er-class sailing) being propelled into the national spotlight. One silver and two bronzes were the total spoils of London 2012 down to just one bronze medal at the Rio 2016 games.

the Finnish wilderness already has a strong, built-in sense of navigation (which comes in useful in the more circuitous rally routes) and may, so the theory goes, have an advantage over someone who comes from a less rugged country.

Finally, one must look beyond the physical features of the country and examine the Finnish personality. There is one feature of the Finnish character which the Finns themselves call *sisu*, a quality so central to their being as to make a dictionary definition nearly impossible. Roughly speaking, the word conjures up an enigmati-

But the Finnish runner whose name has been famous for most of the last century was just under competition age in 1912: Paavo Nurmi

> *Take any group of rally drivers – men and women who drive their cars into a pulp through forest, desert and farm tracks – and among them you are likely to find a puzzlingly high number of Finns.*

Finland's Hannes Kolehmainen crosses the finish line to win the 5,000 metres in the 1912 Stockholm Olympic Games.

cally tough, independent personality. Hand in hand with the toughness is a determined staying power, even under the most adverse conditions.

Sisu has played its role not only in sporting achievement but in Finland's most important pursuit: independence itself. From the republic's very early days – in fact, even before Finnish independence – sport and freedom were inseparably intertwined.

LONG-DISTANCE RUNNERS

As proof of his durability, Jalmari Kivenheimo was still running every day even after his 100th birthday in 1989 (he died five years later). His more famous running mate, Hannes Kolehmainen, won gold in the 1912 Olympics.

(1897–1973). A multiple world record-breaker and medal-winner (with four gold medals), Nurmi first competed in the 1920 Olympics. Variously known as the Flying Finn, the Phantom Finn and the Phenomenal Finn, he is still remembered for his extraordinary running style, speed and tough character.

Nurmi had running in his blood. Although his father, a religious man, did not approve of running, believing it to be a frivolous pastime, Nurmi exerted his independence and spent every spare moment running with boys in his neighbourhood. He ran in competitions at school, and also alone in the woods. It's been suggested that sports competition between Finnish-speaking Finns and Swedish-speaking

Finns was particularly keen in Turku, Nurmi's home town in southwest and heavily Swedish-speaking Finland (see page 179), which may have further fired his ambition. If indeed some of

> *Finland's vast network of lakes frozen into ice for much of the winter means that virtually all Finnish children grow up as comfortable on ice skates as in shoes.*

Nurmi's determination was spurred on by local ethnic competition, it is interesting to note that later, according to his biographer, 'no ambassador could have been more effective than Nurmi' in attracting positive international attention and even investment to the fledgling Finnish republic while it struggled to build a cohesive identity.

SNOW AND ICE

Not surprisingly, skiing is one of the top sports in Finland, and the sport most readily associated with this snow-covered nation. Along with its

Swamp soccer.

⊘ TOP TEN ODD FINNISH SPORTS

For all its reserve, Finland has some of the quirkiest sporting competitions in the world:
Ant-nest sitting; various locations
Air guitar world championships; Oulu
Berry-picking championships; Suomussalmi
Ice-swimming events; various locations
Mosquito-swatting championships; Lapland
Rubber-boot throwing; Savo
Kick-sledding world championships; Multia
Swamp soccer championships; Hyrynsalmi
Wife-carrying championships; Sonkajärvi
Mobile-phone throwing championships; Savonlinna

Scandinavian neighbours, Finland has produced champion cross-country and downhill skiers, who benefit from an extended winter season in which to perfect their skills.

But skiing is not the only winter sport in which the nation excels. Ice hockey is the most-watched sport in Finland, both on television and live at the rinks. Almost all males participate at school, and the elite are filtered through and chosen for the best teams. Finland has an astonishing 60,000 officially registered federation players, and its national team is one of the International Ice Hockey Federation's 'big seven'. Many Finns play in the North American NHL and many foreigners play in Finnish teams as well.

Ice hockey is also highly commercialised and commands large numbers of spectators. The SM-liiga is the top professional league in Finland, with 15 teams competing for the cup. Recent seasons have seen a dramatic shake-up in the league's make-up with Jokerit moving to the KHL, the Espoo Blues going bankrupt, and the promotion of 3 teams (Sport, KooKoo, and Jukurit).

The rivalry between the country's three biggest cities is nothing compared to that between Finland and Sweden. Excitement reached fever pitch during the 2011 IIHF World Cup, when the two teams went head-to-head in the final, and Finland triumphed with a very decisive 6–1 win.

TRACK AND FIELD

The game of *pesäpallo* is a Finnish version of American baseball, first developed by Tahko Pihkala. *Pesäpallo* soon became a 'national' hobby, especially in rural Finland. The best teams now participate in the national Super Pesis League, which is well organised and has become increasingly commercial.

Finns also consider athletics as one of the most 'Finnish' of all sports. 'The Flying Finn' was a common nickname given to Finnish middle- and long-distance runners in the previous century. In addition to Paavo Nurmi's legendary performances, long-distance running flourished in the 1970s when men like Lasse Viren, Juha Väätäinen and Olavi Suomalainen, epitomes of *sisu*, wiped the floor with the competition. Today, sports fields are available for schoolchildren and individuals in every town and village; local governments finance these facilities and the use of equipment is free; and it can surely be only a matter of time before the next batch of athletes emerges.

In the meantime, Finland has had great success in some more unusual sports. Orienteering is a popular occupation in Finland, and Minna Kauppi is one of the sport's heroes. Ranked number two in the world, she has won a total of nine golds, four silvers and three bronzes in the World Orienteering Championships (WOC). Satu Mäkelä-Nummela came first in the women's trap shooting event at the 2008 Summer Olympics.

Although summer sports are not generally associated with Finland, the golf scene has boomed in the last decade. For such a large country, 141 golf clubs may not seem a great number nationwide, but the wealthy Greater Helsinki area has nineteen courses alone. While the summer golf season (May to early October) is relatively short, the smart Rovaniemi enthusiasts will even play golf on ice in winter.

SPORT AND SCANDALS

Joy turned to national shame during the World Skiing Championships in Lahti in 2001, when six Finnish skiers in the cross-country disciplines, including stars such as Mika Myllylä and Harri Kirvesniemi, failed doping tests. Both the men's and women's teams were affected, and

A game of pesäpallo, similar to baseball and considered to be Finland's national sport.

the national mood afterwards was unbelievably sombre. The fact that cross-country skiing plays such a central part in the national psyche, and that Finland is one of the world leaders in the battle against drug cheats, made the shame even greater.

Yet sport continues to dominate even the top level of Finnish society: former presidents Kekkonen, Koivisto and Halonen enjoyed cross-country skiing, volleyball and swimming respectively, former prime minister Paavo Lipponen was an exceptional water polo player in his youth, while Mari Kiviniemi, Finland's second female prime minister, is a keen runner. Who said Finns don't take their sports seriously?

The best way to smoke salmon.

FOOD AND DRINK

Finnish cuisine makes fine use of native ingredients, such as fish and game, washed down by locally brewed beer or strong coffee.

Finland is a land of forests and lakes with abundant possibilities for fine dining. Take the trees – Finns have finally found edible substances in each variety: birch gives Xylitol, a sweetener very kind to teeth; spruce spring shoots are used to make sweet jam, a delicacy served with desserts; pine is a good source of tar, an aromatic substance extracted from the tree in traditional tar-burning pits. The light tar has a soothing aroma, used in Finnish sweets and ice cream. Pine is also raw material for the Finnish-invented Benecol margarine-style spread that has been found to have cholesterol-lowering qualities.

> The changing seasons, endless daylight in summer, deep forests, thousands of lakes and unpolluted environment all help Finland to produce interesting culinary delights.

UNUSUAL VARIETIES

Finnish food is as innovative as Xylitol or Benecol demonstrate – the years of agricultural conformity are over. Be it ostrich farms, strawberry wineries or herb producers, Finnish food is becoming more varied by the day – Finnish restaurants are reinventing the cuisine they serve all across the country – especially in the capital – and rarities such as bear meat or unusual fungi can be found more regularly on menus. Herbs are pleasant surprises, and often the least likely choices of fish yield the best sensations – try tiny vendace (*muikku*) with garlic and cream, an unpretentious fish that has more taste than all tropical varieties combined.

Tasty fare at a Helsinki restaurant.

This is a country that also produces 'non-vegetables' – varieties that are too small to be 'accepted' by EU directives, but that is often the whole point: the 'new' potatoes (the first in the season) are tiny but full of flavour. Small strawberries, blueberries or handpicked mushrooms from the forests all taste better than the fertilised varieties that are produced in bulk in warmer countries.

Finnish food as we know it today has a short history. Traditionally Finnish food comprised largely of fat, and was always home-made. Hamburgers, kebabs and pizzas can satisfy most of the fast-food requirements in modern Finland, but tourists should have no trouble finding genuine Finnish delicacies.

FINNISH FISH

Take fish, for example. Finland has lakes, rivers and the sea, brimming with local species. Fish has always been important in the Finnish diet: bream, burbot, perch and pike are traditional species, and salmon are omnipresent. What isn't available locally can be readily imported from neighbouring countries such as Norway. Smoked fish is the speciality, although it may also be grilled, glow-fired, steamed or basted in the oven. Fried fish is relatively rare in Finnish restaurants.

and eaten whole, it's another fine experience of Finnish haute cuisine.

HUNTING NATION

Much of Finland's tasty elk meat disappears into private deep-freezes during the hunting season, but semi-domesticated reindeer is more common. The Lapland speciality is *poronkäristys* (reindeer casserole), served with mashed potatoes and cranberry (lingonberry). It's an excellent way to fill oneself up after a week-long trek in Lapland's wilderness. The best part of reindeer is fillet steak,

Stall at the Baltic herring market (silakkamarkkinat) in Helsinki.

Salmon soup is another subtle delicacy: only a pinch of salt is added to the liquid, but the main taste comes from the fish. Each way of cooking salmon in Finland gives a distinctive experience, but *graavi lohi* (raw salmon marinated for a day in salt and herbs) is delicious. *Graavi* is the Finnish version of *sushi* – but instead of rice and seaweed, it is served with small potatoes and dill.

While Finnish salmon should not be missed, don't forget to try *siika* as well. This white fish has a more subtle taste, and is also best in the *graavi* variety, with potatoes and dill. *Silakka* (Baltic herring) and *muikku* (vendace) are small fish, typical in Finnish restaurants, but lamprey is not a 'true' fish at all, and is found only in the rivers of western Finland. Charcoal-grilled

> *Rapujuhla (crayfish parties) are by invitation only, although all fine restaurants serve crayfish during July and August. Much of the red delicacy is imported, with each small creature costing several euros.*

usually worth its price, though a real delicacy is smoked reindeer heart, with a cedar aroma and a subtle taste. This latter dish you can find at Juuri in Helsinki (Korkeavuorenkatu 27).

The best restaurants in Finland will also serve rare game birds during the season. Wild duck is most common. Its hunting season only runs from late summer to autumn, and it is worth trying when available. In Helsinki, several restaurants, such as Sea Horse (Kapteeninkatu 11), prepare a number of traditional Finnish game dishes.

Sausage *(makkara)* is also very popular in summer – best grilled with local mustard. Typically, Finnish sausage has more flour than meat, but quality varies. In Tampere, *mustam-akkara* ('black sausage') contains spices, barley and blood in real gut. Blood may also be added to the Åland Islands' *svartbröd* ('black bread'), a distinctively sweet brown bread.

'squeaky' cheese, often eaten with yellow cloud-berries (a sour berry that grows on marshlands).

POTATO AND BARLEY

Potato is the staple food, available all year round, but some restaurants have introduced more tradi-tional barley to replace rice and pasta (which are common in Finland, too). Barley is softer, bigger and, some believe, tastier than rice, but sadly quite rare in restaurants. Barley, oats, rye and rice are all used for porridges, which are typical breakfast items in Finland. Barley dishes can be found, for

A spread of traditional Karelian food.

REGIONAL DISHES

Regional differences are notable around Fin-land. Salted fish, pies and pastries are typical in Karelia (you should avoid the pre-packed Karelian pies at supermarkets, which bear no resemblance to their originals). Rye dough is filled with barley or potato and then turned inwards to create the distinctive Karelian pie, baked in the oven and eaten with mashed four-minute eggs and some butter.

The Lakeland provides plenty of fish, as one would expect, and *muikkukukko* is a typical Savo delicacy, consisting of vendace fish inside a baked rye bread – although it is an acquired taste to some. The northwest coast is renowned for salmon soup and *leipäjuusto,* a baked, bread-like

⊘ WHERE TO FIND SPECIALITIES

Helsinki and other big towns are the best places to look for fresh or smoked fish in supermarkets or markets, as small towns rarely serve culinary delights – there isn't enough demand. An exception is a *smörgåsbord*, or *seisova pöytä* in Finnish, which can be outstandingly good or simply bad. Many theme restaurants, such as Karelian houses along the eastern border, serve an excellent variety of marinated and smoked fish, pickled herring or *graavi* salmon, salads and other vegetables. The larger hotels prepare a great breakfast buffet, and there are also innovative Finnish versions of international buffets.

example, at Restaurant Aino in Helsinki (Pohjois-esplanadi 21), which serves an arctic char with beetroot barley and a blackcurrant hollandaise. Although traditional edible beets such as swede

> Typically, Finns partake of kahvi (coffee) and pulla (wheat buns) after their meals. Cakes are also abundant; cream cakes topped with strawberries are typical.

or turnip are seldom considered 'gourmet food' in Finland, try one that has been on low heat for a day – fully softened swede requires no spices. Finns, in fact, seldom use spices. Many raw, locally farmed ingredients have a naturally strong flavour that may simply be lured out by the right cooking technique.

BREAD

Russians and Swedes produce rye bread, but use different recipes to the unique Finnish kind, which is usually less sweet than its counterparts. It is healthy bread, available in many different

Traditional Finnish Christmas dinner.

⊘ SEASONAL FARE

Christmas food in Finland is very traditional and much loved, despite being rather simple by today's standards. Little has changed on the festive menu over the past century: ham, salmon, casseroles and dried codfish always feature, and there are lots of desserts, including ginger biscuits and the popular star-shaped plum tart, joulutorttu. At Easter, Finns eat mämmi (a malt-based pudding) and drink sima (mead), while tippaleipä pastries are the May Day speciality. Festival times apart, Finnish food varies both seasonally and geographically, making it an endless source of fascination for visitors to the country.

forms, including as a rough crispbread, soft and fresh, or as the slightly stickier and harder jälkiuunileipä. The latter variety keeps edible longer and is good with cheese and cold milk.

FOOD FROM THE FOREST

One special element in Finnish cuisine is the abundance of ingredients that are available free on the forested landscape, including a wide range of berries, fungi and herbs. No one owns these foods, and Finnish law allows free access to the forests. Of course, you have to be certain of your fungi: out of 2,000 varieties, around 500 are edible (although they don't all taste nice). Blueberries are readily available in July, the native sour cranberries (lingonberries) by September. Numerous varieties of mushrooms show up on restaurant menus by the autumn.

WHAT TO DRINK

The Finnish *ravintola* may be a restaurant, bar or pub, and most often people go there to drink. Beer is ubiquitous, and one of the 'big five' is most usually served: Koff, Lapin Kulta, Karhu, Karjala or Olvi (this last is in fact the only major brewery still Finnish-owned). But there are many more, as microbreweries are popping up with more frequency across the country. The same goes for wineries, which for the time being seem

kiosk is another Finnish institution, selling chocolate and groceries when other shops are closed.

Helsinki is the best place to savour Finnish delicacies. Passio Kitchen and Bar (www.passiodining.fi; Kalevankatu 13) offers three- and five-course dinner menus, whereas Spis (http://spis.fi; Kasarmikatu 26) specialises in modern Finnish cuisine. Ora (http://orarestaurant.fi; Huvilakatu 28) focuses on combining local ingredients with modern fare. Helsinki's restaurants are innovative too: Demo (www.restaurant-demo.fi; Uudenmaankatu 9-11), Olo (www.olo-ravintola.fi; Pohjoisesplanadi 5) and Nokka (www.ravintolanokka.

Finnish bar at cocktail time.

unique for Scandinavia; Finland gave up part of the restricting alcohol policy, and there are now around 40 private wineries. Strawberries, blackcurrants and redcurrants, among others, are used to produce a distinctive red wine – not exactly Burgundy, but it is a well-balanced berry drink with 12 percent strength. In the same way, local producers are experimenting by adding other berries to stronger alcohol. However, the law prevents you buying these direct from the winery: you'll have to order the cranberry vodkas and blueberry liqueurs from the Alko store.

WHERE TO EAT

Whether it's culinary delights, fast food, coffee or a pint of lager, you will find it: there is a restaurant or a simple kiosk on practically every corner. The

fi; Kanavaranta 7F) are three haute-fusion places that prepare some excellent modern cuisine. In fact, Demo and Olo have one Michelin star each.

Saaga (www.ravintolasaaga.fi; Bulevardi 36) is a truly Lappish experience, with a rich menu of Arctic specialities, including reindeer. The other end is represented by Zetor (www.zetor.net; Kaivopiha), with a quirky 1950s decor that includes an actual tractor and plenty of typical Finnish home-cooking on the menu.

Creating a buzz, the old abattoir (Teurastamo; Työpajankatu 2) in Helsinki became a foodie centre in 2012/13, with restaurants, a butcher's shop, bakery, coffee roastery and a pasta maker. Food-related events (from picnics to barbecues) occur here frequently.

The Koli Hills in the Lakeland.

IN DEFENCE OF GREENNESS

Despite the familiar images of Finland's pristine lakes and forests, the country is striving alongside the rest of the world towards finding solutions to environmental problems.

Finns have long looked to their country's natural environment for a sense of identity. The national anthem celebrates the country's summer landscape; its blue-and-white flag is said to represent the white snow of winter and the blue lakes of summer; and literature, fine art, design and architecture have all drawn on the environment for a Finnish idiom. Finns love nothing better than to disappear into the countryside, exercising the principle of *jokamiehenoikeus* – the right of anyone to roam at will, wandering through forests, picking wild produce, or paddling along lakes and sheltered coastlines.

As the environmental campaigner Martti Arkko put it: 'We depend on nature and the environment for everything. If we allow our forests and lakes to become polluted, our Finnishness will disappear too. The hearts of the Finnish people lie in the lakes and forests. They are our identity, our capital and riches.'

Finns have brought in many measures to safeguard their environment; however, the landscape is more fragile than it looks, and more could always be done to protect it.

CONSERVATION HISTORY

Finland's landscape seems vast and immaculate, and the country's population density is a measly 18 people per square kilometre. At first glance, you would not imagine that humans could have had much impact on its peaceful forests and snowy wildernesses. However, appearances are deceptive. This long, thin country has diverse biospheres, from temperate European right up to subarctic zones. Its bird and animal species exist in relatively small populations along the narrow strip of land, and are particularly sensitive to environmental change.

Heidi Hautala, Finnish Green MEP.

The fragility of the region's species was recognised as far back as the Middle Ages, when in 1347 King Magnus Ericsson introduced a seasonal elk-hunting ban. From then onwards, various acts restricting hunting were passed, although most were to protect valuable human food sources. The biggest shift towards a modern-day sensibility to wildlife and habitat came with the Nature Conservation Act of 1923, which put legal protection in place for a raft of non-edible species, including crane, heron, jackdaws and bats. It also established the first nature reserves. Finland has since built on this legacy, and today has a total of 40 national parks and many more protected areas, covering nearly 10,000 square kilometres.

CURRENT CONCERNS

Finland's problems are effectively those shared by industrial nations all over the world: air and water pollution, energy conservation, the despoliation of the natural landscape, endangered species and waste management. Finland signed up to the Kyoto Protocol in 2005, but it has sometimes struggled to meet its greenhouse gas emission targets, finishing up as one of the largest emitters per capita in the EU in 2006 and 2007. A marked improvement was achieved in 2012: the total amount of carbon dioxide emitted was 60.9 million tonnes, 14 percent below the commitment level set by the Kyoto Protocol – whose first commitment period ended on 31 December 2012. The second commitment period (2013–2020), known as the Doha Amendment and not yet ratified by all signatories at the time of writing, has a target to reduce the greenhouse gas emissions by at least 18 percent from the 1990 levels.

The biggest immediate concern in the region is the eutrophication of the Baltic Sea – a problem that is not just Finland's to solve. The sea is surrounded by nine countries, and pollution from their

The image of summer that every Finn wants to preserve.

⊘ HUMAN THREATS

The green sanctuaries that are Finland's forests are also the country's recreational playgrounds. The right of common access permits free access to all forests and allows such activities as the picking of berries and mushrooms, and fishing in the lakes, which are national summer pastimes. Of course, there is a trade-off in that the greater use of the forests for recreational purposes also, inevitably, brings problems – litter and other forms of pollution, such as the noise and exhaust emissions of too many vehicles, not to mention selfish drivers who thoughtlessly plough their cars at high speeds through uncharted territory.

combined population of 90 million people flows down numerous rivers and into its shallow water (it has an average depth of just 59 metres/194ft). Toxic run-off accumulates, leading to dying sea life and a desertification of the sea bed. The need for action is acute, and the HELCOM Baltic Sea Action Plan, an intergovernmental organisation of the nine countries and the EU, is seeking to "restore the good ecological status of the marine environment" by 2021. A meeting was held in Helsinki in 2019, which adopted several new recommendations to strengthen the protection of the Baltic.

A similar problem affects Finland's many lakes: pesticides and fertilisers used in agriculture run off into the waters, their phosphorus and nitrogen content causing algal blooms that reduce oxygen and kill aquatic life. Again, shallow water contributes to the problem – the average depth of Finland's lakes is a mere seven metres (23ft).

Lapland has its own specific set of difficulties and paradoxes. Reindeer herds are fundamental to the lives of the Sami, but in the 1990s it became apparent that overgrazing was causing severe erosion problems, as the animals nibbled away moss and lichen that held the sparse subarctic soil in place. In late 2012, the Swedish Mistra Council for Evidence-Based Environmental Management (EviEM) set out to evaluate whether reindeer grazing was still a cause for concern. Today there is still much debate and research as to the degree and severity of the issue.

Apocalyptic as all this may sound, one should remember that, in comparison to extremely polluted areas of Europe, Finland is a model of purity. In the last 20 years, air quality has improved in industrial towns, and many once-polluted watercourses have been cleaned up. In fact, water quality is deemed to be either good or excellent in 80 percent of the country's lakes. Finland generates less than the average EU amount of municipal waste, and the government's 2008 National Waste Plan for 2016 aimed to recycle 80 percent of this by the end of 2016. The 2023 plan has set similarly ambitious targets. Together with Germany, Finland is the biggest recycler of paper in the world, reprocessing around 80 percent of all its paper and cardboard.

For more environmental information, see the website of the Finnish State Environmental Administration (Ympäristöhallinto; www.ymparisto.fi), the state department that oversees nature reserves, protection of wild plants and animals, and even sustainable housing in urban and rural areas.

FOREST THREATS

Driving through Finland, you might feel there is little cause for concern about its endless green forests and lakes, but the Finns nevertheless brought a Wilderness Act into force in February 1991 to defend areas from extensive felling or clearing. Nearly one-third of Lapland's area, for example, is now made up of these protected zones.

Forest accounts for around 75 percent of the total land area, some 230,000 sq km (90,000 sq miles). It is Finland's largest sustainable resource and a source for a major export: forestry and mining provide a large proportion of the country's income. It is indeed ironic, then, that forestry and timber processes (along with mining) cause the most damage to Finland's land environment.

Planting, bog-draining for plantations, fertilising and felling all have severe consequences, changing natural habitats and the balance of Finland's watercourses, and exploiting the soil.

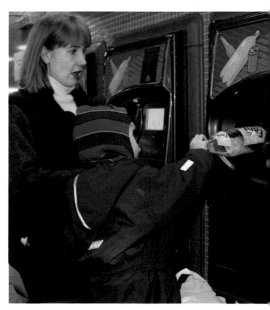

Finland recycles a high percentage of its waste.

⊘ ENVIRONMENTAL PROTEST

The 21st century has seen a growing interest in and enthusiasm for environmental issues. In 2012, the Talvivaara nickel mine in eastern Finland leaked a million cubic metres of unprocessed waste water into nearby watercourses. People took their protest to Helsinki to demand the mine's closure. A few more leaks later, several managers were convicted of criminal environmental offenses. On a positive note, the Nordic Council awarded its 2012 Environment Prize to Finnish activist Olli Manninen for his work in preserving Nordic forests and mobilising environmental NGOs in the region. In 2017, the Finnish company RePack won the prize for its packaging, which can be returned by customers to be reused.

Responsible forest management has been one government solution but, as the state owns only 26 percent of the forests, it has had to offer incentives for private owners to subscribe to the national plan.

GREEN IDEAS

'Green' policies have been part of everyday Finnish life for some time. Recycling schemes and attempts to improve house insulation continue, and the government has repeated its commitment to public transport.

Small-scale Finnish projects that might well solve some of the Western world's ecological problems hit the headlines from time to time. The pioneering idea of constructing a road out of bits of rubber car tyres was intended to have a dual 'green' purpose. Firstly, it gave a use for tyres, which are notoriously difficult to dispose of. Secondly, the experiment was an attempt to find a durable road surface able to resist the strains of the fierce winter ice, which calls for frequent road maintenance and endless resurfacing. Other experiments have involved research into biode-

Wind farms are sprouting up as Finland finds alternative forms of energy.

⊘ NUCLEAR POWER

About 50 percent of Finland's energy comes from burning oil, gas and coal, and the country is dependent on Russia for much of this fuel. A desire to become more self-sufficient may account for Finland's enthusiasm for nuclear energy: a 2010 poll found 61 percent of Finns in favour, and just 23 percent against, making Finland one of Europe's most pro-nuclear countries. Even many supporters of the Green League (which has 15 elected MPs and one MEP) are advocates. Nuclear power accounts for nearly 30 percent of the country's electricity, but this will rise when Finland's fifth nuclear reactor, Olkiluoto 3, goes online in January 2020.

gradable plastic – especially carrier bags – as a by-product of Finland's oil refineries.

From a visitor's point of view, Finland may already represent a supremely unspoilt environment. The Finnish Tourist Board invokes the country's landscape, supported by photographs of summer in Finland's green forests, its blue waters and its leafy towns. Human habitation appears in its proper context, a tiny sprinkling of buildings in a vast forested terrain. This is a true picture of Finland. In a country that is the seventh-largest in Europe, its 5.5 million inhabitants are just a blip on the map: highly influential but outnumbered several thousand to one by trees. For this reason, if for no other, it is in Finland's best interest to secure and protect its natural domain.

LAPLAND: THE HOME OF SANTA CLAUS

Everyone knows that Santa Claus comes from Lapland, and he is now one of the biggest tourist attractions in Finland.

Since the beginning of the tourist boom in the 1950s that played on the legend of Santa Claus and Lapland, well over half a million children from nearly every country in the world write to Finland's Santa every year. Sweden's Jultomten is the biggest competitor to the Finnish Santa, but more than 30,000 letters arrive daily in Lapland in the run-up to Christmas, most often from Finland, the United Kingdom, Italy, Poland and Japan, all expressing their Christmas wishes for that year.

Santa Claus and the Arctic Circle bring half a million visitors annually, and there may be 30 nationalities represented on any day. Fortunately, Santa speaks several European languages – and also the essential phrases in Chinese and Japanese.

PROTECTING A LEGEND

Sinikka Salokorpi is a Santa Claus expert in Finland and has written the official Santa 'thesis' for the Ministry of Trade and Industries, which includes photos of authentic Santa Claus garments. Although written with a tongue-in-cheek attitude, the booklet defines more than the dress code. It tells us, among other things, that while there is harmony with foreign Santas, the 'real' Santa lives in Finland. 'It's a commercial battleground – Santa is big business,' says Salokorpi.

A magical grotto in Santa Park, inside Syväsenvaara Hill at Rovaniemi, the unofficial capital of Finnish Lapland, where it's Christmas all year round.

Santa and his wife in his official home at the Korvatunturi, a 480-metre (1,580ft) hill way up north on the Finnish-Russian border.

There are many Santas in Finland – it's too much work for one man.

Santa Claus is big business in Finland.

Santa Claus theme parks

The Arctic Circle was never an entity until German soldiers marked the spot during World War II, but no one took much notice before Eleanor Roosevelt paid a visit in 1950; a simple shack was built for the occasion. Mrs Roosevelt became an unofficial sponsor for the growing Santa Claus village, which now includes shops, a Santa Claus Office and, of course, Santa's post office.

Santa Park, opened in 1998, is one of the biggest Santa-related tourist traps in Finland. Just 2km (1 mile) from the main Arctic Circle area, the 'park' found an ingenious location inside an artificial cave. You walk 200 metres/yards inside Syväsenvaara hill and find the Magic Sleigh Ride and other attractions. A digitally produced photo with Santa is available in two minutes – a popular, if expensive, souvenir – but other companies want their share: Christmas paraphernalia and Finnish design is also for sale.

The giving of presents at Christmas may stem from the story of the Magi, or Three Wise Men, bringing gifts to the infant Jesus, but Christmas gift-giving was not widespread until the late 19th century, when many of the customs we now think of as traditional were initiated.

...hough Santa Claus sometimes travels by helicopter ...se days, he prefers to use his reindeer, especially ...dolph, to help him get around.

Hundreds of thousands of letters are sent to Santa every year; even those addressed to 'Santa, North Pole' or 'Reindeer Street' still find their way to the Arctic Circle, Finland.

Setting for the Olavinlinna Opera Festival, Savonlinna.

Lakeland dawn.

INTRODUCTION

A detailed guide to the entire country, with principal sites clearly cross-referenced by number to the maps.

Attention to detail in Helsinki.

Nobody has managed to count how many lakes and islands there are in Finland – enough, it seems, for every Finnish family to have an island or lake of its own, with space for visitors, too. No wonder the ideal Finnish summer is based around a wooden cabin at the edge of lake or sea and a wooden steam sauna house nearby. With good fishing, swimming, and a small boat tied up alongside, this is Finnish perfection.

There is a seemingly boundless expanse of untouched landscape, criss-crossed by endless straight roads running between tall trees. As the road extends ever further north, the rolling farmland of the south becomes dense tracts of forests and, gradually, the dark green gives way to the peat and tundra of Lapland, where the midnight sun gives the landscape a red glow in the late evening. This is the territory of reindeer, and the animals of the wilderness areas – bear, wolf and lynx. In the northwest the ground rises to more than 1,000 metres (3,000ft) as it reaches towards the fells and fjords of coastal Norway. Along the west coast of the Gulf of Bothnia, the beaches and surprisingly warm waters are ripe for exploration.

For a country of 5.5 million, Finland has produced an astonishing number of architects, artists, sculptors and designers – and it shows. In Helsinki, in particular, almost every nook and cranny of the city reveals an intriguing detail: an elegantly carved facade on a block of flats, a statue, a curved window, or a tiny figurine full of humour that you nearly miss but laugh out loud once you spot it. Older cities such as Turku or Porvoo, where the Swedish influence was strongest, hold some of the country's most enduring buildings.

A design school in the capital's Arabianranta district.

Even the seasons seem more distinct. In winter, it is time for snow and skiing and also for the great reindeer round-ups in Lapland. In summer, the sea and lakes are full of sails and swimmers. Between the two are the bursts of spring when everything turns green within a few days, and autumn, full of reds and browns as the leaves fall onto the city squares. Finland is emphatically a land for all seasons.

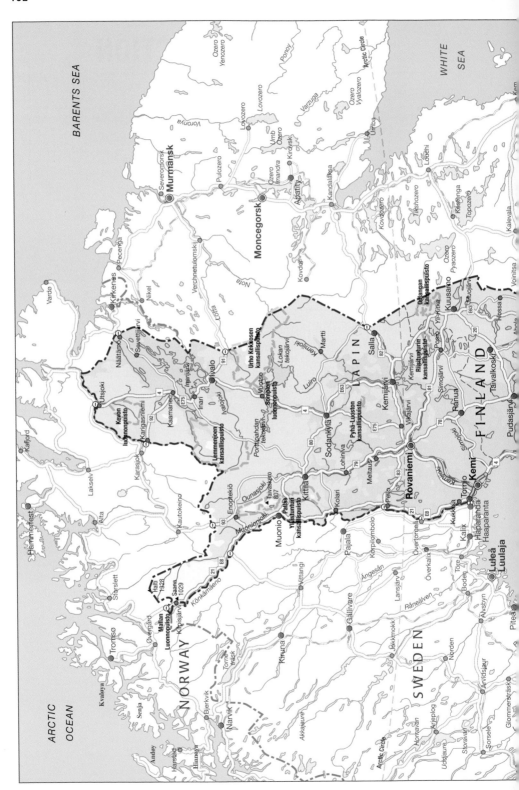

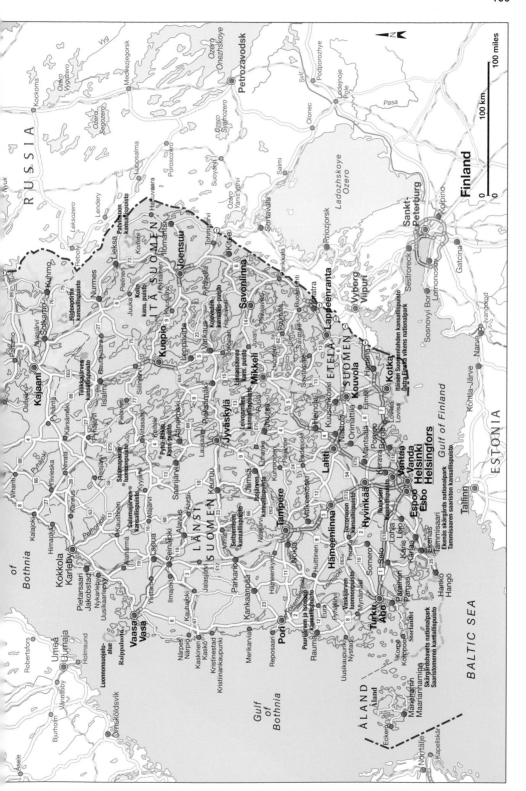

Pier jutting out into the Baltic Sea.

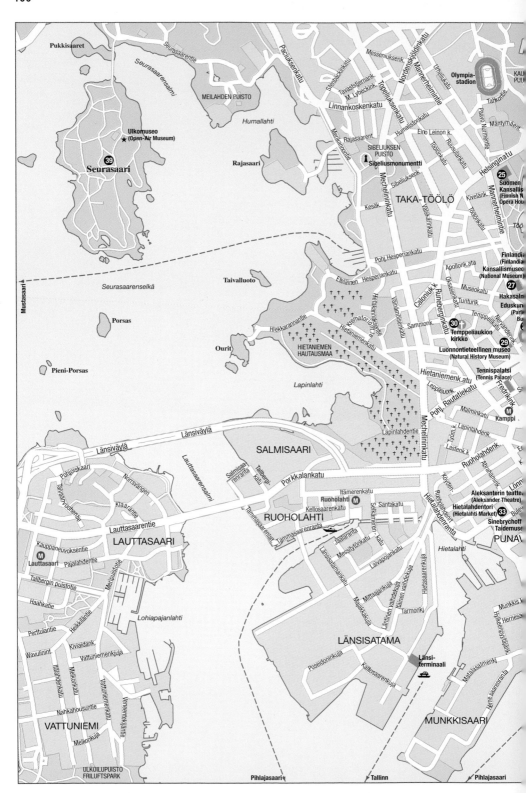

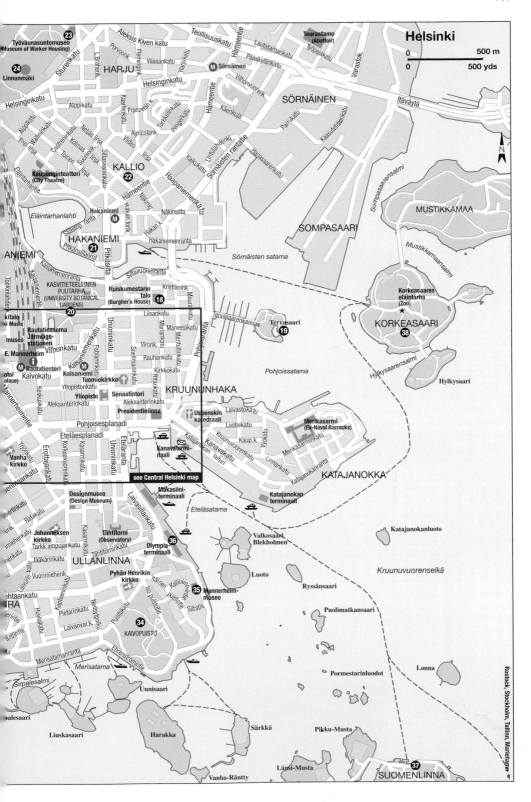

Helsinki

0 — 500 m
0 — 500 yds

N

Työväenasuntomuseo (23)
(Museum of Worker Housing)

Linnanmäki (24)

HARJU

Aleksis Kiven katu

Teollisuuskatu

Teurastamo (Abattoir)

Sturenkatu

Porvoonk.

Viidesk.

Vaasankatu

Sörnäinen (M)

SÖRNÄINEN

Lautatarhankatu

Työpajakatu

Varastok.

Pääskylänkatu

Itäväylä

Helsinginkatu

Helsinginkatu

Alppikatu

Kaarlenkatu

L.Brahenk.

Franzen.k.

Helsinginkatu

Torkkelink.

Vilhonvuoren.k.

Hämeentie

Parruk.

Kaasutehtaankatu

Sompasaarensalmi

MUSTIKKAMAA

Alppikatu

Ensi linja

Wallininkatu

Castreninkatu

Kolmas linja

Neljäs linja

Toinen linja

Suonionk.

Agricolank.

Kaikukatu

Linnanrauhantie

KALLIO

Kaupunginteatteri (22)
(City Theatre)

Hämeentie

Näkink.

Haapaniemenkatu

Sörnäisten rantatie

Hapsasaarenkatu

SOMPASAARI

Mustikkamaansalmi

Eläintarhanlahti

Näkink.

Haapaniemenkatu

Näkinsilta

Hakaniemi (M)

HAKANIEMI (21)

Hakan.torik.

Hakaniemenranta

Sörnäisten satama

Pitkänsillanranta

Saasto-ranta

Hakan.k.

Korkeasaaren eläintarha (Zoo) ★

ANIEMI

Pitkäsilta

Siltavuorenranta

Tervasaarenkannas

KORKEASAARI (38)

Kaisaniemenranta

KASVITIETEELLINEN PUUTARHA (UNIVERSITY BOTANICAL GARDENS) (20)

Ruiskumestarin talo (18)
(Burgher's House)

Kristianink.

Mauritzkatu

Tervasaari (19)

Hylkysaarensalmi

Topeliuksentie

kitalo ki Music

Liisankatu

Pohjoisranta

museo

Rautatieasema Järnvägsstationen

Unioninkatu

Maneesikatu

Mariank.

Vironk.

Meritullink.

Hylkysaari

E. Mannerheim (i)

Vilhonkatu

Fabianinkatu

Snellmaninkatu

Rauhankatu

Kirkkokatu

Pohjoissatama

atsi alace)

(M) **Rautatientori** Kaivokatu

Kaisaniemenkatu

Kaisaniemi (M)

Tuomiokirkko †

Kirkkokatu

Rantakatu

Mannerheimintie

Keskuskatu

Yliopistonkatu

Yliopisto

Senaatintori

KRUUNUNHAKA

Laivastokatu

Aleksanterinkatu

Aleksanterinkatu

Presidentinlinna

Uspenskin katedraali †

Luotsikatu

Merikasarmi (Ex-Naval Barracks)

Pohjoisesplanadi

Kaup.k.

Vyökatu

Merikasarminkatu

Vanha kirkko

Erottajankatu

Korkeavuorenkatu

Yrjönkatu

Kasarmikatu

Unioninkatu

Eteläesplanadi

Eteläranta

Kanavaterminaali

Katajanokan laituri

Kanavakatu

Kruununvuorenkatu

Linnankatu

Katajanokanranta

KATAJANOKKA

see Central Helsinki map

Designmuseo (Design Museum)

Laivasillankatu

Makasiiniterminaali

Eteläsatama

Katajanokan terminaali

Katajanokanluoto

bertinkatu

Ratakatu

Kasarminkatu

imienkatu

Johanneksen kirkko

Tähtitorni (Observatory)

Tarkk'ampujankatu

Olympia terminaali (36)

Valkosaari Blekholmen

Kruunuvuorenselkä

Jääkärinkatu

ULLANLINNA

Tähtitorninkatu

Luoto

Ryssänsaari

Vuorimiehenk.

Pyhän Henrikin kirkko

Iso puistotie

Mannerheimmuseo (35)

Puolimatkansaari

ehtaankatu

Pietarinkatu

Neitsytpolku

Puistokatu

Itäinen puistotie

Kalliolinnantie

Siltatie

IRA

Laivanvar.k.

Huvilakatu

(34)

KAIVOPUISTO

Lonna

Merisatamanranta

Ehrenströmintie

Pormestarinluodot

Merisatama

Sirpalesalmi

Uunisaari

Rostock, Stockholm, Tallinn, Mariehamn

alesaari

Liuskasaari

Harakka

Särkkä

Pikku-Musta

Läpi-Musta

SUOMENLINNA (37)

Vanha-Räntty

HELSINKI

With its intriguing cultural mix of Russians and Scandinavians, the diminutive Finnish capital has a charm as fresh as the breeze that blows across its harbour from the Baltic Sea.

Surrounding the city, the sea appears in Helsinki when you least expect it, its salty tongue lapping at the edges of metropolitan bridges and boulevards, pressing its way into residential areas, forming natural harbours and bays.

In summer, the sea glistens under a tireless sun, driving the light-starved locals wild with its rays and heat. Autumn arrives and, as darkness encroaches and the rains begin to fall, it begins its churn, spawning a world of wet and grey where the borders between sea and land are no longer distinct. Only during the long, cold winter does the sea finally rest, freezing into an endless expanse on which weekend promenaders can walk dogs or try out their cross-country skis.

Long referred to as the 'Daughter of the Baltic', it is to the sea that Helsinki owes its fortunes, its climate and perhaps even the massive, undulating nature of its architecture. It is also to the Baltic that the city owes much of its relatively short but turbulent history.

HELSINKI'S HISTORY

Helsinki was founded in 1550 by King Gustav Vasa of Sweden-Finland to compete with Tallinn, just across the Gulf of Finland, then a port controlled by the Hanseatic League. A first fledgling settlement was erected on the mouth of the Vantaa River at the

Festival, Esplanade Park.

innermost point of the Helsinki Bay – a little northeast of where Helsinki stands today. In order to populate the town of Helsingfors ('Helsinge', the local parish, plus 'fors', Swedish for 'rapids'), Gustav Vasa simply ordered citizens from Porvoo, Ulvila and Rauma to move to the new town.

The new port proved, however, to be not only unpopular but a money-loser as well, once the shallow inner bay became shallower and impossible to navigate. It languished for nearly a century until a visiting governor general

Main attractions
Railway Station
Esplanade Park
Senate Square
Uspenski Cathedral
National Museum
Finlandia Hall
Kiasma
Mannerheim Museum
Suomenlinna

Maps on pages
136, 140

named Per Brahe recommended it be moved further south towards the open sea. On this new site, Kruununhaka, Helsinki finally began to grow, though it still wasn't much more than an outpost for fishermen and farmers. Then the Russian Empire stirred against Sweden, and the town's small fortunes began to go downhill. After battling against the Great Famine in 1696 and the Great Plague in 1710, the city was set on fire in 1713, and reduced to ashes by its own defenders, outnumbered by 17,000 Russian besiegers in the Great Northern War (1710–1721).

HELSINKI PROSPERS

Sweden's decision in 1746 to build Suomenlinna Fortress off the shore of Helsinki (see page 161), to protect what remained of its Finnish territory saved the city. Construction of the fortress drew attention to the port and brought it its first taste of wealth. Merchants constructed a clutch of stone houses and, although streets were still unpaved, some semblance of European cultural life took root.

In 1808, the Russians wrested the fortress from Sweden, annexing Finland the following year and making Helsinki the capital of their new territory. Russian money, and the talents of German architect Carl Ludwig Engel, were poured into the creation of administrative halls and a cathedral. As the city began to enjoy steady prosperity from around 1850, workers' homes were mostly replaced with stone ones. By 1900, Helsinki had grown from a small port with some 20,000 inhabitants into a bona fide capital city. The population soared to 100,000, a railway was built, and gasworks, electricity and water mains all laid down. At the same time, Helsinki became the seat of the nationalist movement. Native architects, such as Eliel Saarinen, then Alvar Aalto, emerged; after independence in 1917, the more Finnish Functionalism replaced Jugendstil (the German version of Art Nouveau) as Helsinki's predominant architectural style.

Unfortunately, nothing could protect the city from the massive Russian air raids of 1944 – nor from fervent, and

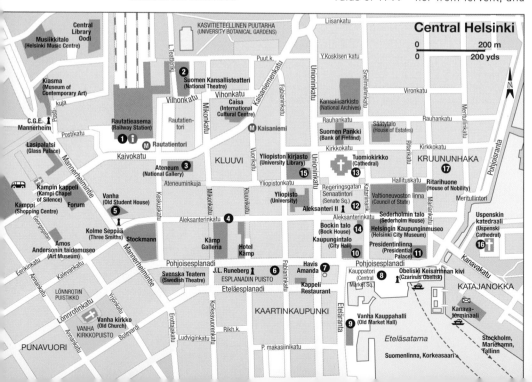

not always aesthetically pleasing, post-war reconstruction. But Helsinki's position on the sea resurfaced to help it regain, and then increase, its stature, not only as a major port but eventually as the important site for shipbuilding, international conferences and tourism that it has become today.

THE CITY TODAY

Modern Helsinki is a tranquil but still growing city with some 643,000 inhabitants – many of whom are second-generation city dwellers. Gone are the marshes and wooden houses, but the fishermen who sell their catch straight from the docks are reminders that this capital's urbanisation is relatively recent. Helsinki isn't a frivolous city but the Finns have let their innate artistry flavour their capital. Statues stand on every other corner, and even the most functional of buildings are notable monuments to Finland's architectural history. The city is not resting on its laurels either: Helsinki was recognised as the World Design Capital in 2012, with €16 million earmarked to enhance

the city through design projects. And in 2016, it was rated 9th in a survey of 140 cities in terms of liveability by the Economist Group.

Consider the **Railway Station** ❶ (Rautatieasema). Finland's most-visited building handles around 200,000 passengers daily and connects Helsinki with numerous commuter cities as well as the rest of the country. It also contains both a metro station stop and an underground shopping complex. The station is a strikingly stylish, round-edged structure in pinkish granite with green trim, a black roof and a 48-metre (160ft) green clock tower.

Designed by Eliel Saarinen in 1905 but not completed until 1919, it links two of Helsinki's most prevalent styles: National Romanticism and Functionalism (see page 76). It also incorporates work by several other well-known Finns. Thanks to Emil Wikström, pairs of solemn-faced, muscular giants hold translucent lanterns on either side of the station's impressive front doors. A large painting by Eero Järnefelt looks over the Eliel Restaurant inside.

Wikström's massive figures adorning Helsinki Railway Station.

⊙ Fact

The SpåraKOFF Bar Tram (www.virginoil.fi/in-english/sparakoff; May–early Sept Mon–Sat, trams leave from the Mikonkatu tram stop at 2pm, 3pm, 5pm, 6pm and 7pm and 8pm, and in July–mid-Aug also 1pm on Fri–Sat) follows a scenic route around the inner city and has two beer taps on board to help you relax. Stops include Kauppatori, Student House and the Opera House.

Trams make it easy to get around.

The railway station has a more metropolitan focus compared to the somewhat rustic harbour. It is a good reference point for a city tour; most places of interest to visitors are within walking distance of here.

EXPLORING THE CITY

The first thing to do before beginning a tour of Helsinki, however, is to find your directional bearings. These are not immediately obvious because much of central Helsinki lies on a peninsula, jutting southward into the Baltic. Being by the sea, therefore, doesn't automatically mean you are in the south of the city. In fact, the peninsula has only a brief southern shore but extended longitudinal coasts on both its eastern and western sides.

Don't rely on geographical names either, which can be deceiving. The 'South' Harbour actually lies on the peninsula's eastern side. It is, however, south of *Kruununhaka* – the old city centre. Keep in mind that the railway station is effectively right in the middle of the peninsula; the tiny *Keskusta*,

or centre, runs east–west below it; and the other neighbourhoods of central Helsinki radiate around them.

More confusing, though, is a visitor's initial glance at the city. Helsinki doesn't follow any of the rules of European capitals. It isn't quaint; it isn't regal; it isn't even terribly old. Nearly every wooden structure that predated 1808 was burnt to the ground, and little more than a century ago, there were still animals wandering the streets.

Step out of the railway station and you'll be greeted by two monolithic commercial complexes side by side: one 'modern' and bedecked with neon signs, a second known for the lengthy tubular balcony winding about its facade. Don't let this put you off: Helsinki is an immensely compelling place for urban exploration, in a quintessentially Finnish way: reserved and modest, enigmatic and stylish.

The **National Theatre** ❷ (Suomen Kansallisteatteri; tel: 010-7331 331; www.kansallisteatteri.fi), to the immediate east of the station and at the northern head of the cobbled railway square

Rautatientori, is visually striking. This small castle in white granite with green trim and a red roof was conceived in National Romantic style. Productions are in Finnish, although the theatre shows some surtitled performances (in English, Estonian and Russian). The pensive statue of Aleksis Kivi, Finland's national writer, in front of the theatre, transcends any linguistic barriers.

Directly across the square from the theatre is the **Ateneum ❸** (tel: 0294-500 401; www.ateneum.fi; Tue and Fri 10am–6pm, Wed–Thu 10am–8pm, Sat–Sun 10am–5pm). Built in 1887, the Ateneum's gilt yellow-and-white facade might seem reminiscent of St Petersburg but it is the site of Finland's National Gallery of Art, one of the first manifestations of Finland's struggle for independence. The museum's collection of Finnish paintings, sculpture and graphic art covers the years 1750 to 1960 and includes works by such famous Finns as Akseli Gallén-Kallela and Albert Edelfelt.

The Ateneum lies on the east side of the shopping centre Makkaratalo (an affectionate nickname meaning 'sausage house', after its tubular balcony). Wedged in between Kaivopiha and the north–south-running **Mannerheimintie** (Helsinki's main thoroughfare and the longest street in Finland) is the handsome though slightly faded Seurahuone Hotel.

SHOPS AND STUDENTS

Behind these buildings stretch three blocks containing one of Helsinki's most important shopping districts. **Aleksanterinkatu ❹** (better known as Aleksi), running parallel to the railway station, is the main thread of this area, but intersecting streets also contain shops. An elegant shopping centre, Kämp Galleria – with its specialised shops, boutiques, cafés and restaurants – is also on Aleksi between Mikonkatu and Kluuvikatu. On the same block sits the legendary five-star Hotel Kämp, originally opened in 1887 and Helsinki's first luxury hotel. It has witnessed important political events, while great Finnish artists such as Jean Sibelius, Eino Leino and Akseli Gallén-Kallela were regular visitors.

⊙ Tip

Helsinki City Ride leads interesting and invigorating Nordic Walking guided tours of the capital. You will be outfitted with Nordic walking sticks, instructed in the art of the sport, and then taken on an active tour of a number of different Helsinki neighbourhoods by a local. Tours depart daily from the city tourist office (tel: 044-955 8720; www.helsinkicityride.com).

Rye bread on sale at the Old Market Hall (Kauppahalli).

The National Gallery of Art is housed in the 19th-century Ateneum.

A classic example of Art Nouveau (Jugend) style in Katajanokka.

Aleksi leads up to Mannerheimintie and **Old Student House ⑤** (Vanha). Built in 1870, Vanha's own stairs are a favourite meeting place for pretty young things on a night out, and its interior now houses a performance hall, café-bar and exhibition quarter. Numerous student organisations are based in the New Student House, located at No. 5 right next to the Old Student House.

Vanha lies on the intersection of Aleksi and Mannerheimintie, and a trio of naked men with fine pectorals – the statue of the *Three Smiths*, or *Kolme Seppää* – dominates the triangular square beneath it. As soon as the snow melts in spring, musicians use this square to serenade the passing crowds, ice-cream stands open for business and even some café tables appear.

Finland's largest department store, **Stockmann**, lies on the other side of Three Smiths' Square from Vanha. Beside it, on Keskuskatu, is Scandinavia's largest bookshop, Akateeminen Kirjakauppa. Upstairs you will find a stylish café designed by Alvar Aalto.

ESPLANADE PARK

The bookshop looks onto another Helsinki landmark, **Esplanade Park ⑥** (Esplanadin puisto), locally known as Espa. Planned by Ehrenström (who was also responsible for the 19th-century city plan), it was first laid out in 1831 and runs east–west between Mannerheimintie and the South Harbour.

The **Swedish Theatre** (Svenska Teatern), an elegant semicircular stone building dating from 1866, commands Esplanade Park's western head on Mannerheimintie. Back to back with it and facing into the long and narrow park is a trendy restaurant complex called Teatteri. Its terrace is always filled with relaxed beer drinkers in warm weather, while the Café Artist, inside the theatre, is a great place to take in some of the theatre-going atmosphere come evening.

An old-fashioned promenade stretches from here across the length of the park: between well-sculpted patches of lawn, past the central statue of J.L. Runeberg, Finland's national poet, to the Kappeli Restaurant at its

⊘ ART NOUVEAU

At first sight they are just city buildings, but the elements are unique: visually striking windows, heavy ornamentation, grey granite, natural colours and castle-like features. Some of the most famous tourist attractions in Helsinki are Art Nouveau – the National Museum, or the Hvitträsk House in Kirkkonummi. Art Nouveau, or Jugend as it is called in Finland, is far more common in Helsinki than first seems to be the case.

Art Nouveau is also called National Romanticism. Its roots go back to the great epic *Kalevala*, which inspired the composer Sibelius and the artist Gallén-Kallela. Architects Gesellius, Saarinen and Lindgren soon followed suit, going back to the roots of Karelianism, forests, bedrock – the key elements of Finnishness.

One of the best areas to look for their designs is Katajanokka, a few blocks east of Senate Square. Eira is another area – see Lars Sonck's Eira hospital at Laivurinkatu 29. GLO Hotel Art (Lönnrotinkatu 29) by Lindahl and Thomé is typically Art Nouveau with a granite facade, as is the Otava House (Uudenmaankatu 10), Pohjola House at Aleksanterinkatu 44 (by Gesellius *et al*) or Tarjanne's National Theatre. Even Saarinen's railway station has hints of Art Nouveau. Arrive in good time before your train leaves and take a look around.

eastern end. This park is still a popular meeting place and is the scene of the Christmas Fair and the Night of the Arts in August. On May Day Eve it is given over to widespread lunacy, gallivanting and inebriation.

Kappeli is also an important spot for a rendezvous, and the tall, lacy windows and a whimsical roof give it a Chekhovian, gazebo-like feel – the older parts of the café date from 1867. The summer terrace allows patrons to enjoy simultaneously fresh air, drinks and musical performances (June–Sept) from the bandstand opposite.

Flanking the bandstand are two pretty little 'ponds' graced by statues of cavorting fish boys and water nymphs. But they cannot compete with the **Havis Amanda fountain ❼** on the small square that separates the eastern end of the park from the South Harbour amid a constant swirl of traffic and trams. The sensuous bronze Amanda created quite a stir when first erected in 1908. Surrounded by four sea lions spouting water, she represents the city of Helsinki rising from the sea, innocent and naked. On May Day Eve, at least, she gets something to wear – a white student cap – while a champagne-happy chaos of human cap-wearers cheer. This square also acts as an extension of the Central Market Square (Kauppatori), with produce, handicrafts and flowers for sale from mid-May to early autumn.

VENERABLE BUILDINGS AND TOURIST OFFICE

Two boulevards stretch east–west alongside either side of the park. Nowadays, the fine 19th-century stone buildings along Pohjoisesplanadi mostly house design shops like Marimekko and Aarikka, with its distinctive wooden jewellery. Still more venerable houses line the Southern Esplanade, most of which function in some type of official or commercial capacity. The oldest is Engel's Empire-style former Council of State, dating from 1824. During the period of Russian rule, it was the palace of the governor general.

The stylish Kappeli restaurant by Esplanade Park.

Esplanade Park.

GOING TO MARKET

The **Central Market Square** ❽ (Kauppatori), across from Havis Amanda on the South Harbour, exudes a much earthier type of appeal. A busy market makes its home here year-round (Mon–Sat 6.30am–6pm, Sun during the summer only 10am–5pm). Going to market is still an important part of the daily routine in Helsinki, and the annual week-long Helsinki herring fair, held here in early October, adds extra excitement.

Helsinki has no fewer than six open-air markets, usually with a stately indoor market hall sitting alongside. Of these, the Central Market is both the one most aimed at visitors and the most expensive, but locals on lunch breaks from nearby shops and offices, and housewives from the affluent southern suburbs, still favour it. A multitude of ruddy-faced merchants gather to serve them and, after the ice melts, boat owners tie their vessels to the end of the harbour and sell fish and vegetables straight from their prows.

The north part of the market square is reserved for Finland's delicious fresh produce. Offerings very much follow the seasons and, in summer, become irresistible: sweet baby peas and mounds of deeply flavoured berries. No wonder that, by July, every Helsinki dweller can be seen clutching a small paper bag filled with something juicy and colourful. The coffee tent attracts locals and tourists; even presidents have been known to pop out from the nearby palace for a quick snack.

HANDICRAFT STALLS

Further down, around the bellicose **Obeliski Keisarinnan kivi** – whose imperial, doubled-headed golden eagle was ripped off during the Russian Revolution and not restored until 1972 – the market veers away from food. Some of these stands proffer interesting goods and handicrafts, but if you are looking for authenticity, be aware that most Finns stopped wearing fur hats quite a while ago. Women wearing high heels might also want to bear in mind that the spaces between the cobblestones can be particularly treacherous here.

The water in this part of South Harbour is overrun by bullying gulls, geese and passenger ferries and while not the cleanest of bays, don't let that stop you from sitting with the locals on its storied docks in the sun, and enjoying a punnet of Finland's fabulous strawberries.

OLD MARKET HALL

However, if it is cold or raining, you might prefer to duck into the yellow-and-red-brick **Old Market Hall** ❾ (Vanha Kauppahalli, http://vanhakauppahalli.fi; Mon–Sat 8am–6pm). Having traded for more than 100 years, the Old Market Hall is not only Helsinki's most centrally located *kauppahalli* but also, as its name suggests, its oldest. It knows its advantage. The renovated interior is polished to the gills, and the price of even a simple *piirakka* (Karelian pie) can be high. As well as

Helsinki Cathedral.

reindeer cold cuts and rounds of Olter-manni cheese, you can buy ready-made snacks from a Russian-style kebab stand or excellent pastry break-fasts at the small outdoor market café.

CIVIC TRIUMPHS

The Central Market sprawls before some of Helsinki's most important administrative buildings. An austere row lies directly across at the end of Pohjoisesplanadi: the long, sky-blue City Hall, designed by Engel in 1833, with a Finnish flag flying above it; the sensible brown Swedish Embassy, importantly placed, and with a Swedish flag; the Supreme Court, dating from 1883; and the Presidential Palace.

The **City Hall** ❿ (Kaupungintalo) started out with a different purpose. Until 1833 it was home to the Seura-huone Hotel (now across from the railway station). Its opening was cel-ebrated by a masquerade ball, so that women could attend – although they had to leave by 4.30am. It is now such an elegant venue that it is used for offi-cial civic functions.

The **Presidential Palace** ⓫ (Presi-dentinlinna) was designed in 1818 as a private home and turned into a tsa-rist palace by Engel in 1843. While the Finnish president no longer lives here, the new official residence, Mäntyniemi, not far from Seurasaari, is occasionally open for visitors.

HELSINKI'S PIAZZA

Helsinki's third major landmark, **Sen-ate Square** (Senaatintori) ⓬, stands one block north of here, back along Aleksi. There is something fateful about Senate Square. As early as the 17th century, the same spot housed a town hall, church and central square. It was flattened by the following century's continuous battles, but the merchants made rich by Suomenlinna soon rebuilt it, erecting the city's first stone build-ings about its southern perimeter. The 1808 fire destroyed everything wooden, but immediately afterwards Russia commissioned architect C.L. Engel to rebuild the square as the municipal centre of their new city plan for Hel-sinki. Eventually, so many important

Helsinki Cathedral dominates Senate Square.

⊘ NEW FINNISH CUISINE

Any gastronomy snobs who think Finnish cuisine is bland, boring and inferior just haven't eaten in the right places. Over the past decades the idea of what comprises typical Finnish food has changed radically. The strongest influence has come from the revolutionary New Nordic Food movement, which sprang up in 2004 and continues to transform dining habits across the Nordic countries. Its focus is on local organic ingredients, gathered in harmony with the seasons, and pre-pared in a fresh, simple and ethical way. There is also a sense of playfulness and experimentation, as old-style 'grandmoth-er's' recipes are revitalised to suit modern tastes.

Which is probably just as well for Finnish food. Unlike countries such as France and Italy, the Nordic nations never maintained a strong bourgeoisie, whose affluence and leisure time allowed for the development of rich culinary traditions. Rather, Finland's austere gastronomic culture developed as a result of the country's isolated rural economy and its unfor-giving climate. Animals were only put out to pasture during the short summers, while long winters meant harvest stores had to last for six or more months. Finns depended on dried,

smoked and pickled meats and fish dishes that would keep for several seasons.

Today, cutting-edge Finnish cuisine goes back to basics, incorporating some of these traditional methods, but using them to create lighter, fresher dishes. Finnish champions of the movement pare back the unnecessary and leave Finland's ingredients to sing out – whether that's whitefish, pike, lam-preys from Pori, blue mussels or Baltic herring; roast elk, reindeer or Karkkila pork; northern grains like spelt, barley and rye; buttermilk and baked cheeses; nutty new potatoes and sweet, earthy swedes; fresh herbs like angelica, woodruff and dill; or sweet wild strawberries, buckthorn, lingonberries and Arctic cloudberries. In Finland, more so than in the other Nordic countries, there is also an emphasis on design: the restaurant interior, the plates, glasses and cutlery – all have to enhance the dining experience.

Naturally, Helsinki is the best city in the country to sample some of the new directions in Finnish food; if your budget allows, try Demo (www.restaurantdemo.fi) or Olo (http://olo-ravin tola.fi), which have one Michelin star each.

Children's Town at the Helsinki City Museum.

Inside the Helsinki City Museum.

institutions made their home here that Senate Square became a national centre for the country – the equivalent of Russia's Red Square or Beijing's Tiananmen.

Encompassing some 7,000 sq metres (75,350 sq ft), this impressive square is covered by no fewer than 400,000 grey and red cobblestones of Finnish granite. Nowadays, the Senate Square functions principally as a byway. The main building of Helsinki University, which occupies the square's entire western border, has a new entrance at the back that lures student activity away. The Palace of the Council of State, directly opposite, receives few visits from the average citizen. The former town hall, on the south side, is used for entertaining official guests, and the boutiques around it cater mostly for visitors.

But the city remembers. Senaatintori becomes the centre of activity on important occasions such as Independence Day in December, when the windswept square is a sea of candles held by students who march here from Hietaniemi Cemetery in the midwinter

dark. Locals gather again one month later to listen to the mayor's traditional New Year's Eve speech and watch fireworks, and again for May Day.

A self-important statue of Tsar Alexander II, erected in 1894, stands in the centre of all this. At his feet, four additional figures tell the square's story: *Lex*, or law (facing the government palace); *Lux*, or light (facing the sun); *Labor* (facing the university); and *Pax*, or peace (facing the cathedral).

Helsinki Cathedral ⑬ (Tuomiokirkko; daily June–Aug 9am–midnight, Sept–May 9am–6pm, subject to services), up a bank of steep steps on the north side, is a point of pride for Finns, and the exterior – with its five green cupolas, white Corinthian columns and sprinkling of important figurines posing on its roof – is decidedly impressive. The interior, in contrast, is severe. Apart from the gilded altarpiece and organ, only statues of Luther, Mikael Agricola and Melanchthon disturb its white symmetry. If you'd like to see the views from the top of the tower you won't be able to walk

up, but you can give the virtual reality headsets a try.

ENGEL'S TRIUMPH

A walk around Senate Square can also reveal a lot about Helsinki's history. The city's oldest stone building, dating from 1757, is the small blue-grey Sederholm House on the corner of Aleksi and Katariinankatu. In 2012 it became **Children's Town** (Lasten kaupunki; tel: 09-3103 6630; www.helsinginkaupunginmuseo.fi/nayttelyt/lasten-kaupunki; Mon–Fri 11am–5pm, Sat–Sun 11am–5pm; free), a hands-on exhibition for kids, where they can scribble on slates in a 1930s classroom, or toil away in an 18th-century cobbler's workshop. This exhibition is part of the revamped **Helsinki City Museum** (Helsingin Kaupunginmuseo; tel: 09-3103 6630; www.helsinginkaupunginmuseo.fi; Mon–Fri 11am–7pm, Sat–Sun 11am–5pm; free), which received a special commendation at the European Museum of the Year awards in 2018, records the city's history through an impressive collection of one million photographs and 450,000 items. The museum complex comprises five buildings of various eras, including a brand new one, and is accessed through the main gate at Aleksanterinkatu 16.

Across the street is the **Bock House ⑭** (Bockin talo), also 18th century, which became the meeting place for Helsinki's City Council in 1818, as a plaque by its door proclaims. It also served briefly as the governor general's residence after Engel had it embellished with Ionic pillars and a third floor.

The rest of the square is pure Engel, making it not only a beautiful but also an unusually consistent example of neoclassical design. In 1832, the oldest part of the main building of Helsinki University (it was extended later to cover the entire block) was completed under the architect, on the western side of the square. Ten years earlier, he had designed the Council of State, along the entire eastern side of the square. The Finnish government still has its seat here. Engel drew the plan for the cathedral as well, although he died 12 years before its completion in 1852.

Across Unioninkatu, the **University Library ⑮** (Yliopiston kirjasto; Mon–Fri 8am–8pm, Sat–Sun 11am–5pm) is decidedly ornate. Not only do white Corinthian columns line every inch of its yellow facade, but inside the splendour continues. In the central room, more columns (now marble with gold tips) support a dark-wood second tier, beneath a painted cupola ceiling. It is the largest university library in Finland and still very much a working library, so visitors are expected to leave their coats at the door, sign in and, above all, respect the quiet and no entry signs. But don't let this discourage you from enjoying the public parts of this most beautiful of Engel's works, dating from 1845.

KATAJANOKKA

After exploring Helsinki's **Keskusta** (centre), venture into one of the

Fresh, garden-grown vegetables are a good buy at Helsinki's Central Market.

Boat restaurant near Uspenski Cathedral in Northern Harbour.

Sailing ship in the harbour at Katajanokka.

surrounding districts, each of which has its own very particular character, though borders are not always clearly defined.

One of the most attractive is **Katajanokka**, which lies on a small promontory sticking out into the sea a few blocks east from Senate Square. Katajanokka is connected to the centre by short bridges where locals like to cast their fishing rods or, as is increasingly commonplace, attach a padlock. A number of restaurants have opened in recent years, injecting new life into this area. After a snowstorm or on a brilliant spring day, its elegant streets are pure serenity. Unfortunately, the first thing you see crossing the Kanavakatu Bridge on to Katajanokka is one of Alvar Aalto's least successful efforts: the dirty white marble Enso Gutzeit Office Building (the 'sugar cube'), dated 1962. Fortunately, Katajanokka has better sights to offer.

RUSSIAN STYLE

The largest Russian Orthodox church in western Europe, **Uspenski Cathedral** ⑯ (Uspenskin katedraali; Tue–Fri 9.30am–4pm, Sat 10am–3pm, Sun noon–3pm), across the street at the top of a sudden grassy knoll, gives supreme proof of this. Completed in 1868, dedicated to the Virgin Mary and undeniably glamorous, Uspenski makes a striking exception to Helsinki's general architectural style. Its red-brick conglomeration of cross-tipped spires and onion-shaped domes has helped convince many film-makers to use Helsinki as a surrogate Moscow (for example, in *Reds* and *Gorky Park*). The cathedral's interior is also both impressive and atmospheric, with a glittering iconostasis. Services in Old Church Slavonic are held at least twice weekly.

Appropriately enough, a Russian restaurant called the Bellevue (http://restaurantbellevue.com) sits at the base of the cathedral, across from Katajanokka Park. The Bellevue, however, has a slightly unorthodox political history. The restaurant was founded the year Finland declared independence from Russia (1917). One of its golden walls also displays a thank-you note

HELSINKI

received in 1990 from America's former First Lady, Barbara Bush.

The Russian motif is echoed elsewhere on Katajanokka, and flirtatious basilic motifs appear over many doorways. Red brick also gets more use, particularly in the recently built residences on the tip of the promontory. But central Luotsikatu is one street where Jugendian (Art Nouveau) style rules. Many of the buildings on this and nearby streets were designed by the architectural team of Gesellius, Lindgren and Saarinen at the turn of the 20th century and abound with little pleasures. Don't miss the beautiful carved door at No. 1.

WATERFRONT

Turning north from Luotsikatu on to Vyökatu takes you to the northern waterfront. A narrow flight of stone steps leads down to an ageing gateway, which until 1968 blocked the way to the **Naval Barracks** (Merikasarmi). These long, yellow Engel-designed buildings have since been restored and now house the Finnish Foreign Ministry.

Walking back along Merikasarminkatu, you'll pass the former **Helsinki county prison** (Helsingin lääninvankila), which housed prisoners from all over southern Finland until 2002, before its transformation into a rather unusual hotel.

The southern side of Katajanokka is where the huge Viking Line ships come in from Stockholm, disembarking crowds of passengers. The block of old warehouses at Pikku Satamakatu, beside the Viking Line Terminal, and the so-called Wanha Satama have been converted into a clutch of eating spots, exhibition halls, stores and a hotel. Even if you don't have business here, it's worth passing by to view the inventive Jugendian-style Customs and Bonded Warehouse, as designed by Gustaf Nyström in 1900, with its grey turrets and round red-brick towers.

THE OLD CITY

Following Kanavakatu back west will return you to Helsinki's oldest district, **Kruununhaka** ⓱, whose name means 'the Crown's Paddock'; not so many centuries ago it was primarily a home

University Library.

for cows. Senate Square is at the lower end of this area, which is now favoured by the well-heeled and offers a large collection of antique furniture, book and clothing shops, as well as art galleries.

Central Helsinki's second-oldest building lies in the southeastern corner of this district, at the juncture of Aleksanterinkatu and Meritullintori. The modest squat structure was erected in 1765 as a customs warehouse, but now houses everyday offices. Other venerable leftovers of an earlier age hover nearby, such as the deep-red residence at No. 12 Aleksanterinkatu (next to Helsinki's City Museum) with its gorgeous blown-glass windowpanes, and the mid-19th-century, neo-Gothic Ritarihuone ('House of Nobility') situated one block north on Hallituskatu.

A few particularly nice pedestrian streets crown the crest of hilly Kruununhaka. Solid stone buildings cut into exposed rock cliffs, insulating the end of the district from the Siltavuori Strait flowing directly below.

They also shelter the city's oldest extant wooden buildings at Kristianinkatu 12, the **Burgher's House** ⓰ (Ruiskumestarin talo; http://ruiskumestarintalo.fi/en; tel: 09-3107 1549; June–mid-Sept and Nov–Dec Wed–Sun 11am–5pm), built in 1818, shortly after the Great Fire, for a sailor's widow. A high wooden fence encloses it, along with a second mustard-coloured house and a weather-beaten red shed, all huddled round a small earthen courtyard filled with the pungent scent of wood smoke. Apart from a few minor improvements made when it became the home of the city's head fireman in 1859 and a recent renovation prior to its re-opening in early 2017, the main house remains exactly as it was when first built, and its gorgeous slats of wooden flooring are completely original. The furniture, meanwhile, has been assembled from different periods starting from 1860. To top off the period atmosphere, guides dress in old-fashioned garb.

TERVASAARI TO THE BOTANICAL GARDENS

If it's a warm day, you may want to head east down to **Tervasaari** ⓳. This little

Helsinki seen from the Tervasaari island.

island, now connected to Kruunun-haka by a man-made isthmus, used to be the city's storage place for tar – an important early export (Tervasaari means 'tar island'). Modern times have turned it into a nice park for summer sunning, with a dog run and laid-back terraced restaurant.

Walking west now brings you down to Kaisaniemenkatu, the street that begins in front of the railway station and frames the west of Kruununhaka. An attractive park squeezes between it, the station and Kaisaniemi Bay. If you choose to continue along the road you'll find the helpful **Helsinki Tourist Information** within the railway station (tel: 09-3101 3300; www.visithelsinki.fi; summer Mon-Fri 9am-7pm, Sat-Sun 10am-5pm, winter Mon-Fri 9.30am-5.30pm), which offers an extensive selection of maps and brochures. During the summer, if you need information away from the station, simply find one of the Helsinki Helpers dressed in green.

Kaisaniemen puisto is a sort of multi-purpose park, with sloping stretches of grass, a variety of playing fields that turn into ice-hockey rinks in winter, an open-air restaurant and the **University Botanical Gardens** ㉠ (Kasvitieteellinen puutarha; Unioninkatu 44; tel: 09-1912 4455; www.luomus.fi; gardens: daily 9am–8pm; free; greenhouses: Tue–Sat 10am–5pm, Sun until 4pm, Thu until 6pm). Designed by a landscape gardener from St Petersburg in the 1830s, these gardens offer a very peaceful place for a stroll right in the middle of the town.

HAKANIEMI AND KALLIO

A long bridge separates the Kruununhaka area and the park from the tiny district of **Hakaniemi** ㉑ and larger Kallio, which were traditionally Helsinki's working-class neighbourhoods. Lenin briefly lived beside spacious Hakaniemen tori (Hakaniemi Square) before the Russian Revolution. Recently, a growing student and boho

population has lent Hakaniemi a bohemian feel. From Monday to Saturday, however, a no-nonsense market takes over the square (Mon–Sat 6.30am–4pm) and the Hakaniemi Market Hall (Mon–Fri 8am–6pm, Sat 8am–6pm) on its edge. Both are noticeably more natural than those at the Central Market. A food market fills the ground floor of the hall, while upstairs is devoted to clothes and fabric, including stands run by the ubiquitous Marimekko and Aarikka companies.

Kallio ㉒ was first built up in haphazard fashion during the early 19th century. It was eventually given a city plan and rebuilt after the fashion of St Petersburg, but you still need to know where to wander to find attractive areas. One of its prettiest blocks, Torkkelinkatu, rises above the whimsical Kallio Library on Viides Linja. The nearby Kallio Church is an important Art Nouveau structure in grey granite from 1912. Its bells ring a tune by Sibelius.

The northern border of Kallio hides the **Museum of Worker Housing** ㉓ (Työväenasuntomuseo; Kirstinkuja 4;

⊙ Tip

Järvenpää, the birthplace of Jean Sibelius, is a popular place to visit on a day trip from Helsinki. The family home was built on a strip of wooded land in 1904, and Sibelius lived and worked here until he died (see page 202). Both he and his wife are buried in the grounds. To get there, take one of the regular trains from Helsinki to Järvenpää, then walk or cycle.

Bookworm's heaven in the town centre.

tel: 09-3107 1548; www.workerhousingmuseum.fi; May–late Sept Wed–Sun 11am–5pm; guided tour; free). This museum comprises four wooden tenements built by the city for its workers and used from 1909 until 1987. Household scenes have been recreated with great effect in nine apartments, using intimate, first-person knowledge from former inhabitants. All the apartments displayed are single stove rooms that housed entire families. This meant that, by day, the beds had to be tucked away in some fashion, but, in flat 9E (1925), the beds of a widow and five of her six children are left unmade. Only the eldest daughter had gone to work, folding her bed against the wall and leaving steel hair curlers on the table. This family's story is particularly poignant; after the woman's husband committed suicide, she saved until she was able to buy a cross for his grave and, with no money left to hire a car, carried it on her back all the way to Malmi Cemetery.

On a more cheerful note, Helsinki's amusement park, **Linnanmäki** ㉔ (access from Helsinginkatu or Tivolitie; tel: 010-5722 200; www.linnanmaki.fi; May–mid-Oct, days and times vary – see website for details) is perched atop a wooded hill a short walk north from here. Half a million people visit every year, attracted by its rides and sideshows, from the famous wooden roller-coaster Vuoristorata to the modern twisting loop-the-loop Ukko. Many of the rides are free; but an all-ride pass costs €42 (reduced to €33 three hours before closing time). Profits go to children's charities.

TÖÖLÖ BAY

Kallio lies north of the railway station along the east side of Töölö Bay. Several other of Helsinki's 50-odd museums lie on the bay's western side, in a neighbourhood called **Töölö**. Like Kallio, Töölö came into its own after the turn of the 20th century. Though not especially chic today, many of its streets offer priceless examples of Jugendian architecture.

To reach Töölö from Kallio, you can walk through the pleasant park around the bay's north end, over the train tracks. This route passes some places

Roller-coaster at Linnanmäki, Helsinki's funfair.

that are important for local people: the City Theatre, the City Botanical Gardens, the Olympic Stadium (scheduled to reopen in 2020) – beside which is an overly popular outdoor swimming pool) and the enormous, ultramodern **Finnish National Opera House** ㉕ (Suomen Kansallisooppera; tel: 09-4030 2211; www.ooppera.fi; contact the box office to arrange guided tours in English), which opened in 1993. It produces around 15 operas and nine ballets per year. Original-language performances are surtitled in Finnish, Swedish and English.

To take the alternative route to Töölö, start by walking one block west of the railway station to Mannerheimintie, as far as the four-storey Forum Shopping Centre, where there are shops, fastfood restaurants, a bar and two cafés. Turn north, and one-and-a-half blocks further on a bronze statue of General Mannerheim on horseback presides over the busy intersection between Mannerheimintie, Arkadian, Postikatu and Salomon streets. Töölö lies directly across the traffic bridge from here.

PARLIAMENT BUILDING AND NATIONAL MUSEUM

The renovated **Parliament Building** ㉖ (Eduskuntatalo; tel: 09-432 2027; guided tours for groups of six can be arranged Mon–Fri), directly across the street, atop an important row of steps, is decidedly less casual. Fourteen columns of red granite mark its stern facade, built 1925–30 after J.S. Sirén's design. The visitors' centre round the corner (Arkadiankatu 3; Mon–Fri 10am–4pm) hands out some information about the parliament building.

Statues of former Finnish presidents scatter the area between the Parliament Building and the **National Museum** ㉗ (Kansallismuseo; tel: 040-128 6469; www.kansallismuseo.fi; Tue–Sun 11am–6pm). The Gesellius-Lindgren-Saarinen trio designed this museum in 1906 to reflect Finnish history in its very construction. Although National

Romantic in style, the heavy grey building also incorporates aspects of old Finnish church and castle architecture. The main tower imitates that of Turku Cathedral (see page 184).

The museum's decoration and permanent collection offer more on Finland. The stone bear by the entrance is the work of Wikström and the frescoes on the foyer ceiling, depicting scenes from Finland's national epic the *Kalevala*, are by Gallén-Kallela. The entertaining jumble of artefacts inside runs from early archaeological finds up to present-day items, and the exhibits are well explained in four languages. The National Museum now also incorporates the Museum of Cultures. Nearby, the fine Hakasalmi Villa (tel: 09-3107 8519; www.hakasalmivilla.fi; Tue–Sun 11am–5pm, Tue until 7pm; free) houses compelling temporary exhibitions, and holds one of the city's most cosy cafés (completely gluten-free).

FINLANDIA HALL AND SIBELIUS ACADEMY

Finlandia Hall ㉘ (Finlandiatalo; tel: 09-40241; www.finlandiatalo.fi; open

Fresh produce at Hakaniemi Market.

You'll find interesting antique shops in Punavuori.

Kiasma.

during events and for guided tours) next door is undoubtedly the most famous building in Töölö – if not all of Helsinki. Alvar Aalto designed it in 1962 both inside and out, right down to the last doorknob.

The striking white building was constructed specifically to blend environmentally with the backdrop of Hesperia Park and Töölö Bay, especially in the winter. Ironically, the bitter Finnish weather caused the Carrara marble facade to warp disastrously. A new, thicker layer of white marble replaced the old one in 1998 – and is being tortured by the elements in exactly the same way. Although it has served as an indisputable bastion for modern Finnish culture, the hall has also had problems in the past with its acoustics. The Helsinki Philharmonic Orchestra has decamped to the Musiikkitalo, which opened in 2011 next to Kiasma, and which has now taken over as the country's pre-eminent venue for classical music. Today Finlandiatalo is used mainly as a unique and highly impressive conference centre.

A number of other important cultural spots are clustered around the Parliament Building. The **Sibelius Academy** (tel: 0600-900 900 for ticket sales; www.uniarts.fi/en/siba), Helsinki's renowned musical conservatory, is just around the corner. Check the website for forthcoming concerts: classical recitals, many free, are given here by some of the top students.

NATURAL HISTORY MUSEUM AND ROCK CHURCH

Across the street at Pohjoinen Rautatiekatu 13 is the **Natural History Museum ㉙** (Luonnontieteellinen museo; tel: 29-412 8800; www.luomus.fi; June–Aug Tue–Sun 10am–5pm, Sept–May Tue–Wed and Fri 9am–4pm, Thu 9am–6pm, Sat–Sun 10am–4pm), whose numerous showcases and vivid dioramas offer a colourful lesson on Finnish wildlife. Pick up a free headset for English explanations. The museum's neo-Baroque building is easily identified by the striking bronze cast of an elk on its lawn.

Nestling, literally, into a small hill behind the winding streets of Töölö

is the ultramodern church **Rock Church** ㉚ (Temppeliaukion kirkko; www.temppeliaukionkirkko.fi/en/index.html; tel: 09-2340 6320 to listen to the recorded opening hours). It is not only an architectural oddity – built directly into the cliffs, with inner walls of stone and a circular coiled-copper roof – but also the site of many excellent concerts during the year. Hugely controversial when it was built in 1969, this understated building now attracts up to 8,000 visitors a day in summer.

CULTURAL HUB

The whole Töölö neighbourhood has evolved based on an original plan by Alvar Aalto, and is still growing and changing. The city's cultural centre is gradually migrating to this area from Senate Square. The **Helsinki Music Centre** (Musiikkitalo; ticket sales tel: 0600-900 900 or 0600-10 800; www.musiikkitalo.fi) is in a prime position on Mannerheiminaukio, just across from the Parliament Building and adjacent to Finlandia Hall. Its understated architecture is deliberate – it was designed to blend in rather than compete with its prestigious neighbours. The acoustics of its six concert halls, however, are second to none – Japanese acoustician Yasuhisa Toyota created each one to host a specific kind of music, from early music to electronica. It's the main venue for concerts by the Helsinki Philharmonic Orchestra, the Finnish Radio Symphony Orchestra and the Sibelius Academy, and puts on frequent pop concerts. Behind it is the **Central Library Oodi** (Keskustakirjasto Oodi; Mon–Fri 8am–10pm, Sat–Sun 10am–8pm), which opened in 2018. Designed to feel like an open meeting place, it is home to over 100,000 books, nine living trees, two cafés, and a number of circular skylights.

Next door to the Music Centre is **Kiasma** ㉛ (tel: 0294-500 501; www.kiasma.fi; Sun 10am–5pm, Wed–Fri 10am–8.30pm, Tue and Sat 10am–6pm), Helsinki's reigning museum of contemporary art. This remarkable machine-like structure by American architect Steven Holl is a symbol of a new Helsinki. The curving asymmetrical building harmoniously interacts

National Museum.

Statue of General Mannerheim, distinguished Commander-in-Chief of the Finnish army in World War II.

Inside the Design Museum.

with its surroundings – the oddly shaped windows afford good views of key landmarks. The bold exhibitions vary from astounding to macabre.

Other Functionalist architecture in the area includes Lasipalatsi ('Glass Palace'), which has been rejuvenated to create a welcoming media centre with an internet library; and Tennispalatsi ('Tennis Palace'), which was used during the 1952 Olympic Games, and now houses Finland's largest cinema complex (14 screens) and the **Helsinki Art Museum** (Helsingin Taidemuseo HAM; tel: 09-3108 7001; www.hamhelsinki.fi; Tue–Sun 11am–7pm). The museum hosts interesting Finnish and international temporary exhibitions, including contemporary art and popular culture and also manages a collection of over 9,000 works of art, almost half of which are displayed in parks, streets and offices throughout Helsinki.

Close to Lasipalatsi, the **Amos Anderson Art Museum** (tel: 09-684 4460; www.amosanderson.fi; Mon, Thu–Fri 10am–6pm, Wed 10am–8pm, Sat–Sun 11am–5pm) is the largest private collection of art in Finland, with the emphasis on 20th-century paintings, prints and sculptures. Its new annex, **Amos Rex**, had to be built underground due to planning permission issues. The result is a spectacular series of underground domes galleries with skylights. Above ground, on Lasipalatsi square, the series of lunar crater skylights create a playful landscape.

Just around the corner, outside the busy Kamppi shopping centre/long-distance bus station, you'll find another of Helsinki's one-of-a-kind churches. The wooden **Kamppi Chapel of Silence** (tel: 50-578 1136; www.kampinkappeli.fi; Mon–Fri 8am–8pm, Sat–Sun 10am–6pm) is an oasis of calm, which won international acclaim long before its opening in 2012.

BULEVARDI

Another district in southwestern Helsinki worth exploring is **Punavuori** ㉜, a bohemian chic area south of Esplanade Park and the city centre. The main street here is **Bulevardi**, one of Helsinki's most beautiful avenues,

which begins at a perpendicular angle from Mannerheimintie (just a couple of blocks before its end) and leads down to Hietalahti shipyard. Most of the buildings date from between 1890 and 1920 and were formerly home to Helsinki's turn-of-the-century patricians. Vanha kirkko (The Old Church), however, between Annan and Yrjön streets, is a stray from Engel. Dating from 1826, it was the first Lutheran church to be built in the new 'capital'.

The former National Opera House – now the Aleksanter Theatre – lies a few blocks further west on Bulevardi. This delightful red building was erected in 1879 as a theatre for Russian officers and for decades it housed the national opera, until the construction of the new opera house (see page 155). The inside is plush and ornate, and the building now functions as a musical theatre and school.

As you reach the end of Bulevardi, you will come to the buildings of the former Sinebrychoff Brewery, which was established in 1819 and is the oldest brewery in Finland. The

Sinebrychoff Art Museum (Sinebrychoffin Taidemuseo; tel: 09-1733 6460; www.sinebrychoffintaidemuseo.fi; Tue, Thu and Fri 11am–6pm, Wed 11am–8pm, Sat–Sun 10am–5pm), which specialises in old European art, is housed at Bulevardi 40, and includes several grandiose rooms containing Old Masters and miniatures.

Don't miss the **Hietalahdentori** ㉝, best known for its flea market. The goods are usually just bric-a-brac and clothes, but this market is one of the best places in Helsinki to watch large numbers of locals in action. It opens daily from June to September, but the weekend (Sat 8am–4pm, Sun 10am–4pm) is by far the best and busiest time to go. On the side of the square, the market hall sells fresh local produce (Mon–Fri 8am–6pm, Sat 8am–4pm, June–Aug also Sun 10am–4pm). Bulevardi holds many fashionable art galleries and boutiques, which spill into neighbouring streets. One of the intersecting streets, **Fredrikinkatu** (known locally as *Freda*) has several trendy boutiques and design shops. One block south and parallel to Bulevardi is

Temppeliaukio church is built into the rock.

The tubular Sibelius Monument by Eila Hiltunen honours Finland's finest composer.

Kaivopuisto Park.

Uudenmaankatu and the pedestrianised Iso-Roobertinkatu, which form a part of the 'bar-hopping' district for the young and trendy. Another two blocks further on is the Johannes Church. This rather regal affair with two piercing stiletto spires is the largest church in Helsinki and a particularly popular place for choral concerts, with excellent acoustics. Across the street, at Korkeavuorenkatu 23, the **Design Museum** (Designmuseo; tel: 09-622 0540; www.designmuseum.fi; June–Aug daily 11am–6pm, Sept–May Tue 11am–8pm, Wed–Sun 11am–6pm) showcases Finland's famed skills in *objets* and furniture design, including Aalto furniture, Lapponia jewellery and many new names (see page 78).

AROUND EIRA AND ULLANLINNA

Heading directly south from here you come upon Eira, historically Helsinki's most exclusive neighbourhood. On the southernmost end of the peninsula the coastline below Eira is lined by parkland. While the sea is still frozen, you can actually walk out over the ice to some of the closer offshore islands. After the ice melts, small boats dock all along the coastline and Sunday cyclists take to the paths. Towards the northeast and the centre, this strip of green grows into Helsinki's oldest and best park, **Kaivopuisto** ㉞. In summer, the city sponsors free concerts here and Kaivopuisto overflows with happy sunbathing locals, strolling, eating ice cream and admiring the fine views across to Suomenlinna.

Embassies fill the well-heeled Ullanlinna district. Most noticeably, the Russian Embassy commands almost a block opposite St Henrik's, one of Helsinki's two Catholic churches. Above them rises **Observatory Hill** (the Finnish name *Tähtitorninmäki* literally means 'star tower hill'), where the tiny, renovated Engel-designed observatory admits stargazers on spring and autumn evenings. It's worth the climb for its views over the city centre and Katajanokka to the north.

The fine **Mannerheim Museum** ㉟ (Mannerheim Museo; tel: 09-635 443; www.mannerheim-museo.fi; Fri-Sun

11am–4pm; guided tour obligatory) is tucked away between embassies at Kalliolinnantie 14. It was the home of Baron C.G.E. Mannerheim, Marshal of Finland, perhaps the most respected figure in the country's history (see page 53). His achievements include a two-year expedition to Asia, when he travelled 14,000km (8,700 miles) on horseback along the Silk Road, and the house is filled with souvenirs and hunting trophies. The engaging guides do a great job of bringing his complex character to life.

Not far away, at Kalliolinnantie 8, is the former home of the **Cygnaeus Gallery**, the tiny, exquisite wooden summer home of local poet and art collector, Frederik Cygnaeus. The gallery closed down in 2014 and its remarkable collection of 19th-century Finnish painting and sculpture has been moved to the National Museum warehouses until it finds a new home.

Directly below to the east is the **Olympia Terminal ㊱** (Olympiaterminaali), the port of call for huge Viking and Silja Line ships and a reminder that the sea has brought prosperity to Helsinki, the 'Daughter of the Baltic'.

SUOMENLINNA

Literally hundreds of islands dot the city's coastline. Some, like Lauttasaari and Kulosaari, have been so integrated by bridges and metro lines that they are almost indistinguishable from the mainland. Others are reserved for weekend cottages, reached over the ice in winter or by motorboat in summer.

Suomenlinna ㊲ ('Finland's castle'; www.suomenlinna.fi), scattered across eight rocky skerries, is an immense sea fort and one of Helsinki's major attractions. It has played an integral part in Helsinki's life since its construction in 1748, under Count Augustin Ehrensvärd. It is a unique architectural monument, listed by Unesco as a World Heritage site.

Suomenlinna has a complicated identity. It began as a naval post,

and still houses Finland's Naval War Academy, but it is hardly just a military enclave. Around 850 people live here year-round in a village-like community: many work at the fortress, and there is also a thriving colony of artists, who use restored bastions as studios and showrooms.

Getting to Suomenlinna is cheap and easy. Waterbuses leave from Market Square one to four times per hour, depending on the season, and cost the same as a metro ticket. Following the 15-minute journey, they dock on Iso Mustasaari and from here, a hilly path leads up through **Jetty Barracks** (Rantakasarmi), which now house art exhibitions and an interesting restaurant and microbrewery by the name of Suomenlinna Panimo Brewery (tel: 09-228 5030).

ISLAND MUSEUMS

Continuing past wooden houses, the Lutheran church sometimes stages concerts. This part of Suomenlinna has permanent residents living both in new houses and Russian-era

Try your hand at dinghy sailing around Helsinki's islands.

Helsinki's shopping area is Aleksanterinkatu.

former military houses. This island also has six museums of interest. The **Suomenlinna Toy Museum** (Suomenlinnan Lelumuseo; tel: 040-500 6607; May–early Oct, times vary so check the main website) contains thousands of dolls and toys from the Helsinki region from the 1830s to the 1960s, collected during the last 30 years. The **Visitor Centre** (tel: 029-533 8410; daily May–Sept 10am–6pm; Oct–Apr 10.30am–4.30pm) houses the large **Suomenlinna Museum** (same hours as Visitor Centre), the main historical exhibition of the islands. A fine, multimedia programme is shown regularly to fill you in on the details. The Military Museum's Manege (mid-June–Oct, times vary so check the main website) exhibits uniforms, heavy equipment – authentic artillery, tanks and other war machines, with roots in Swedish, Russian and Finnish history. Crossing the bridge leads to the rambling remains of the Ehrensvärd Crown Castle (Kruunulinna Ehrensvärd) and gardens. The castle courtyard is the best-preserved section of the fortress and contains the 1788 sarcophagus of the Count himself. His former home is now the Ehrensvärd Museum (May–Sept, times vary so check the main website), with old furniture, arms and lithographs.

The rest of Suomenlinna is split between residences and the fortress fortifications, which spread across Susisaari and the southernmost island of Kustaanmiekka. From the highest outcrop on this windswept last island, close to an atmospheric summer restaurant called Walhalla, it is possible to see Estonia, some 80km (50 miles) away, on a clear day. There is also the restored Vesikko Submarine and the Customs Museum (free).

HELSINKI'S OFFSHORE ISLANDS

Korkeasaari 38 is a popular tourist attraction, with the zoo dominating this rocky outcrop just a few steps away from the mouth of Sörnäinen Harbour. You can reach it by boat from Hakaniemi or from the Market Square. **Helsinki Zoo** (Högholmen; tel: 09-310 1615; www.korkeasaari.fi; daily from 10am, Nov–Feb until 4pm, Oct and Mar–Apr Sat–Sun until 6pm, Jun–Aug until 8pm, Sep until 6pm), perhaps not surprisingly, specialises in 'cold-climate animals', including some big beasts like Asian lions, brown bears and snow leopards. The interesting Amazonia House enclosure is home to South American animals.

Seurasaari 39 is also an atmospheric island, beloved by Helsinki dwellers and visitors alike. A pretty, forested place, its northeastern side has been made into an Open-Air Museum (Ulkomuseo; tel: 29 5336912; www.kansallismuseo.fi; June–Aug daily 11am–5pm; mid-May and early Sept Mon–Fri 9am–3pm, Sat–Sun 11am–5pm), with wooden buildings from provinces all over Finland. The transplanted houses date from the 17th to 19th centuries and include farmsteads and a church. Bonfires are

Boats connect Helsinki with nearby islands.

held near here to celebrate traditional festivities for Midsummer and Easter, during which local Finnish children dress up as 'Easter witches'. The other side of the island is a national park. Seurasaari also has one of Helsinki's naturist beaches. Here there are separate sections for both sexes, whereas on the island of Harakka the beach is shared by men and women.

The island is connected to the shore by a wooden footbridge, so there's no need for a boat. Just take either bus No. 24 from the centre or cycle along the Meilahti coastal drive (which takes you past Sibelius Park and the silvery tubular Sibelius Monument) to the bridge. Admission to the island is free, but to enter any of the houses you'll need to buy a ticket.

Less well-trodden are the smaller islands that form a string around Helsinki's southern peninsula. Across the 'Olympic Harbour' are Luoto and **Valkosaari**, popular restaurant islands with romantic villas as dining spots. A long pier outside Kaivopuisto (see page 160) offers a boat service to Särkkä, another island with a popular restaurant, and Harakka. **Uunisaari** is accessible at the southern end of the street Neitsytpolku. It's a popular recreational island with a beach, a sauna and a restaurant, and is very popular with young Finnish couples.

Helsinki residents' favourite island for swimming is undoubtedly **Pihlajasaari**. Literally meaning 'Rowan Island', Pihlajasaari actually comprises two islands, with a sandy beach, café, sauna and changing cabins on the larger island's western shore. The nudist beach is on the smaller island, which also hides wartime bunkers. Boats to Pihlajasaari depart from mid-May to August every 15 to 30 minutes, just outside Café Carusel in Eira.

The very special **Harakka** ('Magpie') island is now a wildlife reserve but, up until 1990, was reserved for military purposes; this helps explain why it is still absolutely pristine. You can reach Harakka by boat in the summer or, in the winter, by crossing the ice from Eira (see page 160).

The footbridge to Seurasaari.

VISITING RUSSIA AND THE BALTICS

Finland is relatively close to the continental mainland, and a visit to the Baltic nations is surprisingly easy.

Tucked away in the northeast of Europe, Finland is uniquely situated for exploring Russia and the Baltic countries. Estonia, Latvia and Lithuania, with their richly historic capitals, are within a reasonable distance. Tallinn, Estonia's medieval metropolis, is particularly accessible – Finns and foreigners alike enjoy 24-hour mini cruises from Helsinki, with around 20 departures per day in summer. From Tallinn, Riga (Latvia) is a 4.5-hour bus ride; while Vilnius (Lithuania) is a nine-hour drive. Travelling to Russia takes more forethought; but with a bit of planning, you could be exploring

St Petersburg's Winter Palace.

the treasures of St Petersburg's Hermitage within a few hours of leaving Helsinki.

Luxurious car ferries ply the Baltic sea lanes between Sweden, the Åland Islands, Finland and Estonia. The top players – Viking Line (white and red) and Silja Line (white and blue) – are fun, value for money, and cruise through the most beautiful seascapes in the world. See page 271 for further transport details.

ST PETERSBURG

Three-day visa-free round trips across the Bay of Finland to the gorgeous city of St Petersburg are immensely popular (see page 271). Largely built by European architects in the 18th century, St Petersburg is the least Russian of all the country's cities. Situated on 40 islands in the Neva River Delta, its Italianate palazzi and numerous waterways draw comparisons with Venice and Amsterdam.

The city's Hermitage gallery, housed in the Winter Palace, is one of the must-sees on a flying visit to the city. It contains three million works of art, so it's worth working out what you want to see beforehand! Highlights of its Western European collection include masterpieces by Rembrandt, Poussin, Cézanne, Van Gogh and Matisse. You can find floor plans and further information on the museum's website: www.hermitagemuseum.org.

St Petersburg is a rewarding city for walking and absorbing the street life. The city is particularly lively during the 'white nights' of June, when everyone comes out to watch the lingering sunsets. A walk from the Hermitage, through the archway of the General Staff building, will take you to Nevsky Prospekt, the city's main thoroughfare. Men still play chess here and street musicians perform. Also visit the enclosed market off Nevsky for a slice of daily life. The Kafe Literaturnoye (18 Nevsky) has a Viennese atmosphere: coffee and cakes, and occasional poetry readings or chamber concerts. Pushkin ate his last meal here in 1837, before fighting a fatal duel.

Arts Square, round the corner, offers music at the Philharmonia Bolshoy and the Glinka Maly halls, and opera and ballet at the Mariinsky Theatre.

Gostiny Dvor (35 Nevsky) is the largest department store, where home-produced consumer goods sit beside modern Western imports.

PETERHOF PALACE (PETRODVORETS)

Don't miss the stunning Peterhof Palace, a Unesco World Heritage site 28km (18 miles) west of St Petersburg. This is Peter the Great's answer to Versailles – its astonishing fountains and water features are some of the finest in the world. The centrepiece of the Great Cascade is a statue of Samson tearing open the jaws of a lion, which symbolises Peter's victory over the Swedes in 1709. Equally revealing of the tsar's character are the trick fountains scattered around: be careful when choosing a seat – some will send up a shower of water.

TALLINN

Tallinn, the capital of Estonia, is a two-hour ferry hop from Helsinki, just 80km (50 miles) across the water. From here you can set off to explore all three independent Baltic States. Tallinn is a tremendously popular destination for Finnish tourists, drawn by its lively nightlife and inexpensive alcohol; it's a big stag-party destination for Brits, too, for similar reasons. But the beautiful walled medieval Old Town, another Unesco World Heritage site, is a gem in its own right, and one that you could wander for several days. Here, cobbled alleys ascend from the 14th-century castle and the Gothic architecture reminds you that Tallinn was once an important port of the Hanseatic League. A great way to get to grips with the city's long and fascinating history is on a Tallinn Free Tour (www.freetour.com/tallinn). These lively walks set off from outside the tourist office at noon daily. There are fabulous views over the red-tiled roofs from the top of Toompea Hill.

RIGA

Latvia's capital, Riga, a city founded by merchants, is also rich in history but receives far fewer tourists, making it arguably a better option to visit. Its medieval centre is not as well preserved as Tallinn's, but the city is still a Unesco World Heritage site thanks to its amazing proliferation of Jugendstil (Art Nouveau) architecture – there are around 800 buildings from the early 1900s in this compact capital. A walk through Riga is the next best thing to a time machine: fascinating buildings range from the Romanesque St George's Church (now containing the Museum of Decorative Arts and Design) to brutal Stalinist structures like the Latvian Academy of Sciences (with a viewing platform on the 17th floor). The 13th-century cathedral, lined with the tombs of bishops, knights and *landmeisters*, contains the fourth-largest organ in the world: most evenings you can hear performances of Bach or Mozart here.

VILNIUS

Lithuania's capital, Vilnius, also has a Unesco World Heritage-blessed Old Town, with a strong Jewish history. Its medieval streets cluster below the squat, redbrick Gediminas' Tower, high on its hilltop. Gothic and Renaissance buildings greet you at every step, as do the ubiquitous jewellery shops selling amber, for which Lithuania has long been famous. The festive atmosphere that prevailed when independence arrived is summed up by a bust of Frank Zappa, raised after those of Lenin came down.

The skyline of Tallinn, Estonia.

📷 THE TRADITIONAL FINNISH SAUNA

An old Finnish proverb says: 'First you build the sauna, then you build the house'; even today, there's nothing so uniquely Finnish as a sauna.

There are some things along the way that a traveller does not forget – and a real Finnish sauna is one of them. Although its origin is obscure, the sauna came to Finland over 2,000 years ago, and it is a rare Finn who admits to not liking one. Official statistics estimate that there are over 3 million saunas in Finland – that's more than one for every two Finns – and many of these are in the summer cottages and cabins that dot the shoreline of the country's lakes (see page 222). The sauna is a national institution and a way of life.

BUSINESS AND PLEASURE

The sauna outgrew its rural roots long ago. Today, be it in a city or a village, you will find public saunas everywhere, and it is fairly safe to assume that every new apartment block has a sauna for its tenants. Many companies also maintain saunas for their employees.

A Finnish sauna is not a meeting place for romance or sexual encounter, as it may be in some countries; codes of behaviour are strict. Titles and position are, they say, left hanging in the changing room with the clothes. It is not unusual for board meetings and government cabinet meetings to be held in a sauna – perhaps because swearing or raising one's voice is a cultural no-no once inside.

Soaking up the heat in a sauna is a refreshing and revitalising experience, good for the skin and the psyche.

A Helsinki sauna.

Typical Finnish sauna by a lake.

Some brave souls dive into icy water or jump through holes in the ice – not recommended practice for people with high blood pressure.

How to take a sauna

Being invited to a Finnish sauna is an honour. It's polite to take a shower first, and to put a towel on the bench prior to sitting down. The ideal sauna temperature is 80–100°C (175–210°F): a good host tries to find the right amount of steam for everyone. A common practice is to brush oneself with a wet birch switch, called the *vihta*, which gives off a fresh fragrance and increases blood circulation.

How long you sit in the sauna is entirely up to you. When you have had enough, you move on to stage two: cooling off. A cold shower is the most common way but, if the sauna is by a lake or the sea, a quick plunge into the cool (or often freezing) water is stimulating. Most Finnish people repeat the heating and cooling process at least twice, but there is no 'right way' – do what is comfortable for you.

The final stage is to dry off, which should be done naturally, to avoid further perspiration. It is also time for a thirst-quenching drink and a snack to complete the ritual.

But there is more to the sauna than just getting clean. It is a social event and a ritual – a time to meet friends or family, to share gossip and news.

...nish musician M. A. Numminen giving a concert in ...e country's largest sauna, at the Naval Academy ...Suomenlinna.

...oling off after a sauna in Lapland.

Birch leaves, cut in early summer when they are green, are tied up in bundles and used in the sauna as switches to increase blood circulation.

Bengtskär lighthouse, near Hanko.

SOUTHERN FINLAND

From Swedish-speaking farming communities to bastions built to protect the Finnish-Russian border towns, the south coast has an atmosphere quite distinct from the rest of the country.

To follow the south coast of Finland from west to east is to follow a route once travelled by Nordic kings and princes to St Petersburg, known appropriately in Finnish as *Kunikaantie*, or the King's Road. It is mainly flat, coastal country covered with farmland and densely grown forest. And, because proximity to the coast has always given extra value to land – in addition to the beneficial, warming effects of the Gulf of Finland – this area has traditionally been heavily settled by Finnish peasants and manual labourers.

It is also heavily Swedish-speaking. From Pargas, south of Turku at the head of the Turku archipelago, through Ekenäs (Tammisaari), Karis (Karjaa), and further east through a cluster of small villages on the approach to Kotka, you will hear a great deal of Swedish and see it as the first language on signposts. This is all part of the democracy of bilingualism in Finland: in any town with a majority of Swedish-speakers, the Swedish name will take precedence.

FARMS AND FORTRESSES

The landscape changes only very subtly from west to east. The low farmland tends to be misty in the early morning and late evening. While not as rich in lakes as the country north of here, it is sufficiently irrigated by local meandering rivers and streams, and there are plenty of good walking trails.

The green of ripening wheat and the golden hue of rapeseed dominate in late spring, after which the wheat matures and the wild flowers explode into bloom. The grassy strips at the roadside are first overrun with cowslip and lupin, a midsummer flower with tall purple, pink and white spindles. When the lupin fades, the landscape is overtaken by *maitohorsma,* a tall, spindly flower, its magenta petals filling not just the edge of the road but entire

Main attractions

Hanko
Ekenäs
Fiskars
Hvitträsk
Espoo
Tarvaspää
Porvoo
Loviisa
Kotka
Hamina

Map on page 170

Ekenäs.

The harbour at Hanko, Finland's southernmost town.

forests and fields. Autumn is slightly more colourful in the west, where the linden adds bright colour to the golden hue of the birches. The west is also hillier than the east, and set against this backdrop are clusters of attractive old farm buildings, stained dark red, and manor houses painted a rich ochre or brilliant yellow.

The eastern section of the coast, beyond Helsinki, is scattered with fortifications, a telling reminder of Finland's chequered past. For the Swedes, then the Russians, and finally the independent Finns, the Russian border has served as a critical dividing line, for centuries separating nations, cultures and peoples.

The Finnish-Russian borders still have a no-man's land running between them, and although travel between the two countries has become far simpler and more popular since the break-up of the USSR, there is a definite change in atmosphere after you've crossed from west to east: a somewhat sterner attitude in Russian customs guards and a noticeable change in road conditions and

land upkeep. Plan ahead if you intend to travel into Russia as you'll need a visa.

SALO

From the ancient city of Turku (see page 179), the country's former capital, the King's Road heads east, past the turn-off to Pargas and Turku's archipelago. It continues through farmland to **Salo ❶**, in the heart of the apple-growing Salojoki Valley. The town centre is dominated by a triad of churches – the Lutheran Uskela (Engel, 1832), the Greek Orthodox Tsasouna at its foot, and the stunningly modern Helisnummen (Helisnummi Church) about 4km (2.5 miles) outside the town. Salo still has a very lively market, held every day except Sundays. Along the Uskela River there are some beautiful residential garden districts.

From Salo, the post route swoops south, following Road 52 back towards the sea. It originally curved eastward again at Tenhloa, but modern visitors should take a detour south and west, to where the land dips a cautious toe into the waves.

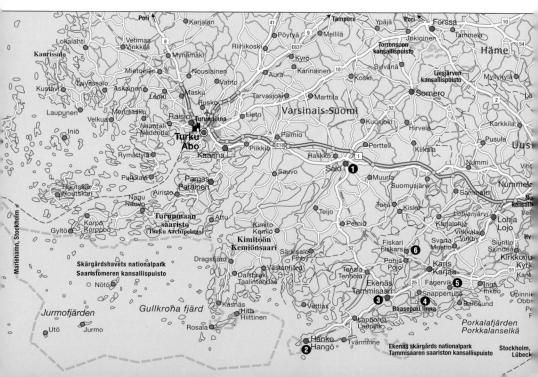

HANKO

Right out on a peninsula tip is the super summer resort **Hanko** ❷ (Hangö), Finland's southernmost town. Known for its large, lively marina, its annual July regatta and its 30km (19 miles) of sandy beaches, Hanko also has some of the most playful architecture in Finland. A long parade of turreted and deeply eaved villas, built at the turn of the 20th century when Hanko was a popular spa town, follows the stretch of beach. In summer, Hanko is the place to bask in sunshine and good cheer: if swimming and sunbathing aren't enough, all kinds of activities are on offer here, from gambling your cash away in the town's casino to kayaking, surfing, scuba diving, birdwatching, cycling, tennis, horse riding, boat trips and guided seal safaris.

Yet Hanko hasn't always been a joyful summer playground. It was also the port from which 300,000 Finns emigrated between 1880 and 1930 to escape raging epidemics and famine – the Emigration Monument, on Merikat, commemorates these unhappy years.

At the end of the Winter War, the Hanko headland became a Soviet naval base under the terms of the Moscow Peace Treaty – Hanko's inhabitants had just 10 days to evacuate their homes. The small **Front Line Museum** (Hangon Rintamamuseo; Hankoniementie, Lappohja; tel: 050 5666-223; Sept–Dec and Apr–May Sat–Sun noon–5pm, June–Aug daily 11am–6pm), 17km (10.5 miles) along the peninsula, has exhibits relating to this period.

EKENÄS

Ekenäs ❸ (Tammisaari) is the next main coastal stop, a finely laid-out old town with cobbled streets (named after different craft trades) that are great for a stroll. Just to the south is the Ekenäs Archipelago National Park, resplendent with marshes, forests and water birds.

There is an extremely active boating life in and around Ekenäs, and numerous outdoor concerts in summer: Ekenäs is considered by many to be the major cultural centre of Finland's Swedish-speaking people. The Knippan boardwalk restaurant and

The Monument of Liberty in Hanko, erected in 1921.

the steeple of the old granite church (1680) are the town's main landmarks. There's also a pretty seaside camping ground within walking distance. For historical background to the town including historical interiors and artifacts from prehistoric to modern times, visit the **EKTA** museum (Gustav Wasas Gata 11; tel: 019-289 2512; Jan–late Aug Tue–Sun 11am–5pm, late Aug–Dec Wed–Sun 11am–5pm).

Just north of Ekenäs along Road 52 is the Teijo hiking area, where marked trails cut through gorgeous lakes and forests, offering plenty of scope for interesting exploration.

AROUND RAASEPORI CASTLE

A few kilometres eastward is **Snappertuna** (no connection with fish), a farming village of Swedish-speaking Finns and the town closest to the splendid 14th-century **Raasepori castle** ❹ (Raseborg; May–mid-June daily 10am–5pm, mid-June–early Aug daily 10am–8pm, rest of Aug 10am–5pm, Sept Sat–Sun 10am–5pm), enfolded in a wooded valley. Most of the fortification is in good condition, and you can freely tour its ramparts and impressive interior spaces, refurbished in wood.

The Outdoor Theatre in the Raseborg dale stages dramatic and musical evenings, and if you visit in July you may catch a re-enacted medieval duel. (These tend to be comic rather than serious historic re-enactments, with British factions often featured.)

Further east beyond Snappertuna is **Fagervik** ❺, the site of a tremendous old manor overlooking a protected sea inlet. Its granite and wood buildings, which once oversaw the local 18th-century ironworks, make a fine backdrop for a picnic or horse ride. The French garden alone is worth a visit.

The most famous ironworking village in Finland is **Fiskars** ❻, 30km (19 miles) northwest of Fagervik. The village grew up around a single blast furnace, established in 1649, and today is a centre for Finnish arts and crafts. Its beautiful early 19th-century buildings, many of which were designed by C.L. Engel, contain the studios and workshops of local artisans. The original Fiskars company still exists, producing its iconic orange-handled scissors as well as other perfectly designed tools, and has a store here, too. Most of the studios, smithies and shops are open daily from 11am to 5pm in summer; check the village's website (www.fiskarsvillage.fi) or call tel: 020-439 2099, for other times.

ART NOUVEAU AT HVITTRÄSK

Back on Road 51, heading towards Espoo, make time for the must-see artistic Mecca **Hvitträsk** ❼, some 20km (14 miles) west of Helsinki in Kirkkonummi municipality (tel: 029 533 6952; www.kansallismuseo.fi; May–Sept Wed–Sun 11am–5pm; guided tours by arrangement). The house can also be reached by train on an excursion from Helsinki (E, L, S, or U train: Helsinki–Kauklahti, then a quick taxi ride from the station.

Fiskars.

Three of Finland's most famous architects – the hallowed trinity of Herman Gesellius, Armas Lindgren and Eliel Saarinen – designed this to be their joint studio home. Built in National Romantic style, the stone and timber buildings blend right into the forest, the great cliffs and the lake (White Lake) that gives the house its name. The inside is a harmonious song of architecture, interior designs and furniture, with breath-catching detail in every item.

Hvitträsk celebrated one of the architectural partnership's earliest triumphs, the Finnish Pavilion at the Paris World Exhibition in 1900. The dining-room ceiling, like the pavilion decoration, is the work of Gallén-Kallela. Saarinen, who disliked long meetings, designed the hard black table and chairs; reproductions of his furniture designs are still on sale today.

The harmony of working partnerships did not always extend into the private lives of the little community, however. Proximity, perhaps, turned the gaze of Saarinen's first wife, Matilda, towards his partner, Gesellius, and she simply crossed the garden and changed houses. Apparently bearing her no grudge, Saarinen married Gesellius' sister, Loja, two years later. But the triumvirate broke up in 1906, and by 1916 Saarinen was working at Hvitträsk on his own.

In 1922, after winning a major prize in a competition in New York, Eliel Saarinen moved to the United States, was made Dean of the Cranbrook Academy of Art and became as well known abroad as he was in Finland. He continued to visit Hvitträsk each year until his death in 1950, and his grave now overlooks the lake.

PORKKALA PENINSULA

The whole Kirkkonummi municipality was once a large rural Swedish-speaking area. However, at the end of World War II, Finland was forced to lease the Porkkala Peninsula in the south to the Soviet Union as a naval base, a situation that remained until 1955. The Russian cemetery here, in typical Soviet scale, is an ageless

Hvitträsk interior.

⊘ SUMMER RESTAURANT

On a craggy island 2km (1.2 miles) east of Hanko is the summer restaurant the House of the Four Winds (Neljän Tuulen Tupa; Pieni Mäntysaari; tel: 019-248 4060; www.makasiini.fi; May Sat–Sun 11am–5pm, June–Aug Wed–Sun 11am–5pm). The building dates back to the early 1900s and is a pleasant place to dine. During Prohibition (1919–32), Little Pine Island was the place to come for 'hard tea'. The drunkenness and merrymaking so displeased one neighbour on next-door Big Pine Island that in 1927 he bought the café to put an end to the rowdiness. That neighbour was Marshal Mannerheim. Far from being a hands-off owner, the future war leader chose the café's theme and sent to France for crockery. There is even a photo of him at the cash register, counting the day's takings.

Tip

You can reach the Finnish Nature Centre Haltia from Espoo via buses 245, 245(A) or 245(K). Get off at the Haltia stop, from there the centre is only a 30-metre walk.

reminder of that time – 7,000 Finns had to leave their homes at 10 days' notice to make space for it.

Today Porkkala has a Finnish naval garrison in the village of **Upinniemi**, with a remarkable sea chapel, designed by Marianne and Mikko Heliövaara, which is shaped like a boat with open sails and overlooks the sea. An impressive number of bird migration routes pass over the Porkkala Peninsula, and spring and autumn draw ornithologists here to gaze at flocks of cranes, swans and geese. In summer, sailing boats and beach cabins dot the spectacular Baltic coastline.

ESPOO: A GARDEN 'CITY'

The next settlement of any size you come to is **Espoo ⑧**. While Espoo is, strictly speaking, a 'city', it feels much more like a huge, spread-out municipality. Populated largely by wealthier Finns who commute to Helsinki, Espoo is a strange mix of rural farm areas and genteel, leafy suburbs that offer a large and colourful palette of Finnish residential architectural styles.

Hvitträsk was designed in National Romantic style.

Espoo's Tapiola area is renowned as the planned garden suburb of the 1950s, in which leading architects of the age aimed to create a harmonious mix of housing, from flats to family houses, set around a central pool. The area is under ongoing construction. Despite all the sleek Modernism, the area has been settled since 3500 BC, and Espoo's parish church dates as far back as the 15th century. In addition, many artists and architects have made their homes in the area. The artistic feel is concentrated at the worthwhile **Espoo Museum of Modern Art** (EMMA; tel: 043-827 0941; www.emma.museum; Tue, Sat–Sun 11am–5pm, Wed–Thu until 7pm, Fri until 9pm), featuring a permanent collection of post-war Finnish art and changing exhibitions with the 2020 exhibition of Tatsuo Miyajima being one of particular interest.

Some 32km (20 miles) west of Espoo off Road 1 (E3) is the town of **Lohja**, full of pretty gardens and with a medieval church at its centre. It's well known for its apple trees – 136,000 at the last count – and celebrates them with a sweet little Apple Carnival in late September.

NUUKSIO NATIONAL PARK

Around 16km (10 miles) north of Espoo is **Nuuksio National Park ⑨** (Nuuksion kansallispuisto), a great place to come for a short hiking trip of a day or two. The park is one of the most important conservation areas in Finland, with cool, herb-rich forests, lakes and mires that are home to a number of threatened species, including the woodlark, European nightjar and various flying squirrels. The spectacular **Finnish Nature Centre Haltia** (tel: 040-163 6200; www.haltia.com; May–Sept daily 10am–6pm, Oct–Apr Tue–Sat 10am–5pm), which opened in 2013, is the first public building in Finland made entirely of wood. Its main exhibition shows off the glories of Finland's 37 national parks, and its dedicated Outdoor Information Service offers tailor-made advice on planning hikes throughout the country. A 4km (2.5-mile) trail links the centre to Nuuksio National Park's main entrance at Haukkalampi.

TARVASPÄÄ

At the end of the route from Turku to Helsinki is **Tarvaspää** ⓾, the home of Finland's national artist, Akseli Gallén-Kallela (see box). To get there by car, leave Road 1 (E3) at the Ruukinranta junction, from where the museum is signposted. Alternatively, as a day trip from Helsinki, take tram 4 (to Munk-kiniemi) and enjoy the scenic 2km (1-mile) walk from the last stop.

Gallén-Kallela dreamed of escaping into the countryside to 'a crenellated castle, with a tower of grey stone and timbers of pine and oak.' With the help of his friend Eliel Saarinen, he made the dream a reality when, between 1911 and 1913, he converted an existing villa into his new studio-home, complete with octagonal turret. It now forms

the **Gallén-Kallela Museum** (Gallén-Kallenlatie 27; tel: 010-406 8840; www. gallen-kallela.fi; mid-May–Aug daily 11am–6pm, Sept–mid-May Tue–Sat 11am–4pm, Sun 11am–5pm; guided tours by arrangement), a peaceful oasis of a place, set in a park and overlooking the sea. The artist's forceful personality is etched throughout.

The museum holds some 100 illustrations for the *Kalevala*, which decorated the Finnish Pavilion at the Paris World Exhibition in 1900. The paintings are on display at the Ateneum in Helsinki (see page 143) and Turku Art Museum, where Gallén-Kallela's work sometimes features in temporary exhibitions. Also on view are paintings for his frescoes in the Juselius Mausoleum in Pori (see page 214), which commemorated Sigrid Juselius, the 11-year-old daughter of a Pori businessman. Working on these frescoes was a poignant task for the painter, because his own young daughter had died a few years earlier. There are also relics of his time spent in Africa, Paris and further afield.

Main street, Porvoo.

Nuuksio National Park.

⊙ AKSELI GALLÉN-KALLELA

Akseli Gallén-Kallela (1865–1931) is considered by many to be Finland's greatest national artist. After studying at the Finnish Society of Fine Arts, he made his debut in the 1880s to popular acclaim, with his realistic images of everyday Finns. From 1884 to 1889 he lived in Paris and painted images of Parisian bohemian life, but he was soon to be drawn back to his native country. Gallén-Kallela had become fascinated with Elias Lönnrot's epic collection of poetry, the *Kalevala*, and wanted to capture in paint its mythical heroes. Returning to Finland, he devoted his time to researching themes from the epic poems.

In 1890 Kallela married Mary Slöör and they honeymooned in eastern Finland and Karelia, the regions in which the folk poems were set. The *Kalevala* paintings were to become the best known of Kallela's works. In 1909–10 the family lived in British East Africa (now Kenya), where he painted some 150 works and gathered ethnographic and zoological material. In 1911, Kallela designed and built his studio at Tarvaspää, and in 1918 he was appointed aide-de-camp to General Mannerheim. During the 1920s, the family lived in the United States for three years, during which time Gallén-Kallela created the *Great Kalevala*, a lengthy series of illustrations based on the mythology of the *Kalevala*, which he continued to work on throughout his life.

Winter scenery near Kotka.

Old cottages in Porvoo in winter.

EAST OF HELSINKI

Northeast of Helsinki is **Vantaa** ⓫, another city with endless open spaces, although the place is actually best known as the site of the international airport. The Vantaa River Mouth, a wide wash of water just to the east of the capital, is the home of the *Vanhakaupunki*, or 'Old City', upon which Helsinki was founded in the 16th century.

Porvoo ⓬ (Borgå) is one of Finland's most important historical towns. It was a busy trading post from 1346 and, ultimately, was where the Diet of Porvoo (1809) convened to transfer Finland from Swedish to Russian hands (see page 39). The striking **Porvoo Cathedral** (tel: 019-661 1250; May–Sept Mon–Fri 10am–6pm, Sat 10am–2pm, Sun 2–5pm, Oct–Apr Tue–Sat 10am–2pm, Sun 2–4pm; free), where this momentous event took place, dates to the 15th century. The church lost its roof in 2006 when it was set on fire by a drunk teenager, but has since been restored.

Porvoo's rich history made the town important; **Holm House** (Välikatu 11; tel: 040-838 0556; May–Aug Mon–Sat 10am–4pm, Sun 11am–4pm, Sept–Apr Wed–Sun noon–4pm) is a 1763 merchant's house now converted into a museum that shows how well-off tradesmen lived at the turn of the 18th century. It contains several spacious rooms – a living room, salon, smoking room and bedroom – with many antique furnishings.

For scenery, Porvoo also has few rivals: its trim riverbanks are lined with red-ochre fishing cottages, and the pastel-coloured houses of the Old Town provide a charming backdrop. Furthermore, the town has a palpable artistic energy, alive with the work of artists and writers who live here.

East of Porvoo, the landscape becomes more rural and less populated, with only the occasional village to break up the vast spread of forests, wheat fields, hillocks and wild-flower beds (in spring and summer). There are just two more towns and one sizeable city, all in fortification country.

Loviisa ⓭, a pretty, provincial town with an esplanade headed by the neo-Gothic Church, is the smallest of these. A town museum tells of local history, including the role of the Rosen and Ungern bastions, built in the 18th century to safeguard the important trade route between Vyborg and Turku.

KOTKA

Further east, the frequency of rivers (originating in the great lake area immediately to the north) and Orthodox churches begins to increase. After the old villages of Ruotsinpyhtää and Pyhtää is the broad Kotka Delta, at the centre of which is Kotka – an industrial port that nevertheless has some worthwhile sights for visitors.

It is around **Kotka** ⓮ that the Kymi River divides into five branches before emptying out into the sea, creating salmon- and trout-fishing conditions good enough for royalty. Tsar Alexander III had his famous fishing lodge at **Langinkoski** ⓯ (4km/2.5miles north

of Kotka, signposted from Langinko-
skentie). Its tremendous log building
and furnishings are now preserved
as a museum (tel: 029-533 6991; www.
kansallismuseo.fi/en/langinkoski/frontpage;
May daily 10am–4pm, June–Aug daily
11am–6pm). The cabin was crafted by
the Finns for the tsar, who spent his
summers here.

Within Kotka, the biggest attraction
is the **Maritime Centre Vellamo** (Tor-
natorintie 99; tel: 040-350 0497; www.
merikeskusvellamo.fi; Tue–Sun 10am–
5pm, Wed until 8pm), a spectacular
maritime museum at the port. The
building, wave-shaped and covered in
glinting panels, is dazzling in itself;
the interior contains a wealth of information on Finland's seafaring history.
Interactive displays and an outside pier
full of historic vessels (the latter open
summer only) make this fun for adults
and kids alike.

Children will also appreciate the
Maretarium (Sapokankatu 2; tel: 040-
311 0330; www.maretarium.fi; hours vary
greatly), a large aquarium of Finnish
fish. It is located on the other side of
town at the pleasant Sapokka harbour,
which has a high (artificial) waterfall
and fine park.

Sapokka harbour is also the departure point for **summer cruises** to
nearby islands such as Haapasaari,
Kaunissaari and Varissaari, the latter scattered with the remains of an
18th-century fortress. Contact the
tourist office in the Spa Hotel Hamina
(Sibeliuskatu 32; tel: 040-199 1330;
www.visitkotkahamina.fi/en/tourist-infor
mation; Mon–Sat 8am–8pm) for more
information.

On the adjacent peninsula, Santa-
lahti beach is a popular Finnish holiday
resort, with a five-star campsite and
holiday cottages, and activities including nature trails, mini-golf and fishing.

TOWARDS RUSSIA

Hamina ⑯ is the last of the large Finnish towns before you reach the border.

Its concentric plan is part of a huge fortification, and its military nature is also
preserved by the many young Finnish
men based here for national service.
Pastel-coloured wooden houses contrast prettily with red-brick barracks
and magazines. Three old churches are
to be found in Hamina, as well as several quaint museums. One of the large
bastion sections has been turned into
a covered concert venue; the vaulted
fortress walls have excellent acoustics.

Further east lies Virolahti, a small
town with a great collection of charming waterfront cabins at Hurpun Tila.
Finally, there is **Vaalimaa**, the busiest
border station on your way to Russia. The E18 takes traffic across (foot
passengers are forbidden), although
queues can be horrible – more than
3.5 million people cross the border
here annually. The Zsar Outlet Village
(www.zsar.fi) opened in 2018 in Vaalimaa just 500 metres/yards from the
Finnish-Russian border. And along
with a casino (still under construction)
locals are hoping to entice Russians
across the border.

*The town hall
of Hamina.*

*This is big-sky country.
The Kotka tourist
board can point out
nature-protected paths
and rivers, as well as
arrange other trips
and activities (with
guides, if needed).*

SOUTHWESTERN FINLAND

The southwestern area of Finland is known by many as the 'essential triangle'. It encompasses three major cities and various tributes to the industries and artists that have formed much of the modern Finnish nation.

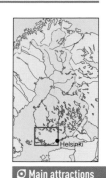

A round trip of some 500km (310 miles) from the capital Helsinki to the west of Finland takes in the three largest cities and is one of the best ways to get a feel for the country in a couple of weeks. Our route leads to Turku, the old capital at the heart of Swedish-speaking Finland, and then on to Tampere, the industrial capital, where water set the first 18th-century mills rolling.

LAKES, HISTORY AND CLEAN AIR

Along the way are most of the elements, past and present, which make Finland what it is today. In the south, there are coasts and lakesides, some lakes so vast that it is difficult to decide whether they are lake or sea. Beautiful old houses restored as museums and hotels lie along the route, as do historic castles with magnificent banquet halls and dungeons, and statues that reflect Finland's history, sometimes warring, sometimes at peace. Further north, the lakes become more prevalent, and it may be tempting to leave the car and travel as local Finns once did, using waterways such as the Silverline route, which winds through the lake system between Tampere and Hämeenlinna. You can go north by the Poet's Way to Virrat, and swim, fish or sail on lake or sea.

This is a good opportunity to get to know something about Finland's arts

Ship navigating the Turku Archipelago.

and culture, remarkable in a country of only 5.5 million, and glimpse the Finns' famed skill in design at glassworks and studios; here, visitors are welcomed and offered the opportunity to buy distinctive articles that could only be Finnish. Above all, between the cities lies the long Finnish road through forests and old villages, to make it a tour filled with flowers and fresh air.

TURKU

Turku ❶ is the 'other' face of Finland, the view from the southwest, closest

⊙ Main attractions
Turku
Turku Archipelago
Naantali
Tampere
Valkeakoski
Hämeenlinna
Riihimäki
Ainola

⊙ Maps on pages
180, 182, 192

In Finland you are never far from nature's beauty.

to Scandinavia and the rest of Europe, not just in trade but also in culture. The Aura River divides the modern city in two; the Baltic Sea, curling round the river mouth, has countless islands in an archipelago stretching southwest until it explodes into the collection of islands known as Åland, splayed about the Baltic Sea halfway between Finland and Sweden (see page 205).

Turku (Åbo in Swedish) is also a city of paradoxes. It may feel like a capital, but it only ever held that title in the Swedish-Finnish kingdom. It is Finland's oldest city, and yet many of the buildings date back only to 1827,

when the Great Fire destroyed a town then largely made of wood. Islands, river and sea make Turku a summer paradise for laid-back boating, yet it is also the cornerstone of the Finnish shipbuilding industry.

A BRIEF HISTORY OF TURKU

Legend has it that in the 1150s, saintly King Erik sailed up the Aura River with an English bishop in tow, on a mission to convert the heathen Finns (the bishop, Henrik, later became Finland's patron saint). However, the first proper evidence shows that the Swedes founded the settlement in the late 13th

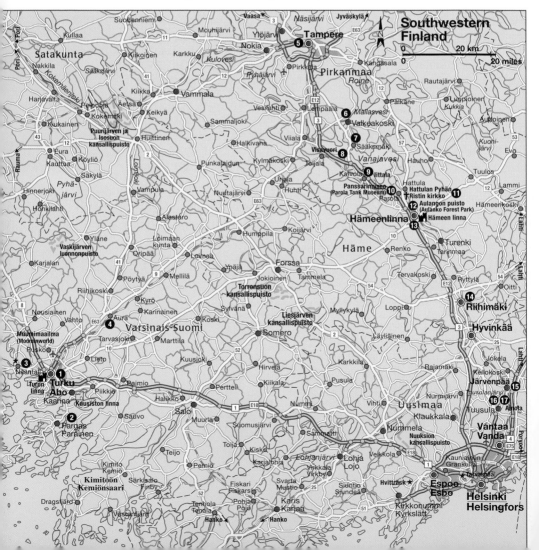

century, calling it Åbo. At this time, the solid lines of a castle began to rise near the mouth of the Aura River, where the Swedish governor lived and visiting dignitaries paid their respects. Åbo became the seat of royal power, and was soon Finland's spiritual centre, too, when its great cathedral was built in 1300.

TURKU CASTLE

Turku Castle  (Turun linna; tel: 02-262 0300; www.turku.fi/turkucastle; early June–early Sept daily 10am–6pm, early Sept–early June Tue–Sun 10am–6pm) is one of the most impressive in all the Nordic countries and stands as a testament to the historical importance of the city, with beautifully preserved halls, rooms, alleyways and corridors that together tell the story of Turku in the Middle Ages.

Often on the defensive, the castle was besieged six times during the medieval era. Its most colourful phase came in the mid-16th century, when Gustav Vasa named his son, Johan, Duke of Finland. The castle was greatly expanded, and Duke Johan settled here with his new wife, the Polish princess Katarina Jagellonica. Katarina brought glamour to the castle, introducing a splendid court life that was already common in most of Europe but had not yet reached Finland.

After Gustav Vasa's death, feuds broke out between his three sons, and the eldest, Erik XIV, besieged the castle and bundled Johan and Katarina into captivity. Later, as Johan III, Duke Johan gained his revenge: visitors can view the austere room in which King Erik XIV was imprisoned, along with his wife Karin Månsdotter, the only queen that Finland ever produced.

In 1614, a huge fire destroyed most of the wooden sections of the building, and the castle was more or less abandoned as a defensive structure, serving variously as a governor's residence, a granary and a prison until its 20th-century restoration.

TURKU'S UNIVERSITY

Turku was the first city in Finland to have a university, founded by the

Turku is the former capital of Swedish-speaking Finland.

Turku Castle.

17th-century governor general of Finland, Count Per Brahe. After its ceremonial opening in 1640, **Åbo Akademi** Ⓑ made Turku the centre of culture and learning, as well as religion. When Finland became a Russian Grand Duchy, the tsar ordered the Academy to be transferred to the new capital to become the University of Helsinki, but the old Academy building remains. In 1918, independent Finland created a second Akademi as Turku's Swedish-language university, and also founded the University of Turku.

EXPLORING THE CITY

After the Great Fire in 1827, market and town moved away from the cathedral to the west bank of the Aura, much of it designed and built to the plan of that industrious Finnophile German, Carl Ludwig Engel, who visualised a city of rectangular blocks intersected by broad streets, a plan still clear in modern Turku. The best start to a walking tour is among the bright stalls, piled with fruit and flowers, in **Market Square** Ⓒ

(Kauppatori; market Mon–Fri 7am–6pm, Sat 7am–3pm). On one side, the Hotel Hamburger Börs has busy bars, cafés and restaurants packing its ground floor. The hotel faces the green, cap-like dome of the Orthodox Church, another Engel design built in 1838 on the orders of Tsar Nicholas I. The yellow building to the southwest is the Swedish Theatre, yet another Engel construction.

During the days of the Grand Duchy, the **Orthodox Cathedral** Ⓓ (Ortodoksinen kirkko; tel: 02-277 5440; Mon–Fri 10am–3pm, Sat 10am–3pm, 5.30–6.30pm, Sun 9.30–11.30am) served a Russian community, and its present congregation of 2,000 includes converts and several families who moved from Karelia during the World War II resettlement. Inside, it has all the rich beauty one would expect. The dome is held up by ornate pillars, and paintings tell the story of St George and the Dragon, and Empress Alexandra (wife of the Roman Emperor Diocletian), to whom the church is dedicated. Continue on Aurakatu away

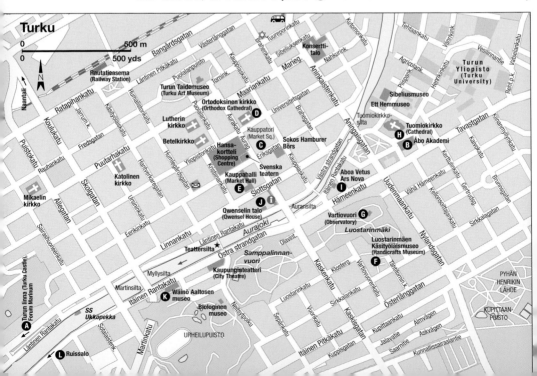

from the market square and you arrive on Puolalanmäki.

Atop the hill is the imposing building that houses **Turku Art Museum** (Turun Taidemuseo; tel: 02-262 7100; www.turuntaidemuseo.fi; Tue–Fri 11am–7pm, Sat–Sun 11am–5pm), with a collection of Finnish classics and exhibitions.

HANDICRAFTS AND SWEETS

Yliopistonkatu (Universitetsgatan) to the west is a happy hunting ground for gifts and mementoes, with a selection of shops selling handicrafts, wood and chinaware and other typically Finnish goods. Between here and Eerikinkatu (Eriksgatan) is the **Hansa Shopping Centre** (Hansakortteli; Mon–Fri 7am–9pm, Sat 7.30am–7.30pm, Sun 10am–7pm), enticingly weatherproof in a Finnish winter.

More exciting is the 19th-century **Market Hall** ❸ (Kauppahalli; www.kauppahalli.fi; Mon–Fri 8am–6pm, Sat 8am–4pm), across the street in Eerikinkatu. There is something about the smell of a market hall that lures you in, a mixture of cheese, meat, fish,

sweets and a tang of exotic spices. The stalls stretch along the entire length, with tempting arrays of *munkki,* a sweet doughnut, and *pulla,* a cake-like bread. At Turun Tee ja Mauste, you can breathe in the aroma of some 200 teas before you buy and pick up oddities such as a Christmas ginger tea or tea spiced with cloves – perfect for cold weather, the Finns say. Nearby, a stall sells typical wooden tulips and leaves, painted in bright colours. Made by a sheltered workshop, they are half the usual cost.

Turning down Aurakatu towards the Auransilta (bridge) you pass the **tourist information office** (tel: 02-262 7444; www.visitturku.fi; daily Mon–Fri 10am–6pm, Sat–Sun Apr–Sept 9am–4pm, Sat–Sun Oct–Mar 10am–3pm). The bridge gives the first view of the numerous restaurant boats. Along the banks, people sit at open-air restaurants and, below the bridge, there is dancing on summer evenings.

Over the bridge, on the right-hand side, is a statue of long-distance runner Paavo Nurmi, one of Turku's most famous sportsman.

The clock tower of Turku Cathedral.

CLOISTER HILL

The entrance to one of Turku's most interesting areas is just a short walk from here. This is **Luostarinmäki** (Cloister Hill), the site of an early convent. There's a certain rough justice in the fact that the only part of the wooden city to survive the Great Fire of 1827 was this hill, for it gave a home to those too poor to buy houses in the 18th-century city. That escape has left Turku with a unique inheritance: the 200 houses stand exactly where they were built, rather than being relocated from various areas, as at other Nordic open-air museums.

The name **Handicrafts Museum** (Luostarinmäen käsityöläismuseo; tel: 02-262 0350; www.turku.fi/en/handicraftsmuseum; early June–early Sept daily 10am–6pm, end April–early June and first two weeks of Sept Tue–Sun 10am–6pm, late Nov–early Jan Tue–Sun 10am–6pm) is a slight misnomer because this old area is much more; the woman spinning today in the dark interior of a wooden house is a museum worker, but she is spinning in the same way and in the same place as the early inhabitants, and the 18th-century costumes seem quite natural. There are traditional sweets, every sort of craft, a tin, copper and goldsmith's, and a baker's that sometimes sells pretzels made in the traditional way. Seamstresses and tailors sew and the old way of life is revealed in the community houses where different families lived in the same building, sharing their kitchen and their bathhouse.

Coming down the hill, detour via the Observatory on **Vartiovuori**, another Engel building, which has been used as a museum and school building. Nearby is an anti-aircraft gun memorial from World War II, when ordinary Finns raised money for defensive guns – Turku bought nine.

TURKU CATHEDRAL

Also on the east side of the river is **Turku Cathedral** (Tuomiokirkko; daily 9am–6pm, subject to services; free), the focal point of old Turku. Look down from the balcony for the best view of the high arches of the

Take a step back in time to 18th-century Finland at Luostarinmäki.

main aisle, with its side chapels. The balcony is also where you'll find the Cathedral Museum (charge), with valuable collections of religious artefacts. Among the most interesting chapels is the Kankainen Chapel, where the stained-glass window by Wladimir Swertschkoff shows Queen Karin Månsdotter, wife of the luckless Erik XIV, who was eventually poisoned after his imprisonment.

Don't miss the statue of Mikael Agricola near the cathedral's south wall. The architect of the Reformation in Finland, he was born on a farm in Pernå, east of Helsinki, and took the name Agricola, meaning 'farmer's son', when he went to study in Rome. In the Cathedral Park, Count Per Brahe stands in a classically proud pose, not far from Åbo Akademi, a block or two to the north. The main buildings of the Swedish-language university and the University of Turku are also nearby.

MODERN ART MUSEUM

Not far away stands the magnificent **Rettig Palace**, formerly a secretive residence of Hans von Rettig, tobacco industrialist, shipowner and one of the richest men in Turku. The estate has now been converted into one of southern Finland's best museums. **Aboa Vetus Ars Nova ❶** (Itäinen Rantakatu 4–6; tel: 0207-181 640; www.aboavetusarsnova.fi; daily 11am–7pm; guided tours in English offered July to Aug daily at noon) holds hundreds of compelling works of modern art – the name is Latin for 'Old Turku, New Art'. But it's not just art that people come to find here. During building work in the 1990s, engineers stumbled upon the remains of medieval alleyways and stores from when the Finnish nation was only a twinkle in the eyes of a few Finns. You can now descend underground into the darkly lit streets of the subterranean Convent Quarter of the medieval town, and wander past the ruined walls of its once-grand merchants' houses. Many of the 37,000 artefacts unearthed during the excavations are on display, bringing 15th-century Turku to life.

⊙ Eat

Numerous boat restaurants dot the riverside in Turku – up to a dozen during the summer, with many serving a variety of beers and fully packed on sunny days. In the winter, too, some boats occasionally hold session.

The bustling university town is a good base from which to explore.

ALONG THE RIVER

In Turku you are never far from the Aura River, which you can cross using one of its five main bridges or by taking the little ferry that still carries pedestrians and cycles free of charge.

For a riverbank tour, the first stop is **Qwensel House** , Turku's oldest wooden building, named after and built by Judge W.J. Qwensel, who bought the plot as long ago as 1695. Perhaps the best-kept secret in town, the backyard has a café with 18th-century decor and recipes. Qwensel House now contains the **Pharmacy Museum** (Läntinen rantakatu 13; tel: 02-262 0280; www.turku.fi/en/pharmacymuseum; June–Aug daily 10am–6pm, Sept–May Tue–Sun 10am–6pm), which keeps traditions alive by growing aromatic herbs in the garden. You can also see fine 18th-century furnishings, and old pharmaceutical items.

TOWARDS THE HARBOUR

The leafy riverside path takes you past a clutch of bridges: Teatterisilta, a civilised people-and-bicycle footway that links the downtown area to the city theatre; Myllysilta (Mill Bridge); and Martinsilta, where you'll find the SS *Ukkopekka*, the last steamship to sail Finland's coastal waters, and a buzzing summer restaurant, Vaakahuoneen Paviljongin, with quayside dancing and live jazz bands (typically from May–July, however there is the occasional show in April and August). Depending on how far you care to walk, you can continue on this side as far as Turku Castle and the modern harbour areas that show how important the sea still is to Turku, with merchant tugs and tankers and the terminals of the Viking and Silja Lines.

On your way to the harbour at Linnankatu 74 is the **Forum Marinum** maritime museum (www.forum-marinum.fi; tel: 02-267 9511; exhibitions June–Aug daily 11am–7pm, Sept–May Tue–Sun 11am–7pm; museum ships late May–Aug daily 11am–7pm). Turku has been a shipbuilding centre since 1737, so exhibitions naturally focus on this region's connection to the sea. There's also a section about the *Suomen Joutsen*, the 'Swan of Finland': once you've

Authentic 18th-century costume at the Pharmacy Museum.

read up on the ship, you can wander out to the riverside and admire her sleek white hull and complicated rigging. The riverbank here is lined with fascinating museum ships, including the barque *Sigyn*, the Postineiti post boat and the minelayer Keihässalmi.

WÄINO AALTONEN

Heading back towards the centre you come to the austere outlines of the **Wäinö Aaltonen Museum** Ⓚ (Wäinö Aaltosen museo; Itäinen Rantakatu 38; tel: 02-262 0850; www.turku.fi/en/waino-aaltonen-museum-art; Tue–Sun 10am–6pm). Aaltonen was one of Finland's best-known sculptors and artists, and a national icon. He has famously sculpted a number of likenesses of famous Finns, including Paavo Nurmi and Jean Sibelius. The building contains much of his work, including the massive statues of *Peace*, hands raised, and *Faith*, a mother and child. In a self-portrait, this private man placed a text in front of his face to hide his feelings. Outside the City Theatre is Aaltonen's statue of Aleksis Kivi,

one of the first authors to write literature in Finnish.

The windmill on Samppalinnan-mäki overlooking the river is the last of its kind in Turku. Here Paavo Nurmi, stopwatch in hand, trained against his own best times. The polished granite stone on the slopes is Finland's independence memorial, unveiled in 1977 on the 60th anniversary. On this river walk, you will notice the waterbuses by Auransilta Bridge and below Martin-silta Bridge. A sightseeing cruise is the best way to get a feel for this water city.

RUISSALO ISLAND

Boat services run several times daily to **Ruissalo Island** Ⓛ; it's also a nice cycle ride, or take bus 8 from opposite the Market Hall. Ruissalo is a green and leafy island, a place for botanists and birdwatchers as well as cyclists and walkers. It is famous for its verdant oak groves (a woodland species found only in southern Finland) and its pretty 'lace villas' (so called because of their latticed balconies and windows). The oldest examples of the latter were

The nave of Turku Cathedral.

Ø SHIPBUILDING GIANT

Meyer Turku (formerly STX Finland) makes specialist boats, including car ferries, ice-breakers and enormous luxury liners. Its Royal Caribbean cruise ships *Oasis of the Seas* (2009) and *Allure of the Seas* (2010) are the second- and third-biggest vessels ever to have been built – French-built *Harmony of the Seas* (2016) is number one – each one is 361 metres (1,184ft) long, has a cruising speed of 22 knots, and is able to carry an incredible 6,360 passengers and 2,100 crew. Turku is quietly proud of these mighty vessels: both were made right here in its shipyard, 6km (4 miles) west of the city centre. The Forum Marinum (see page 186) can arrange guided tours for groups to the Meyer Turku yard, which give an insight into how these massive liners are built, as well as a sense of how important shipbuilding is to Finnish industry.

built by wealthy merchants in the early 19th century. Choose one of several nature trails or rent a bicycle to explore the flora, fauna and beautiful villas on the island. Ruissalo has the area's best beaches, including a small nudist beach – something still rare in Finland, not because of any national prudery but because the Finns, with their isolated cabins on lonely lakesides, had not realised one might actually need permission to bathe without a swimsuit.

A good café and restaurant is Honkapirtti, a Karelian-style pinewood building constructed in 1942–3 by infantry soldiers near the front during the Continuation War. In summer, the island is home to Ruisrock, the world's oldest annual rock festival (see page 89). There is also a spa hotel and a camping site, as well as the **University Botanical Gardens** (daily 10am–5pm; free).

One of the most civilised ways to see the archipelago is a supper cruise aboard the SS *Ukkopekka* (tel: 02-515 3300; www.ukkopekka.fi), which retains something of its steamship past and

its original engine. As the passengers strive for window tables, the *Ukkopekka* moves smoothly down the river and out to sea. If the timing is right, a fisherman may sail out to the *Ukkopekka* with the fish he has caught and smoked that day.

EXPLORING THE ISLANDS

Richly vegetated but sparsely populated, the **Turku archipelago** (Turunmaan saaristo) is quieter than the Ålands in terms of tourism (see page 205). Its islands and skerries – some 20,000 in total – outnumber the people who live on them. In the west, the five main islands (Pargas, Nagu, Korpo, Houskar and Iniö) form the curving Archipelago Trail, easily accessed from the mainland as they are linked by a series of bridges and ferries. Boats also service some of the smaller islands that spin off south from the main chain, while local buses connect the larger towns.

Pargas ❷ (Parainen), the capital of the archipelago, is a hard-working town famous for Finland's largest limestone quarry. It contains a

Cycling in Naantali.

stunning medieval grey-stone church dedicated to St Simon, with unusual spreading brick columns that support the interior and contrast with the light-blue trim of the pews. A short walk away near the quarry, a charming series of wooden buildings form the local **history museum** (www.pargashembygdsmuseum.fi; June–Aug Tue–Sun 11am–4pm); one of its houses sheltered Lenin when he was on the run in 1907.

As you approach Pargas from west or south you come to **Sattmark** (tel: 044 970 2599; June–mid-Aug daily, hours vary), on the island of Stortervolandet. This tiny log cabin, which was once a sailor's quarters, now serves light meals, including home-smoked fish. It also offers overnight cabin accommodation.

The archipelago's finest harbour is on the northeast spur of **Nagu**. With its charming wooden boardwalk, little shops and cafés, walking trails and happy holiday atmosphere, it's the place to be in summer. An old wooden house overlooking the marina is now a guesthouse-style hotel, with a French brasserie and a chic restaurant, L'Escale, next door. Nagu also contains the beautiful 14th-century St Olof's Church (June–Aug), with primitive frescoes and Finland's oldest Bible.

NAANTALI AND MOOMINWORLD

Naantali ❸, around 20 minutes' drive west of Turku, is now a famous sailing harbour, packed with visiting boats. It is also a historic 200-year-old town, with old houses that are still lived in today. There is a beautiful grey-stone convent church, with a new organ that attracts famous organists, particularly during the June Music Festival, when some 18,000 visitors crowd into the tiny town. At its start in the 1980s, the sceptics thought that little Naantali's festival 'would die in 10 years'. Now it is proving everyone wrong as it celebrates more than 40 seasons. The harbour is also popular with artists, and galleries include the Purpura, which specialises in Finnish artists and supports an artist-in-residence scheme.

◉ Fact

Perched above a rocky coast in Naantali is Kultaranta, the summer residence of Finland's president. The extensive gardens, which supply the president's household with flowers and vegetables year-round, are open to guided tours (early-June–Aug Tue–Sun) – contact the Naantali tourist board (tel: 02-435 9800; www.visitnaantali.com/fi) for further information.

Many tiny islands surround Ruissalo Island.

Moominworld.

Tampere Orthodox Church, showing the Russian influence in Finland's second city.

However, the city's main draw is **Moominworld** (tel: 02-511 1111; www. moominworld.fi; daily late June–mid-Aug 10am–6pm, late Aug noon–6pm), an outstanding theme park based on the beloved characters of Tove Jansson. It is perfect for a day out for the young and the young at heart. The park is focused around the five-storey, blueberry-hued Moomin House, and visitors can meet any number of Moomin characters and visit Moominmama's Kitchen, Hemulen's yellow house, Snufkin's Camp and Moominpappa's boat, among other favourite places from the books. This world isn't just for summer fun, as in February (typically) the park hosts a Winter Magic festival. They build a ski circuit, curling track and a track for hobby horse booble. Or you can enjoy their famous snowshoe trail or their thrilling downhill slide.

GLASSWORKS AND MOBILE PHONES

For the most direct route to Tampere, leave the city on Road 40. This leads to **Aura** ❹, some 30km (20 miles)

north, where from Road 9 you have a fine view of the Aurakoski (rapids). Road 9 continues northeast through rich farmland with a possible detour right at the Helsinki-Pori crossroads (Road 2) for a short drive to the Iittala Group Humppila Glassworks, where at a glass-walled demonstration forge you can watch glassblowers at work. The Glass Village at Nuutajärvi (tel: 020-439 3527; www.nuutajarvi.fi, daily from 10am–6pm), a little further north on the left of the road, was formed around Finland's oldest glassworks, dating from 1793, and is famous for producing the glass birds designed by Oiva Toikka. While the factory was moved to the Iittala site in Visavuori in 2014, you can still visit the workshops and the glass museum, buy some lovely glassware at the shop, and have a lovely lunch. Accommodation is also available.

An alternative route, Road 41, slightly to the west, goes through Oripää, a gliding centre, where the Moorish-style building is the studio-home of sculptor Viljo Syrjämaa,

⊘ INDUSTRIAL TAMPERE

With its abundance of forests, Finland is at the forefront of international paper production. It is still a thriving industry – worth $8 billion per year in paper exports – and factories lining the waterways are a familiar sight. Textiles, shoemaking and wood production are other industries for which Tampere has been well known since the 19th century. While the 20th and early 21st century saw mobile technology dominate.

One excellent way to take in Tampere's industrial heritage as well as its natural surroundings is a local lake cruise. In summer, various boats ply the beautiful Lake Pyhäjärvi, with cruises from Tampere to Virrat and to Hämeenlinna, the oldest town in Finland. A popular day trip is out to Viikinsaari, a wooded summer recreation area, where many locals venture to enjoy the sun and a beer.

and from Vammala, the road plies its way along the flat, fertile land of the Loimijoki Valley. About 25km (15 miles) to the northeast is **Nokia**, a pleasant little town on the shores of Lake Pyhäjärvi that is the original site of the Nokia telecommunications company. Boat cruises from Tampere regularly stop at Nokia. Just north of here are more magnificent rapids at the start of the waterway system that leads to Tampere.

TAMPERE

Officially Finland's second city, its residents may call Tampere 'the Manchester of Finland', but anything less like a classic industrial city is hard to imagine. It is one of the loveliest places to visit in the country, not least for its waterways and lakes, which are easily explored in a day.

Tampere ❺ lies on a narrow neck of land between two lakes, great stretches of water so large that you feel you are close to a sea rather than way inland. Linking the lakes, the rushing waters of the Tammerkoski

River first brought power, industry and riches to Tampere. Though it still provides some energy, the Tammerkoski is so clean nowadays that it attracts growing numbers of anglers, out for the season's trout. On weekends, the two lakes are bright with rainbow sails, while the shores are packed with picnickers.

Despite a changing pattern of industry, Tampere has managed to retain factories and workers' houses without allowing them to turn into slums, and the tall red-brick chimneys that do remain are symbols of both past and present, for Tampere's factories are still high on the list of Finland's leading manufacturers and exporters.

There are some 200 lakes in and around the city. The two largest, Näsijärvi to the north and Pyhäjärvi to the south, are the meeting point of two famous waterway routes. To the south, the Silverline threads its way through a labyrinth of lakes towards Hämeenlinna, passing Valkeakoski, another industrial town in a splendid rural setting, and stopping at

On board a ferry leaving Turku for the Åland Islands.

Aerial view of Tampere from Nasinneula Observation Tower.

Tampere's neo-Renaissance Finlayson Palace now serves as a restaurant.

the beautiful Aulanko Forest Park, among other places (see page 200).

The romantically named Poet's Way boat, SS *Tarjanne,* steers north through narrow, winding waters to Ruovesi and Virrat. The trip takes eight hours in one direction; and the return journey gives a two-day taste of Finland's lakes, with an overnight stay at either Virrat or Ruovesi. A little further north, Ahtäri has one of Finland's best native zoos (www.ahtarizoo.fi). The national poet J.L. Runeberg began his best-known work, *Tales of Ensign Ståhl,* in Ritoniemi Mansion at Ruovesi and, near the village, Akseli Gallén-Kallela (see page 76) built his first 'Kalela' studio-home.

TAMPERE'S HISTORY

Tampere was officially founded in 1779 by King Gustav III of Sweden-Finland but, since the Middle Ages, the Pirkkala area to the south of the centre had been settled by farmers, attracted by the waterways that made transport easy. From around the 13th century, when the Swedes granted them rights to collect taxes from the Lapp people,

they prospered richly. These earliest *tamperelaiset* (Tampere residents) are commemorated on the Hämeensilta Bridge in a series of statues by Wäinö Aaltonen. Also clear from the bridge is the tall chimney of one of Tampere's earliest industries, Frenckel, the paper-makers, dating back to 1783.

EXPLORING THE CENTRE

The Tammerkoski has largely lost its working factories, and hotels, shopping centres and museums have taken their place. The venerable and well-restored Radisson Blu Grand Hotel Tammer, the Scandic Tampere Koskipuisto and Sokos Hotel Ilves all have splendid views of the Tammerkoski rapids, and, from the top of the Ilves's 18 storeys, the panorama takes in the quay where the Silverline boats berth, the leisure craft, the red brick of the old factories and the magnificent stretches of lake. A minute or two away on the riverside, the **Verkaranta Crafts Centre Ⓐ** (Taito Pirkanmaa/Taitokeskus Verkaranta; Vuolteentori 2; tel: 050-496221 409;

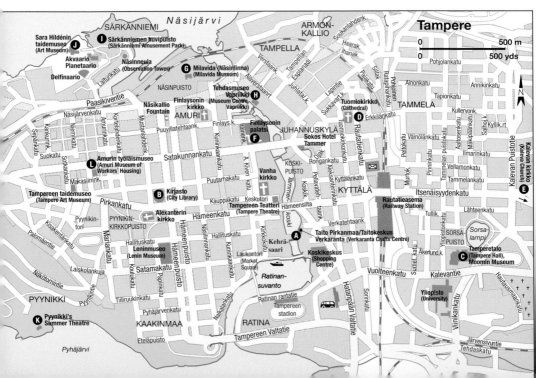

Mon–Fri 10am–5pm) sells good-quality craftwork and knitting and weaving materials. Nearby are the Tampere Theatre building (Hämeen-katu 12) and the Koskikeskus covered shopping centre, which is home to 80 shops; the market hall, for fresh produce, is at Hämeenkatu 19.

CITY LIBRARY AND TAMPERE HALL

Across a footbridge over the rapids, one of the oldest factory areas stands on Kehräsaari (Spinning Island). In the Independence (civil) War, the victorious White Army crossed the Tammerkoski here to capture Tampere. Today, its factories and boutiques are grouped around cobbled courtyards. Nearby, the only factory still working on the river, Tako, makes carton paper. Keep an eye out, too, for the old factory chimney with a bomb shield on the top, a reminder that Tampere was bombed fiercely in the 1918 civil war, when it was an important 'Red' stronghold, and again during World War II with eight heavy raids.

Tampere's architecture is largely 20th-century, typified by the **City Library** Ⓑ (Kirjasto; Pirkankatu 2; Mon–Fri 9am–8pm, Sat 10am–4pm, Sun 11am–5pm), an astonishing building said to be based on the open wings and spread tail feathers of a wood grouse, though you might see it more as a series of mushrooms. In the mid-1980s the library and the Tampere City Building Office won several awards for its husband-and-wife architects, Reima and Raili Pietilä. Finns are great readers and library fans – around 80 percent regularly use a library.

The **Tampere Hall** Ⓒ (Tampere-talo; www.tamperehall.com) is Tampere's pride, a spectacular blue-white event hall designed by Esa Piiroinen and Sakari Aartelo in 1990. Streams of light illuminate the main foyer's fountains, which commemorate the Tammerkoski rapids as the source of local prosperity. The main hall holds 2,000, while a smaller auditorium seats 500. If you arrive on a festival morning you can catch the sound of a choir or orchestra rehearsing on stage. Lit for an opera

Interior of St Michael's at Messukylä.

such as *Parsifal*, the large hall is magnificent. The hall is used for conferences and congresses and there is a café. The **Moomin Museum** (Tue–Wed 9am–5pm, Thu–Fri 9am–7pm, Sat–Sun 10am–5pm; www.muumilaakso.tampere.fi) also resides here. The museum exhibits Tove Jansson's original works in a modern, multi-sensory way. There is also a Tove Jansson library and a Moomin shop.

TAMPERE'S CHURCHES

Lars Sonck was only 30 when he won a national competition with his design for the **Tampere Cathedral** ⓓ (Tuomiokirkko; daily May–Aug 10am–5pm, Sept–Apr 11am–3pm), which was then St John's Church, completed in 1907 at the height of the National Romantic movement. It stands in its own park at Tuomiokirkonkatu 3, a few blocks east of the river, and contains some of the best of Finnish art, including Magnus Enckell's altar fresco of the Resurrection and his circular window that forms a cross and wreath of thorns. Hugo

Simberg painted *The Wounded Angel*, a shattered form carried by two boys, and *The Garden of Death* – despite its name, not a gloomy picture. His note on the back of a working sketch reads: 'A place where souls go before entering heaven.' Around the gallery, his *Garland of Life* shows 12 boys carrying a green garland of roses, symbolising humanity's burden of life. This great church seats almost 2,000 and, softly lit, makes a beautiful setting for a Sunday evening concert.

The **Kaleva Church** ⓔ (Kalevan kirkko; Liisanpuisto 1; daily Jul–Aug 11am–5pm, Sept–June 11am–3pm, guided tours are available at tel: 03 2190 705), east on the Kalevan Puistotie road, is a curving concrete structure that rises tall and narrow out of a field. No wonder it's nicknamed 'the silo of souls'. Inside, the stark appearance changes to dramatic, with a soaring light that pulls your gaze upwards. A striking feature of this church, another Pietilä design from 1966, is the organ, its 3,000 pipes shaped like a sail. Behind the altar the wooden statue is

Modern Tampere.

intended to be a reed – 'a bruised reed He shall not break'.

Tampere's oldest church is the 15th-century **St Michael's at Messukylä** (Kivikinkontie 2; June–Aug Tue–Sun noon–6pm; free), around 5km (2 miles) east along the Iidesjärvi (lake) on the old Lahti road. The oldest part is the vestry that once stood beside an even earlier wooden church. A moment of high excitement in 1959 revealed extensive wall paintings, now restored, from the 1630s. The church's most valuable wooden sculpture is believed to be that of the royal saint King Olav of Norway, whose tomb in Trondheim became a place of pilgrimage during the Middle Ages.

FINLAYSON AREA

Tampere's rich industrial heritage illustrates how international the city was nearly two centuries ago. One of the most important industries, textiles, was founded by a Scotsman, James Finlayson. He arrived in 1820 from Russia to build a heavy engineering works at the north end of the Tammerkoski, with the first water-powered spinning mill. When he sold to Rauch and Nottbeck in 1836 it grew to become one of the biggest textile factories in the Nordic countries, but in those early days Mrs Finlayson was not too proud to sell the mill's products in the market. James Finlayson was an industrialist in the Quaker mould and Finlayson's became almost a town within a city, with its own police, health programme and hospital, factory school and a church. Visitors now find a completely refurbished area of bustling activity, with a microbrewery, restaurants, a 10-screen cinema complex and several museums, including a small **Spy Museum** (Vakoilumuseo; Satakunnankatu 18; tel: 03-212 3007; www.vakoilumuseo.fi; June–Aug Mon–Sat 10am–6pm, Sun 11am–5pm, Sept–May Mon–Sat noon–6pm, Sun 11am–5pm), which is good fun for kids.

After Finlayson returned to Scotland, the new owners continued the traditions and the name, and lived in a mansion house nearby, known as the **Finlayson Palace 𝐅** (Finlaysonin

Särkänniemi Amusement Park.

⊘ Shop

You can pick up iconic Finnish houseware objects at bargain prices at the Iittala outlet at Pirkkala, 10km (6 miles) from Tampere. There is even a larger selection at the Iittala and Arabia outlet in northern Helsinki, half an hour from downtown (tram 6).

palatsi; Kuninkaankatu 1) and built by Alexander von Nottbeck. It became a famous house, visited by Tsar Alexander II and his court, and there are portraits of both Alexander I and II on the central staircase, grand enough to feel you should be sweeping down it in full evening dress. The palace is now a restaurant (Tue–Fri 11am–midnight, Sat from noon), with live music in the evenings. The restaurant serves food during the day and is also popular for art exhibitions and social functions. The surrounding park is open daily, admission free.

Another Nottbeck home is in **Näsinlinna**: the **Milavida Museum** Ⓖ (www. museomilavida.fi; May–Sept Tue–Sun 11am–6pm, Jan–Apr and Oct–Dec Fri–Sun 11am–6pm), an old mansion on a hill in Näsinpuisto Park overlooking the lake, an easy walk from the Finlayson buildings. The museum presents the history of the von Nottbeck family and also stages temporary fashion and design exhibitions.

On the edge of the park, at the top of Hämeenpuisto, is Wikström's

interesting Näsikallio Fountain. To illustrate how knowledge and skill are passed from generation to generation, on one side a grandmother explains handiwork to a little girl, on the other a boy shows an old man how water power has made work easier. On top is the Maid of the North from the *Kalevala* sitting on a rainbow, spinning golden thread.

MUSEUM CENTRE VAPRIIKKI

The other main company, Tampella, on the eastern side of the river, began as a foundry in 1850. This enormous edifice housed some of the EU meetings during Finland's presidency. It has now been renovated and renamed **Museum Centre Vapriikki** Ⓗ (from the Swedish word fabrik, or factory). The main museum (tel: 03-5656 6966; http:// vapriikki.fi; Tue–Sun 10am–6pm) contains permanent collections (focusing on Finnish ice hockey, dolls, shoes and natural history) and changing exhibitions, often large international ones.

One former Tampella factory, on a peninsula above Lake Näsijärvi, is now a spa hotel (Holiday Club Tampereen Kylpylä), which concentrates on healthy living, and offers massage and other treatments in a comfortable atmosphere.

TAMPERE'S AMUSEMENTS

From Näsinlinna, across the northern harbour entrance, is an even higher viewpoint: the Näsinneula Observation Tower at the centre of **Särkänniemi Amusement Park** Ⓘ (Särkänniemen huvipuisto; tel: 020-713 0200; https://sarkanniemi.fi; opening times vary so check website), with its aquarium, dolphinarium, planetarium and children's zoo. The tower is the highest free-standing structure in Finland, and there is no better way to get an overview of Tampere than while chewing a sugary doughnut at the café, more than 120 metres (400ft) up, or from the revolving restaurant a

Sara Hilden Art Museum, Tampere.

storey above it. Looking immediately below, the funfair's railways, Ferris wheels, roller-coasters and water park rides look like children's toys. The restaurant is good, but on the expensive side; it takes 50 minutes to complete a revolution and is open until midnight.

If your tastes run to modern art rather than funfairs, or if you like both, don't miss the **Sara Hildén Art Museum** ❶ (Sara Hildénin taidemuseo; tel: 03-5654 3500; Tue–Sun 10am–6pm), in a beautiful building close by, which claims to have Tampere's best lake view. Sara Hildén was an art collector who specialised in Finnish and foreign art of the 1960s and 1970s, and there are also visiting exhibitions and concerts.

Between the lakes, the western part of the isthmus rises to form the Pyynikki Ridge, born 10,000 years ago during the last Ice Age, around the old bowl of an ancient sea. It was once the home of the town's bishop, and its old viewing tower is a popular place for looking over both lakes and towards

the **Pyynikki's Summer Theatre** ❸ (Pyynikin kesäteatteri; www.pyynikinke sateatteri.fi) down near Lake Pyhäjärvi. In a remarkable example of lateral thinking, the theatre auditorium revolves rather than the stage – truly theatre in the round, as the audience turns to face each new scene, with perhaps fairies from *A Midsummer Night's Dream* perched high in the trees. It is the oldest revolving auditorium still in use in the world. The theatre (mid-June–mid-Aug) is especially beautiful when the trees are drenched in white blossom.

AMURI MUSEUM OF WORKERS' HOUSING

Further west is Pispala (Bishop's Village), now considered a very prestigious place to live. In fact, it was built in the late 19th century by factory workers. As a sign of progress, their children left and went to live in central Tampere, but now the grandchildren of the original builders are eager to return and restore. The **Amuri Museum of Workers' Housing** ❶

Dusk in Tampere.

(Amurin työläismuseo; Satakun-nankatu 49; tel: 03-5656 6690; www.museokortteli.fi; mid-May–early-Sept Tue–Sun 10am–6pm) shows how these houses would have looked up until 1970, when the city stopped old-style construction and began building terrace houses. There are 25 houses and two shops, all giving the impression that the owners might return at any moment. Nearby, Café Amurin Helmi, decorated in the 1920s style, sells traditional biscuits for dipping, and the Amuri shop offers treacle-sugared sweets and caramel cones.

ART AND LENIN

Just down the street, **Tampere Art Museum** (Puutarhakatu 34; tel: 03-5656 6577; www.tampere.fi/english/art museum; Tue–Thu 9am–5pm, Fri–Sun 10am–6pm) displays mainly 19th- and 20th-century Finnish paintings, prints, drawings and sculptures. It no longer houses the Moomin Museum, which has now moved to Tampere Hall.

If you have time to spare, the unusual **Lenin Museum** (Hämeenpuisto 28; tel: 010 420 9222; http://lenin.fi; June–Aug daily 11am–6pm, Sept–May Tue–Sun 11am–5pm) is also worth a visit. Exhibits document Lenin's stays in Finland after the failed 1905 revolution, and the museum itself is based in the Workers' Hall of Tampere, where Lenin and Stalin first met. Whatever else you miss in this water city, do not miss a boat journey. VisitTampere has details on trips out to various islands and beaches where you can birdwatch or relax under cool forest trees, and enjoy a picnic away from everyone else. It's hard to believe that, strictly speaking, you are still in Finland's leading industrial city.

BACK TOWARDS HELSINKI

The first stops along Road 3 from Tampere to Helsinki are Valkeakoski and Sääksmäki, yet more of those Finnish industrial centres that contrive to place themselves in beautiful surroundings. These happen to be set between two lakes. In the Middle Ages, **Valkeakoski** ❻ was no more than a hamlet, later a mining village

Worker making an Aalto vase in the Iittala glass factory.

in the important parish of Sääksmäki; but even then, it harnessed its powerful rapids to grind corn and make paper. Later, the 19th-century National Romantic movement brought artists to Sääksmäki. For a feeling of Valkeakoski's industrial history, go to the wooden outdoor museum of **Kauppilanmäki** (tel: 040-563 6017; end of June–mid-Aug Wed–Sun noon–4pm), with five houses typical of the early paper-mill workers' homes up to 1920. The workers' hall, with its union flags, was the centre of political thought as well as home to the community entertainment.

The old **Voipaala Manor** (Voipaalan kartano; June–Aug Tue–Sun 11am–6pm, Jan–May and Sept–Dec Tue–Fri 11am–5pm, Sat–Sun noon–6pm) on Rapola Hill has become an art centre. The museum was once the studio of the sculptor Elias Ilkka, who owned the manor and the farm where the Valkeakoski Summer Theatre performs. Today exhibitions are held here. On the hill above is an ancient hill fort and a view of the church of **Sääksmäki** ⑦, a short walk away. This early parish had an even older church, but the present grey-stone building dates back to the 15th century. A fire on April Fool's Day, 1929, destroyed much of the church, but a 1932 restoration preserved some wall paintings, as well as the altarpiece and two wooden statues.

ART AND GLASSWARE

Just over the bridge, detour right towards Toijala and then right again to **Visavuori** ⑧ (Kirkkovainiontie 80; tel: 03-543 6528; www.visavuori.com; June–Aug daily 11am–6pm, Feb–May and Sept–Dec Tue–Sun 10am–4pm, Jan Tue–Fri 10am–4pm), the studio home of one of Finland's best-known sculptors, Emil Wikström (1864–1942). Aged 29, he had just won a competition to design the frieze for Helsinki's House of Estates, when he designed his house

on the peninsula overlooking the lake. Here he worked in the wood-lined studio, spending his nights observing the stars in his rooftop observatory. The studio is a stopping place for the Silverline boats.

Of all Finland's well-known glass-makers, **Iittala** ⑨ (Könnölänmäentie 2, Iittala Glass Capital; glass factory June, Aug Mon–Fri 9am–8pm, July Mon–Fri 9am–5pm) is probably the most famous, with austere designs, beautiful functional glassware, and *objets d'art* such as glass birds and fruit shapes so perfect that you immediately want to hold them – a practice not to be recommended in the museum, on the same site (May–Aug Tue–Sun 11am–5pm).

Inside you will also find past and present designs by such eminent Finns as Alvar Aalto and Timo Sarpaneva, designer of the 'i-collection', which became Iittala's trademark. Helped by an expert glassblower who does most of the work, you can try your talents on a misshapen paperweight. Even better is the Iittala shop,

Häme Castle, Hämeenlinna.

where seconds – often indistinguishable to the naked eye from the real thing – are regularly less than half the price of a perfect work.

MILITARY HARDWARE

There is no escape from modern history at the **Parola Tank Museum** ❿ (Panssarimuseo; tel: 040-568 1186; www.panssarimuseo.fi; daily May–Sept 10am–6pm, Oct–Apr 10am–3pm), set up by the Association of Armoured Troops and Veterans, survivors of the Finnish campaigns during World War II. Some Winter War tanks go back to 1910, and the Continuation War terrace has some captured Soviet tanks, their hammer and sickle replaced by the swastika, after Finland found itself fighting on the same side as the Germans. For military historians this little-known museum is a fascinating tribute to the Finnish tank operators, but even the most casual visitor will be intrigued by the armoured train in the woods above. To reach Parola, take Road 57, marked Hattula, off the main road, and then, just past the next crossroads, branch left again to Parola.

ANCIENT CHURCH AND FOREST

Continue back on Road 57 to the **Hattulan Church of the Holy Cross** ⓫ (Hattulan Pyhän Ristin kirkko; mid-May–mid Aug daily 11am–5pm; free), one of Finland's best-known and oldest churches. It was built beside the lake of Hattula, probably in the 14th century: some of its construction details appear similar to those of Turku and Häme castles. Inside, your eyes are immediately drawn upwards by the delicate colours of the intricate 16th-century frescoes that cover ceilings and walls and are the most extensive of any Finnish church. They were later lime-washed and hidden until the mid-19th century, when they were restored. Today, Hattula has regained the atmosphere of a medieval church, and its most valuable statue is a wooden St Olav, the 11th-century Norwegian royal saint.

Aulanko Forest Park ⓬ (Aulangon puisto), just off Road 3, is ideal for a

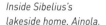
Inside Sibelius's lakeside home, Ainola.

break. The forest had a fortress long before the days of Christianity, but the man who made Aulanko what it is today was Colonel Hugo Standertskjöld, in the 1930s the governor of Häme province. He had made his fortune as an arms dealer in Russia and returned to build a new manor and beautify the forest park with ornamental lakes, follies and the observation tower overlooking Aulankojärvi (lake). The Bear Cave nearby has an appealing family group of bears carved by Robert Stigell. Jean Sibelius, born in Hämeenlinna, is said to have commented on Aulanko: 'I was thinking of these scenes from my childhood when I composed *Finlandia*.' Aulanko is a stopping place for the Silverline boats and has an outdoor theatre and a modern spa hotel, with golf courses and tennis courts. It attracts more than a million visitors a year.

CASTLE AND COMPOSER

Hämeenlinna ⑬ has two claims to fame: as the home of **Häme Castle** (tel: 029 533 6932; Sept–Apr Tue–Fri 10am–4pm, Sat–Sun 11am–4pm, May Mon–Fri 10am–4pm, Sat–Sun 11am–4pm, June–Aug daily 10am–5pm) and the birthplace of Jean Sibelius.

In the 13th century, when Earl Birger led the first Swedish foray into this ancient countryside, Swedish governors were ever-conscious of the proximity to Russia and obsessed with the need for defensive measures. Birger's first task was to build a square-walled defensive camp with towers at its corners – still the heart of Häme Castle. Over the next 700 years, Häme was remodelled to suit the moods of various countries' rulers, and its red-bricked walls now intertwine Swedish, Finnish and Russian history. The castle area also includes a worthwhile **prison museum**, plus changing historical and archaeological exhibitions.

Hämeenlinna itself was granted town status in 1639 by Count Per Brahe, but it was already an important settlement on the Oxen Trail between Turku and Häme Castle. This centuries-old route has served soldier, merchant and traveller alike, though pack animals and carts have given way to

motorcars and the track has become a modern road. With its busy centre and shady park, Hämeenlinna makes an excellent base for touring.

Sibelius was born in December 1865 in the little timberboard house of the town physician, Christian Gustaf Sibelius. The **Birthplace of Sibelius** (Hallituskatu 11; tel: 03-621 2755; www.hmlmuseo.fi; May–Aug daily 10am–4pm, Sept–Apr Tue–Sun noon–4pm) is decorated in 1860s style, and contains memorabilia from the composer's childhood. This includes Sibelius's upright piano from 20 years later and an early photograph of the composer and his brother and sister performing at the Loviisa Spa Casino, where they gave summer concerts. The dining room is used for occasional recitals.

RIIHIMÄKI

The **Finnish Glass Museum** (Suomen Lasimuseo; Tehtaankatu 23; tel: 019-758 4108; www.suomenlasimuseo.fi; Feb–Dec Tue–Sun 10am–6pm) is the most popular place in **Riihimäki** ⓮, just off Road 3 some 35km (26 miles)

Armoured vehicles at the Parola Tank Museum.

south of Hämeenlinna. The building is an authentic glassworks from 1914, still active in the 1930s. The ground-floor exhibition traces the history of glassmaking, from the early days of Finnish independence, when the industry concentrated on mundane items such as window panes, to the 1930s, which saw both the beginning of glassmaking as a fine art and, later, its mass production.

LAKE DWELLERS

Heading south through Hyvinkää to Järvenpää, you are only 45km (30 miles) from Helsinki. The area's lake attracted artists away from their city haunts to build studio-villas on the eastern side, just beyond **Järvenpää** ⓯.

The first of these late 19th-century artist-intellectuals to arrive were writer Juhani Aho and his artist wife, Venny Soldan-Brofeldt. Within a year they were followed by artist Pekka Halonen, whose work had already been inspired by the beautiful **Lake Tuusulanjärvi** ⓰ and by the farming life around him, as was another incomer, portrait painter Eero Järnefelt, famous for his rural and folk scenes. When Sibelius and his wife Aino moved to the lake shores, the Halonens' home, **Halosenniemi** (tel: 09-8718 3461; Tue–Sun May–Aug 11am–6pm, Sept–Apr noon–5pm), became a meeting point for convivial saunas, recitals and the drinking of Halonen's home-made rhubarb wine.

Ainola ⓱ (tel: 09-287 322; www.ainola.fi; May–Sept Tue–Sun 10am–5pm) was the Sibelius home for 53 years. Designed by Lars Sonck, it is still furnished as it was in Sibelius's time – the drawing room holds the composer's piano. Outside in summer, the garden is quiet and peaceful. Sibelius died at Ainola in 1957 at the age of 91; his wife died in 1969 aged 97. Underneath the apple trees their grave is a square flat stone, with always a few floral tributes close by.

Sunset by a frozen lake in winter.

Sculpture by artist Juha Pykäläinen on the island of Kobba Klintar.

THE ÅLAND ISLANDS

Although separated from the mainland and inhabited by Swedish-speakers, the Åland Islands remain very much a part of the Finnish landscape and heritage.

Helsinki

Map on page 206

Map on page 206

Main attractions
Mariehamn
Eckerö
Geta
Kastelholm
Bomarsund
Föglö
Degerby
Kökar

The Åland Islands (Ahvenanmaa in Finnish) are a collection of granite-bound skerries scattered out to the west of the Finnish coast. Most people outside Scandinavia have never heard of them, though they are part of a unique, autonomous political structure that gives the 26,000 Swedish-speakers here their own particular identity. They have had their own flag since 1954 and their own postage stamps since 1984.

GEOGRAPHY AND CULTURE

In 1917 the islands demarcated the western limit of the Grand Duchy of Russia that Finland then was, and the Russians began sending reinforcements to the islands. But, while Finland was celebrating independence from Russia in 1918–19, Ålanders were petitioning to become part of Sweden. Although the League of Nations assigned the islands as a demilitarised, semi-autonomous entity to Finland (with Swedish as the official language), today's Ålanders hold few grudges. Like mainland Finns, Ålanders take tremendous pride in a Finnish athlete or team beating the Swedish competition. But they do not think of themselves as ordinary Finns. Ålanders have inhabited their islands for thousands of years, and have a strong sense of cultural identity and pride in their traditions. The fact that they never became part of Sweden

seems, if anything, to have nurtured even greater pride in their uniqueness.

From June to August, the archipelago is a place of breeze-ruffled inlets edged with tiny, sun-kissed beaches of glacier-worn granite and fishing villages that huddle at the edges of rocky promontories. Winters here are sodden and windy and involve less snow than Sweden or Finland, although temperatures can still drop to -10°C. Although the islands attract fleets of oversized sailing and motor yachts, and with them a well-to-do crowd, the sentiment here is never elitist – merely restful.

The island of Sund.

Tip

You can easily make your way around the Åland archipelago by renting a bicycle or moped in Mariehamn from Ro-No RENT (tel: 018-12820/21; www.rono.ax). Bikes can be taken on ferries and buses for a small fee.

The Ålanders have scraped a living from the soil and extracted it from the sea for centuries. In the days before motorised sailing, it took six weeks to ply the rough waters to Helsinki, where Ålanders traded sealskins and oil. They also profited from local apples, herring and loaves of sweet black bread known as *svartbröd*, which goes especially well with herring.

Today, Ålanders earn their living in a slightly less gruelling fashion; a high percentage of the population is directly employed in tourism and tourist-related services. Seal hunting has dropped out of the picture, but shipping, farming and construction remain fundamental to the local economy. One unique Åland product you'll see is the Finnish potato crisp, made from island-grown spuds.

The grand-scale shipbuilding that once took place here has largely died out, but a big part of Finland's merchant navy is still owned by Åland shippers, and the Maritime Quarter has a marina and traditional boat harbour for small ships and traditional wooden boats that make for a great visit while in Mariehamn. The Finland-Sweden ferries provide hundreds of jobs

– locals have worked in the marine industry since old Åland grain ships once plied worldwide routes as far as the Antipodes.

Ålanders also continue to follow old customs. Many of these centre on weddings: until very recently, brides from certain islands wore black and a few brides still wear the traditional high crown of birch leaves and wild flowers. A proper Åland wedding can go on for days. At Midsummer, every tiny hamlet sets up its own distinctive Midsummer pole. Looking something like a sailing ship's mast, the poles are garlanded with birch leaves and mountain-ash blossom, and topped by different symbols (a sun, a crown, a fish, a rooster or the wooden Fäktargubbe figure, wildly waving his arms).

MARIEHAMN AND AROUND

An enjoyable way to visit the Åland Islands is by taking a Viking Line or Tallink Silja ship from Turku (see page 179) to Mariehamn, which provides a scenic cruise through the thousands of islands and skerries. The main ring of islands includes Åland, Föglö, Kökar, Sottunga, Kumlinge and Brändö.

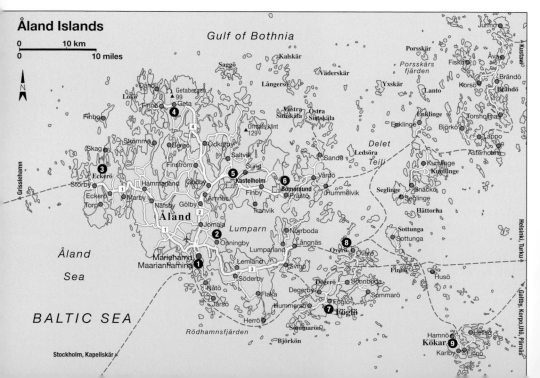

Åland Islands

Mariehamn ❶ is the capital of the main island, Åland, and has 11,700 inhabitants; the original town on this site was called Ytterna, and some of its old buildings can still be seen in south Mariehamn.

Near the west harbour is the **Maritime Museum** (tel: 018-19930; www.sjofarts museum.ax; daily June–Aug 10am–5pm, Sept–May 11am–4pm). Designed in the image of a ship, the museum has plenty of excellent exhibits on the seafaring history of Åland's peoples – the islands once maintained the largest number of wooden ships in the world. Your ticket also admits you aboard the four-masted museum ship *Pommern* (May–Sept daily, same hours), moored below the museum. Built in Glasgow in 1904 and since restored to its original condition, this stately tall ship has a fascinating history.

On the cultural side are the **Ålands Art Museum** and **Ålands Cultural History Museum** , both located at Stadshusparken (tel: 018-25426; www.museum.ax; Sept-Apr–Sept daily 10am–5pm, Oct–Jan Tue–Sun 11am–5pm, Thu until 8pm; combined ticket). The first of the two museums is dedicated to the art of the Åland Islands, including paintings, sculptures and modern video installations while the second focuses on the history of the islands, from Prehistoric times to modern times.

ONNINGBY AND ECKERÖ

Mariehamn is the only town-sized settlement on the islands, but there are dozens of villages, many dating back centuries, such as **Onningby** ❷ at Jomala, much favoured by painters, including the acclaimed Finnish artist Victor Westerholm, who had a summer house here. The smallest islands are either wholly uninhabited, or perhaps only by a single family.

On the main island, the countryside stretches out for miles in all directions from Mariehamn, alternating between wide-open fields and sea vistas to dense, aromatic forests crowded with pines and birches. The scenery is particularly beautiful along the straits that cut into **Eckerö** ❸, straits which resemble rivers at

their narrower points. Eckerö Harbour is set off by the cherry-red boathouses clustered along its bays and promontories. Due to its western exposure, you can watch the midnight sun in Eckerö from its evening dip towards the sea until its early dawn rising.

The huge Russian-era **Post House** (Posthus) dominates this tiny settlement. Eckerö was once known as the Island of Widows, as so many of its farmers and fishermen, pressed into delivering mail between here and Sweden, drowned in the icy seas. A small exhibition, open daily in summer, details the dangerous voyages. In mid-June, the **Postrodden** or mailboat race leaves from Eckerö, a re-enactment of the once arduous journey. Participants sail over in 18th-century costume, and stay at the old postal workers' hotel at Storby.

Along the attractive fishing harbour, the **Hunting and Fishing Museum** (Jakt och Fiskemuseum; tel: 018-38299; www. jaktfiskemuseum.ax; mid-May–mid-June and early Aug–end Aug Mon–Sat 10am–5pm, mid-June–early Aug daily 10am–6pm) has exhibitions on the subject, and a shop selling local handicrafts.

Traditional wooden houses in Mariehamn.

Making hand-crafted boats.

Nowhere is very far on the Åland Islands.

Medieval church in Eckerö.

Eckerö is closest to the Swedish mainland (Grisslehamn) and so is the main harbour used by Swedish holiday-makers. The journey takes two hours.

Moving across the north to **Geta ❹**, you'll find a superb landscape of shelves of granite laced with natural grottoes dug out aeons ago by glaciers and then eroded by the sea. There is a small café at the end of the Geta road; the grotto path is to the right. The teetering piles of stones that line the path are said to be remains from age-old bread ovens.

EAST ÅLAND

Saltvik, Sund, Lumparland, and Lemland, on the east side of the main island, are farming areas. With its numerous, forest-fringed inlets and natural protection from the open sea, Lumparland Sound is a fine spot to fish, picnic or plan a cottage stay.

There aren't many 'big sights' as such on Åland. In the northeast, the medieval stronghold Kastelholm and the 19th-century Bomarsund fortifications are the most impressive structures on the island.

Kastelholm ❺ in Tosarby Sund (tel: 018-25 000; www.kastelholm.ax; daily May,

June, Aug and early Sept 10am–5pm, July 10am–6pm), dating from the 1300s, was once the administrative centre of the islands. It's in a picturesque spot, raised up on a bluff and protected by waterways and a (now dry) moat. One small, claustrophobic tower was the prison of Erik XIV, locked away here by his brother Johan in 1571. Ultimately the site was destroyed by fire in the 18th century, but it has undergone extensive restoration and today is an interesting spot to visit. Adjacent is the **Jan Karlsgården Open-Air Museum** (May–mid-Sept daily 10am–5pm; free), a charming collection of 19th-century cottages, windmills and farm buildings. Around 5km (3 miles) to the north of Kastelholm is the 13th-century granite church of Sund.

About 13km (8 miles) east of Kastelholm is **Bomarsund ❻**, which was built by the Russians as a huge fortified area, surrounded by a stone wall and then knocked out by British and French firepower during the Crimean War. The 1856 Peace of Paris that ensued included Tsar Alexander's declaration that the islands would have no more military reinforcements. Ålanders are, even today, exempt

⊘ VINTAGE BUBBLY

Åland's thousands of islands, skerries and submerged rocks have always made it a treacherous place for sailors – the archipelago contains more than 500 known shipwrecks. In 2010, there was huge excitement when divers found a 19th-century sunken schooner, which possibly met its fate while bound for the Tsar's court in St Petersburg. Its cargo included 168 bottles of bubbly, dated to around 1841, making it the oldest champagne in the world. The divers raised 145 bottles to the surface. The first bottle of Veuve Clicquot was auctioned the following year for €30,000, with proceeds going to charity. Further down in the wreck was another surprise – five bottles of the world's oldest beer. It has since been analysed, and in 2015 the local brewery started producing its own version, the Stallhagen Historic Beer 1843 .

from military service in Finland although they are required to serve within institutions like the coast guard.

BIRD ISLAND

Southeast of Åland lies the second-most populated island, **Föglö** ❼. The ferry takes about 30 minutes from Svinö (a bus from Mariehamn to Svinö takes about 40 minutes) and lands at the enchanting port town of **Degerby**, once a popular vodka smugglers' destination as well as an important customs post. In the eastern part of the island is a natural bird reserve, inspiration for the three golden birds on Föglö's coat of arms.

Degerby's cross-shaped Maria Magdalena Church used to be a key landmark for sailors crossing the north Baltic. It dates from the 12th century and was renovated at great expense in 1859. On the altar is a precious silver crucifix from the 1500s (excavated in the 1960s), preserved in a lucite casing. The church's sacristy holds a fascinating collection of priests' robes.

The Maria Magdalena cemetery has many headstones carrying the name Perón; any Föglö resident named Perón is related to the family of the late Argentinian president. One version of the unlikely story explaining this link claims that an Argentinian seaman became involved in work at the Degerby customs station, found a Degerby wife, and never left.

Föglö has wonderful possibilities for touring by bike, with its empty roads and lack of steep terrain. From Degerby you can ride to **Overö** ❽, the northernmost island in the Föglö group, in just over an hour, using a series of car bridges that stretch to the last strait before Overö. To cross this, you must go on board the cable ferry, which, like the inter-island ferries, is considered an extension of the road system so is free (small charge for bicycles).

Unless you decide to rent a private cottage along the Föglö Straits, the only choice for accommodation will be the charming **Enigheten Guesthouse** at Degerby, a preserved farmhouse manor (tel: 018-50310; www.enigheten.ax).

ARCHAEOLOGICAL TREASURES

Kökar ❾ is a bare island and most of its vistas look towards the open sea. By the rocky coast at Hamnö is a fascinating medieval church, founded by Franciscan fathers and renovated in 1784. The soil around the church has yielded rich archaeological treasures, including ancient Estonian coins and the church's original baptismal font, now located near the altar. Other finds are displayed in the stone chapel in the churchyard.

The **Kökar Museum** (tel: 0457-524 4077; mid-June–mid-Aug daily noon–5pm; rest of the year by previous arrangement) has a collection of old photos whose captions have been hand-corrected by discerning locals. There are also farm tools, costumes and narratives about the Germans' failed attempts to shoot down Kökar's beacon tower in World War II.

The amenities here include only two food shops, one café, one bank, two taxis and a good campsite. However, Havspaviljongen in Hälsö has cabin accommodation, miniature golf and a restaurant with a great view over the Kökar archipelago (tel: 0457-5555 800; www.havspaviljongen.ax).

⊙ Tip

Mariehamn has very few hotels and accommodation in the rest of the islands is in cottages, campsites, guesthouses and picturesque rural farmhouses. For more details, contact the tourist information office **Visit Åland** (Storagatan 8, Mariehamn; tel: 018-24000; www.visitaland.com).

Bucolic summer scene on a lake jetty.

THE WEST COAST

Sprinkled with islands, the beautiful Gulf of Bothnia preserves its rich maritime heritage and retains a harmonious blend of Finnish and Swedish culture and language.

Main attractions
Uusikaupunki
Rauma
Pori
Vaasa
Nykarleby
Oulu

The west coast of Finland is a fascinating mixture of past and present. There are plenty of reminders of days gone by: old wooden houses; museums that focus on the great days of sailing ships and the export of tar; and monuments to fierce battles when Sweden and Russia tussled over the body of Finland, caught fast between its powerful neighbours. The present is represented by modern industry, which, fortunately, is usually well clear of historic town centres. The hinterland is either flat or gently undulating, largely an area of farms and forest with a sprinkling of lakes – in other words, typically Finnish.

As this is the part of Finland which is closest to Sweden, Swedish was the language of many communities during the centuries when Finland was dominated by the Swedes – especially on the southern part of the coast. Even today, many still speak Swedish as a first language, and some towns are even better known by their Swedish name than their Finnish name.

LOUHISAARI MANOR

An important site of near-pilgrimage for Finns, 30km (19 miles) northwest of Turku, is **Louhisaari Manor** ❶ (Louhisaarentie 244, near Askainen;

tel: 0295-336 971; mid-May–Aug Tue–Sun 11am–5pm), the birthplace of the Marshal of Finland, C.G.E. Mannerheim. Access is by guided tour only, every half hour: the information desk is accommodating about arranging English-language tours. The house is a rare example of late-Renaissance palatial architecture, and contains some grand old rooms. The one that every Finn scrambles to see, though, is the modest bedroom where the great general himself was born.

Map on page 212

Street view of Rauma.

West Coast

0   50 km

0   50 miles

UUSIKAUPUNKI

The first main town north of Turku (see page 179) on Road 8 is **Uusikaupunki** ❷ (Nystad in Swedish), typical of this coastline. At the end of the 19th century, it boasted Finland's second-largest sailing fleet. An earlier high point came on 30 August 1721, when the Peace Treaty of Nystad ended the 'Great Hate', a particularly bloody period in Russo-Swedish hostilities. The town's fortunes declined with the arrival of the steamship, along with the decline of the tar industry, but revived with the advent of new industries in the 1960s. The Saab-Valmet car assembly plant offers a motor museum (tel: 020-484 8068; daily Jun–Aug 10am–6pm, Sept–May 11am–5pm) exhibiting the world's largest collection of Saabs. The small-boat harbour is a delight in summer, full of people and pleasure boats, and the old salt warehouses are now antiques shops and restaurants.

Nevertheless, maritime memories remain. The **Uusikaupunki Museum** (Ylinenkatu 11; tel: 044-351 5447; https://uusikaupunki.fi; mid-June–Aug Mon–Fri 10am–5pm, Sat–Sun noon–3pm, Sept–mid-June Tue–Fri noon–3pm) is in the house of F.W. Wahlberg, a former shipowner and tobacco manufacturer, and has an attic exhibition dedicated to Uusikaupunki's seafaring history. Vallimäki Hill has a pilot's cottage, in use from 1857 to 1967, which is now a small museum.

The gorgeous **Uusikaupunki Old Church** (Rantakatu; Koulukatu 6; tel: 02 840 4100), completed in 1629, is Uusikaupunki's oldest building. Its unusual wooden ceiling resembles an upturned boat, and it contains many original 17th-century details and artefacts, including a votive ship, a horse-drawn funeral carriage and two biers.

After investigating the town's serious historical sights, pay a visit to the frankly crackers **Bonk Museum** (tel: 02-841 8404; www.bonkcentre.fi; late June–mid-Aug daily 10am–6pm, June and late-Aug Tue–Sat 11am–3pm). Established in 1893 (so the museum will have us believe...), Bonk Inc. began producing machines for the betterment of mankind, all powered by anchovy oil. Many of the mythical Pär Bonk's inventions are on display, and a touching mausoleum commemorates this ingenious man, who, we are told, was sadly vaporised by a meteorite in 1908. In the children's workshop they are building a giant Time Machine and they need everyone's help. Artist Alvar Gullichsen, a sometime Bonk spokes-person, is the creator of this tongue-in-cheek alternate reality.

WORLD HERITAGE SITES

Rauma ❸ (Raumo in Swedish) is one of six Finnish towns founded in the Middle Ages. It is listed as a Unesco World Heritage site thanks to its perfectly preserved Old Town (Vanha Rauma), an outstanding example of traditional Nordic wooden architecture. Its 18th- and 19th-century buildings, painted in traditional pastel shades, form a large, handsome, lived-in town: most of its 600 buildings are still homes and working businesses.

Like most west-coast towns, Rauma expanded and prospered in the days of sailing ships, and the **Marela Museum** at Kauppiaankatu 24 (tel: 44-567 9183; www.rauma.fi/museo/marela; Jan–mid-May and Sept–Dec Tue–Fri 12pm–5pm, Sat 10am–2pm, Sun 11am–5pm, mid-May–Aug Tue–Sun 10am–5pm, Lace Week daily from 10am–5pm) is the home of a former merchant and master shipper, Abraham Marelin. Much of the interior – panelling, stoves and doors – is original, and the museum has an interesting display of period costumes. Kirsti's, an early 20th-century sailor's home, provides another maritime connection, continued by the Rauma Museum in the Old Town Hall.

The museum's other main attraction is lace; bobbin lace-making has been associated with Rauma since the mid-18th century. Nobody knows how lace came to the town, but by the 1850s it was a major industry,

The clock tower of Rauma's Town Hall. Built in 1776, the building now houses the Rauma Museum.

Pori Jazz Festival.

and almost every woman in the town was a skilled lace-maker. The bubble burst when lace bonnets went out of fashion. Today, the old skills have been revived: lace is sold in specialist shops, and the industry is celebrated in Lace Week at the end of July.

Around 20km (12 miles) out of town, near the village of Lappi, the 36 Bronze-Age burial cairns of **Sammallahdenmäki** ❹ are the region's second Unesco World Heritage site. Visitors are few – the graves have far more archaeological importance than visual impact; but their setting in a rustling pine forest, where the only sounds are the peeping calls of unseen birds, is undeniably atmospheric.

PORI AND JAZZ

Pori ❺ (Björneborg in Swedish), 47km (30 miles) north of Rauma, was founded by Duke Johan of Finland in 1558 as a port at the mouth of the Kokemäenjoki River. Since then the sea has receded and the land has risen, a phenomenon common to the Gulf of Bothnia coastline; so today Pori is marooned some 10km (6 miles) from the sea. In the intervening years, the town burnt down nine times – something of a record even for Finland. The last conflagration, in 1852, led to the stylish rebuilding of the present centre. With a population of almost 85,000, it is, above all, an industrial centre and port, accessed through a series of canals and inlets that lead from the city centre out to the sea.

Post-1852 buildings include the Jennélius Palace, now the Town Hall, built in the style of a Venetian palace. The Pori Theatre, completed in 1884, is one of the most beautiful in Finland. More offbeat is the strange **Juselius Mausoleum** (tel: 04-0030 9779; May–Aug daily 11am–4pm, Sept–Apr Sun noon–5pm) found at the Käppärä Cemetery, and built by a Pori businessman in memory of his young daughter. Its interior is one of Akseli Gallén-Kallela's masterpieces (see page 76), restored by the artist's son in the 1930s.

The **Satakunta Museum** (Satakunnan museo; Hallituskatu 11; tel: 02-621 1063; www.pori.fi/smu; Tue–Sun

Vaasa market.

11am–6pm, Wed until 8pm), dating from 1888, is Finland's largest cultural history museum, with over 60,000 items on display, plus an archive of 110,000 photographs and 10,000 books. The museum has a particularly fascinating section on Pori itself. The **Pori Art Museum** (Porin taidemuseo; Eteläranta; tel: 02-621 1080; www. poriartmuseum.fi; Tue–Sun 11am–6pm, Wed until 8pm), in a skilfully converted warehouse, is also worth a visit.

The great annual **Pori Jazz Festival** (www.porijazz.fi), one of Finland's best-known summer festivals, has been luring in musicians (not solely jazz ones) from all over Europe and beyond for a hectic week in July since 1966. During the festival the town is alive with music day and night: by the riverside, food stalls and temporary stages pop up along 'Jazz Street'. Across the river on Kirjurinluoto Island, the biggest stars of the festival play on a huge summer stage – past performers have included James Brown, Bob Dylan, Isaac Hayes, Tom Jones, Alicia Keys and Kanye West. More than 150,000 people come to enjoy the merry atmosphere and floods of music.

The 20km (12-mile) peninsula leading from Pori to Reposaari (island) has a long sandy beach, **Yteri**. It is one of Finland's best resorts, with a big hotel and congress centre. A golf course illustrates the huge surge of interest in the game in Finland.

KRISTINESTAD

Kristinestad ❻ (Kristiinankaupunki in Finnish) was founded by the enthusiastic Swedish governor, Count Per Brahe, in 1649. A master of tact and diplomacy, he gave the town the name of both his wife and Queen Kristina of Sweden-Finland. This Swedish influence is still noticeable, as even today almost 60 percent of the population is Swedish-speaking and uses the town's Swedish name.

Despite its illustrious beginnings, Kristinestad remained quiet until the 19th century, when it became the home port of one of the country's largest merchant fleets and a shipbuilding centre. The importance of this is shown

Yteri beach.

The market square,
Vaasa.

St Birgitta's Church at
Nykarleby.

clearly in the **Merimuseo** (Kauppatori 1; tel: 06-221 2859; mid-June–Aug Tue–Sun noon–4pm), in the house of former shipowner S.A. Wendelin, and displaying his maritime memorabilia. But, as elsewhere, the shipowners were caught out by the switch from sail to steam. Many citizens emigrated to the United States, and today Kristinestad is a modest town, quiet even at the height of summer.

At the top of the town, the older quarter contains some interesting 18th- and 19th-century wooden buildings. Ulrika Eleonora's Church (1700), named after another queen of Sweden-Finland, is a perfect example of a typical coastal church, with numerous votive ships, donated by sailors, hanging from the ceiling. Its roof is made of wooden shingles, and a separate bell tower stands in the grounds.

During Swedish rule, every traveller into the town had to pay customs duty: the town boasts not one but two old customs houses, dating back to 1680 and 1720. The **Lebell Merchant House** (Lebellin Kauppiaantalo; Rantakatu 51–53; tel: 06-221 2159; June–Aug Mon–Fri 11am–5pm, Sat–Sun 11am–2pm and by appointment) is worth seeing. Lebell was a Polish aristocrat and soldier who married the mayor's daughter and took her name. He lived in the Lebell family home, which was gradually extended, with the result that its 10 rooms now represent a variety of styles spanning the 18th and early 19th centuries.

VAASA

Vaasa ❼ (Vasa in Swedish) is an obvious division between north and south, at the heart of the region of Ostrobothnia. Its origins lie in Old Vaasa, established in the 14th century when the present site was below sea level. It has had a history of devastation by wars and fire, the last of which in 1852 left little but smouldering ruins.

Today, Vaasa (population 67,000) is a handsome ensemble of wide, attractively laid-out streets and a large market square, a mixture of Art Nouveau and modern architecture. Axel Setterberg designed

the Orthodox church, which is surrounded by late 19th-century buildings of the Russian Grand Duchy, and the Court of Appeal (1862). The Town Hall (1883) is the work of Magnus Isaeus and is equally imposing. For the best view of the town, clamber up the 200 steps in the tower behind the police station headquarters.

Vaasa is well endowed with museums reflecting the region's life, the most important being the **Ostrobothnian Museum and Terranova** (Pohjanmaan museo; Museokatu 3; tel: 06-325 3800; www.pohjanmaanmuseo.fi; Tue–Sun 10am–5pm), which covers local history and art; downstairs, Terranova is an excellent exploration of the region's natural history, also covering the nearby Kvarken Archipelago.

The town contains several art galleries: one of the best, not least for its unusual setting in the old customs house, is **Kuntsi** (Sisäsatama; tel: 040-183 0440; http://kuntsi.vaasa. fi; Tue–Sun 11am–5pm), with changing exhibitions of modern paintings, sculptures and installations.

Culture aside, what really draws the summer visitors to Vaasa is family entertainment. On an adjoining island, Vaskiluoto, linked by a causeway, is the 'spa paradise' **Tropiclandia** (tel: 020-796 1300; www.tropiclandia.fi), with indoor and outdoor water slides, waterfalls, jacuzzis and different kinds of sauna. Vaskiluoto is also where ferries leave en route to Sweden.

Offshore islands, reached by a short ferry crossing, add to the charms of Vaasa, as does the collection of some 60 relocated old farm buildings at Stundars, 16km (10 miles) from the town. North of Vaasa, the flat, farming country recalls parts of Sweden, with the Swedish influence being especially clear in the architecture.

LAPUA AND SEINÄJOKI

This area is also rich in political history. In the civil war of 1918 the whole area around Vaasa was a stronghold of the 'White Guard' (right-wing government troops with German military support). Nearby **Lapua** ❽, on Road 16 inland from Vaasa, was the birthplace of the

Boats near Vaasa.

⊘ KVARKEN ARCHIPELAGO

The Unesco-listed Kvarken Archipelago is geologically part of Sweden's 'High Coast' area, where the land, freed of its crushing Ice-Age burden since the glaciers melted, is now springing back upwards. The area is rising at 8mm per year, one of the fastest rates in the world. New land – the size of 150 football pitches – materialises every year from the Gulf of Bothnia, slowly joining Finland to Sweden.

The 5,600 low islands exhibit unusual geological features, and the many sheltered pools and shallow bays attract plenty of birdlife. The archipelago is linked to the mainland by Finland's longest bridge (1km/0.6 miles long), Replot: cycle over to explore, or take a two-hour summer boat cruise (tel: 050-026 0751; www.berny.fi) from Restaurant Berny at the far side.

anti-Communist Lapua movement, which reached its zenith in 1930, when 12,000 people from all over Finland poured into Helsinki on the 'Peasants' March' and forced the Finnish government to outlaw Communist newspapers and public displays of Communist sentiment and sympathy.

Architecture fans should consider a quick trip to the working city of **Seinä-joki** ❾, 20km (12 miles) south of Lapua. At its heart lies an ambitious Alvar Aalto scheme: the city hall, library, theatre and administrative buildings were all built to his design from 1957 to 1987, as was the astonishing **Lakeuden Risti church** (Koulukatu 24; tel: 06 418 4260; Mon–Fri 2–5pm, tower closed in winter, otherwise by appointment). You can ascend its 65-metre (213ft) tower for breathtaking views. Seinä-joki is generally pretty tourist-free, but hundreds of thousands of people flock here for three major festivals: Provins-sirock, held at the end of June, is one of Finland's biggest rock festivals; equally popular is Tangomarkkinat, a tango festival held in July. July also sees motor racing and music combined at the Vauhtiajot festival.

TRAVELLING NORTH

St Birgitta's Church at **Nykarleby** ❿ (Uusikaarlepyy), built in 1708, is one of the most beautiful in the Ostroboth-nia region. Its ceiling paintings are by Daniel Hjulström and Johan Alm, while the windows behind the altar are much more recent, painted by Lennart Segerstråhle in 1940. The 1876 Thelin organ is another prized possession. The town, founded in 1620 by Sweden's great warrior king, Gustav II Adolf, faces a beautiful archipelago.

Nykarleby also has its place in history. On 13 September 1808, a Swedo-Finnish force beat off an attack by a Russian army at the battle of Jutas just outside the town. The event is com-memorated by a monument to Major General G.C. von Döbeln and in a poem by J.L. Runeberg, Finland's national poet. After this brief fame, Nykarleby did not develop to the same extent as some other coastal towns, and today the population is just 7,500. Though a

Oulu's market square.

narrow-gauge railway line opened at the turn of the 20th century, it did little to promote trade and industry and closed in 1916. Today the 60 year-old steam engine *Emma* puffs along the remaining track during the summer.

PIETARSAARI

Pushing further north, **Pietarsaari** ⓫ (Jakobstad in Swedish) takes its Swedish name from a famous military commander, Jakob de la Gardie, and was founded by his widow in the mid-17th century. Much of the town was destroyed in the Russo-Swedish War of the early 18th century. Nevertheless, Pietarsaari became the pre-eminent Finnish shipbuilding centre, producing ships that opened new trade routes around the world. In the 18th century, no shipowners were more powerful in the town than the Malms. One of the family was reputedly Finland's richest man, who, on his death, left 6.5 million gold marks – a vast fortune in those days. **Malmin talo**, his house, is now the local history museum (tel: 06-786 3373; Tue–Sun noon–4pm).

One of the town's best-known sailing ships, *Jakobstads Wapen*, a 1767 galleass, was designed by Fredrik Henrik af Chapman, one of the most famous naval architects of the 18th century. An exact copy of the ship has been completed from original drawings; unfortunately, she has been beset by problems due to deteriorated woodwork and has been undergoing continual repairs in dry dock for a number of years. In **Skata**, the older part of the town, proud owners have carefully restored some 300 or so wooden houses.

KOKKOLA

From Pietarsaari to Kokkola, take the attractive route called the 'road of seven bridges', which runs from island to island across the archipelago.

Like Nykarleby, **Kokkola** ⓬ (Karleby) was founded by King Gustav II Adolf in 1620, and became prosperous in the 18th century largely down to the work of one man. Anders Chydenius (1729–1803), a clergyman, Member of Parliament and one of Finland's first exponents of economic liberalism,

⊙ Fact

Until it was closed in 1998, Pietarsaari was home to Europe's oldest tobacco factory. Now, the former office block maintains another superlative, holding what locals claim is Finland's largest clock.

19th-century interior of the Nykarleby Museum.

succeeded in breaking Stockholm's monopoly of the tar trade. From 1765, Kokkola and its neighbours gained 'staple' rights – the all-important freedom to sell and ship tar directly to foreign customers.

Today Kokkola is an important port town with a population of 47,700, of which 13 percent speak Swedish as their first language. The most charming area is the former fishermen's quarters, **Neristan**, full of wooden 19th-century houses. Kokkola's Town Hall was designed by C.L. Engel, who has left his mark on so many Finnish towns, but the town's most unusual trophy is in a small building in the English Park. It relates to a bizarre episode during the Crimean War known as the 'Skirmish of Halkokari' (1854), during which British marines were repelled by local civilians, armed with hunting rifles. The marines' small gunboat was captured by locals – who still refuse to return it, despite the occasional request from the UK.

On the 230km (140-mile) road running north from Kokkola to Oulu, the most visited place is **Kalajoki** . Kalajoki is the most popular summer-holiday spot in Finland, thanks to its long, sandy beaches, which stretch for almost 10km (6 miles). There are fishing, bathing and sailing opportunities, and big new developments including a spa hotel, amusement park and a waterpark.

OULU – TAR CITY

Oulu (Uleåborg in Swedish), with a population of more than 203,000, is the largest city in northern Finland. It owes its existence to the Oulu River and King Karl IX of Sweden, and its fortunes to tar, essential for wooden sailing ships. After excessive Central European tar-burning in the 18th century led to a decline in the number of coniferous forests, the industry moved to the Baltic, with Ostrobothnia soon becoming one of its most important areas.

Making tar occupied the entire northern area; every village east of Oulu had its smouldering pits, and barrels by the thousand came down to the coast in long narrow boats. In

Oulu's marina.

1781, Oulu merchants set up a Tar Exchange, and in the 19th century the town was the leading tar exporter in the world. Prosperity ended abruptly in 1901 when the Tar Exchange went up in flames.

Old tar pits and tar boats can be found at the **Turkansaari Open-Air Museum** ⓯ (Turkansaaren ulkomuseo; tel: 044 703 7191; daily June–Aug 10am–5pm, extended hours until 6pm from late June–early August), accessed via a footbridge to a small island in the Oulujoki (river) 14km (8 miles) east of Oulu, off Road 22. Established in 1922, this is an interesting collection of 40 Ostrobothnian buildings, including a church, farm buildings and windmills. If you want more detail, the **Northern Ostrobothnia Museum** (Pohjois-Pohjanmaan museo; tel: 044-7037 161; Tue–Fri 9am–5pm, Sat–Sun 10am–5pm) in Ainola Park has historical and ethnographic exhibits on the region.

MUSEUMS AND ISLANDS

After the era of tar and sail, Oulu languished in the doldrums, but the establishment of a university in the 1960s was a major turning point. It attracted high-tech companies to the area and led to the creation of the Finnish Technical Research Centre.

This emphasis on the latest technology has been responsible for one of Oulu's notable attractions, **Tietomaa Science Centre** (Nahkatehtaankatu 6; tel: 050-3166 489; www.tietomaa.fi; Mon–Fri 10am–5pm, Sat–Sun until 6pm). Taking a hands-on approach, with excellent interactive displays, the museum appeals to children and adults alike. Exhibits range from a low-gravity simulator to a means of checking on the world's weather and population. In all, Oulu has seven museums, from those concentrating on geology and zoology to the oldest wooden house in the city (1737). The elegant **Oulu Art Museum** (Oulun taidemuseo; Kasarmintie 9; tel: 044-703 7471; Tue–Fri 9am–5pm, Sat 10am–5pm, Sun noon–7pm) has a permanent exhibition of Finnish contemporary art plus regularly changing temporary exhibitions.

An 1822 fire led to the construction of a new city centre and cathedral, designed by Engel. The city's aesthetic also benefits from the presence of a number of islands linked by bridges, the Oulu River and some green oases, such as Hupisaaret Park. Visit Koskikeskus on the mouth of the Oulujoki River, with 12 fountains and surrounding islands. The island of **Linnansaari** has castle ruins, and there are recreational facilities on Raatinsaari and Mustasaari.

TOWARDS SWEDEN

From Oulu to Tornio on the Swedish frontier, the road and railway cross numerous rivers draining into the Gulf of Bothnia and the scenery undergoes a subtle change. This is no longer the west coast but the approach to Lapland.

Statue in Oulu.

📷 ENJOYING THE FINNISH SUMMER

Summer is the best time in Finland, and many Finns who live abroad return annually for the long evenings, warm weather and cool lakes.

On Friday afternoons in summer nearly all Helsinki denizens leave the city in the weekly rush hour. But once in the heartland of the country, the traffic eventually thins out as cars turn off at intervals onto what might seem to outsiders like invisible dirt tracks, each leading to a *mökki* (summer cottage). Here, Finns live their parallel lives.

LIFE AT THE SUMMER COTTAGE

There are almost half a million summer cottages in Finland – that's one for every 10 Finns. Daily life at a *mökki* is a mixture of bohemian, Chekhovian and Finnish lifestyle aesthetics. Families visit relatives and friends; food is eaten leisurely and coffee (and beer) drunk over the long days, and everyone spends time in the sauna before jumping into the lake. Cottage gardens yield salad vegetables and new potatoes, but the nearby *kyläkauppa* (village shop) is a steady source of bottled drinks and ready-made food. So important is the influx of summer visitors in small villages that in summer months sales (and population) may triple.

But Finns rarely stay at the cottage every day: aside from summer sports, such as fishing, cycling, swimming and sailing, summer festivals are always on the agenda (see page 88). Nearly every town and village in Finland has tried the same formula – pick a theme and build its reputation as a 'must-do' event.

A summer in Finland is a totally different experience from winter snow; it is Finnish comfortable living at its best.

The countryside in summer offers a sense of space and freedom that can't be found in the city, as well as the chance to fill your lungs with clean, fresh air.

For those who can't escape to the country, city parks provide space to soak up the summer sun.

The simple canoe has a variety of uses: ideal for leisurely fishing trips that may take half a day, or just for simply crossing from one edge of the lake to the other.

A good mökki should be rustic, yet equipped with modern amenities. The simple life is very attractive to city dwellers, but electricity is a must.

Paying for a room with a view

Many Finns rent rather than own their *mökki* – a lakeside location is preferred but it is not cheap, and buying a nice house near water is impossible for the majority of Finns. Many cottages are inherited, and the oldest log cabins, painted with red ochre, are actually known as *mummonmökeistä* ('Grandmothers' Cottages'). These tend to be more primitive dwellings, with two or three rooms and a well for fetching water.

Less than an hour's drive from big towns such as Tampere, Finns may enjoy unrestricted freedom, with no noise and no pollution. Finnish law stipulates that no new houses be built on the lakeshore, so most cottages are hidden and the lake view remains unmarred by unscrupulous investors.

However, wealthy urbanites masquerading as jovial country people do not always impress the locals – the cultural gap between town and country is ever-widening.

Summer breaks may involve energetic activities, or they can be leisurely affairs. A gentle woodland walk with the family may be all that is needed after a hard week in the office.

...hing near Kuopio in the Lakeland.

...st tracts of forest provide berries and mushrooms for ...mmer cooking, as well as great opportunities for trekking.

LAKELAND

Finland's central region of lakes, surrounded by lush pine forests, matches the image most people have of the country, and a tour of the waterways will not disappoint.

Helsinki

Main attractions

Lappeenranta
Imatra
Punkaharju
Savonlinna
Valamon luostari
Kuopio
Lahti
Jyväskylä

If you could flood the whole of Scotland and dot it with some 33,000 islands and peninsulas, you would have the equivalent of the Saimaa Lake area. Add to that the Päijänne system and you could cover Wales as well.

The Great Lakes of Saimaa and Päijänne in central Finland are among the best known and most popular places to visit in the country and are the target for thousands of visitors who long only to be in, on, or beside them. But despite the number of visitors, this watery landscape never appears crowded, simply because there is so much of it – lakes large and small, smooth curving bays with yellow-grey beaches or ragged and broken shores, rushing torrents squeezed between high banks or flooding over hidden rocks, and rivers linking the different waters.

CANALS, SEALS AND SUNBATHING

Where the land intervenes, Finnish engineers turned their skills as long ago as the 19th century to building canals to connect the stretches of water. Today, boats can journey the length and breadth of both lake systems, calling at the small, strategically placed towns, and the even smaller villages, and stopping along the endless lakesides.

Sometimes, the land is flat beside the water or crunched up into ridges where rocks and trees point upwards. This varied landscape owes its beauty to the Ice Age, when glaciers carved out the shape of lake and ridges, the most famous being at Punkaharju, an 8km (5-mile) chain of ridges which winds between the lakes. Far inland, Saimaa has its own resident species of seal, the Saimaa marble seal, whose ancestors were trapped in the lake system long ago when the glaciers cut off the route to the sea.

Map on page 226

Fishing in the Lakeland.

◎ Tip

In the summertime, Saimaa Travel (Ratakatu 23, Lappeenranta; tel: 05-541 0100; www. saimaatravel.fi) organises canal boat trips to Vyborg along the Saimaa canal, as well as package tours to St Petersburg.

There are two perfect ways to get to know the Great Lakes: from the water by passenger steamer or smaller craft, or by doing as the Finns do and renting a lakeside cabin, to fish, swim, canoe, sauna or simply sunbathe.

THE SAIMAA SYSTEM

The Saimaa waterway was the historic buffer zone between the kingdom of Sweden-Finland and tsarist Russia, at times changing hands with dizzying frequency. Subsequently, it became part of the frontier with the Soviet Empire. The social and geopolitical effects of these shifting borders are recurring themes as you travel the area.

It would be hard to visualise landscapes more fragmented or more liquid than the Saimaa waterway. A series of large and lesser lakes are linked by rivers, straits and canals, and framed by an amazing complexity of headlands, ridges, bays, islands and skerries, to form Europe's largest inland waterway system. Up to a quarter of the Saimaa region's total area of 70,000 sq km (27,000 sq miles) is covered by water.

Saimaa's waters provided natural highways for goods and people long

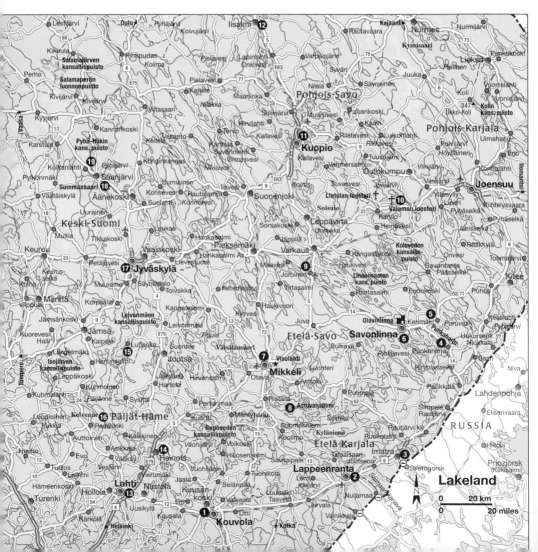

before railways and, especially, roads probed into its remoter reaches. To a large extent, they still do. No lakeside home is without its rowing boat, usually with outboard engine. Tugboats hauling their floating timber trains, up to 500 metres (1,600ft) long, from forest to factory, are common sights.

Embryonic tourism dates from the 19th century, as the well-to-do of tsarist St Petersburg boarded the then new-fangled railway to explore the Grand Duchy of Finland on the fringes of their empire. They went to take the waters in the handful of newly created spas, to marvel at such natural wonders as the foaming cascades of Imatra and to hunt and fish in the richly stocked forests and lakes.

The best approach to the lakes region from the south is via industrial **Kouvola** ❶, about 140km (85 miles) northeast of Helsinki and a junction of road and rail routes into Saimaa. Although not the most interesting town in Finland, Kouvola's Kaunisnurmi quarters, formerly a railway staff colony, house quaint handicraft shops and several museums. Kouvola is also a jumping-off point to the unspoilt lake regions of Iitti and Jaala, northwest of Kouvola. Jaala's Unesco-listed World Heritage site **Verla** (tel: 02041-52170; www.verla.fi; early May–late June and Sept Tue–Sun 11am–4pm, late June–Aug daily 10am–6pm) is a perfectly preserved cardboard factory, dating from the 1880s and in operation until 1964. Craft shops and boutiques occupy the mill grounds; the mill itself is accessible only by on-the-hour guided tours.

From Kouvola road and rail routes lead north into the heart of the lakes region. Yet to capture the spirit of Saimaa, we suggest heading east on Road 6. About 80km (50 miles) on, and close to the Russian border, you reach Lappeenranta, South Karelia's main town.

Café in Lappeenranta.

LAPPEENRANTA

Like almost every Finnish community, **Lappeenranta** ❷ combines work and play. There is a great deal of industry and some excellent holiday facilities – for most kinds of water sports, for

Sailing in Lappeenranta harbour.

☉ THE OPERA FINNISHED

The intact medieval Olavinlinna in Savonlinna is possibly the most splendid setting to hear opera in Europe, whether for *Aïda* in Italian, *Faust* in French or *The Magic Flute* in Finnish.

Tickets for these world-class performances sell out months in advance. Opera-goers from all over the continent often come dressed to impress, the wisest of them armed with blankets, for Finnish summer nights are predictably cool. After the performance, with daylight fading at last, Olavinlinna is softly illuminated to provide a memorably romantic backdrop as you stroll back past the town's elegant restaurants and cafés, many still open and welcoming. You can see the programme and buy tickets at the Savonlinna Opera Festival website: www.operafestival.fi.

A flea market is held in Lappeenranta's main square on Sunday mornings.

Reindeer in autumn.

example. Its spa amenities have undergone a recent renaissance too, though their origins lie in the Tsarist 1820s. The town is the southern terminus for Saimaa's venerable lake fleet.

In the past Lappeenranta was a major military town, heavily fortified by the Swedes in the 18th century, only to be rebuilt by the Russians after they destroyed it. The Linnoitus (fortress) is the oldest and most interesting area, where you will find Finland's oldest Orthodox Church (1785), the **South Karelia Museum** (tel: 05-616 2255; Jan–early June and late Aug–Dec Tue–Sun 11am–5pm, early June–late Aug Mon–Fri 10am–6pm, Sat–Sun 11am–5pm), with a fascinating exhibit on the old city of Vyborg (now in Russia), and the **Cavalry Museum** (Ratsuväkimuseo; tel: 05-616 2257; early June–Aug Mon–Fri 10am–6pm, Sat–Sun 11am–5pm), detailing the history and distinctive red uniforms of Finland's proud soldiers. There are also a number of handicraft workshops and a great deal of military hardware. The museum, at the time of writing, was undergoing renovations so

do check ahead to confirm it is open. The town is a popular destination for families with young children, drawn by its shallow beach and to admire the giant Sandcastle (Hiekkalinnan; mid-June–Aug daily 10am–8pm) built here every year from 3 million kilos of sand.

These days Lappeenranta is just a few miles from the Russian border, but back in the days of the Grand Duchy and the first decades of the Republic, Finnish territory extended east beyond Vyborg (Viipuri) and included substantial portions of huge Lake Ladoga. In 1856, when the 43km-long (27-mile) Saimaa Canal was completed, Saimaa was linked with the Gulf of Finland entirely through Finnish territory. Victorian travellers hailed the canal as one of the greatest engineering feats of the 19th century, and its construction encouraged the development of a string of inland ports, Lappeenranta among them.

Post-World War II, the borders changed, and half of the canal fell within the USSR. The waterway lay disused and in growing disrepair

until the 1960s when, after lengthy negotiations and the privilege of paying for its restoration, the Finns regained use of the canal in 1968. The canal is still leased from Russia: a new 50-year agreement was signed in 2010, and Finland pays a basic rent of €1.22 million per year to use it.

'NIAGARA OF FINLAND'

Despite the overwhelming predominance of lake and forest, parts of Saimaa's southern shores are undeniably industrial. Just a few miles beyond Lappeenranta, **Imatra** ❸ lies in the midst of the most concentrated industrial area of Finland. It also has some claim as a famed beauty spot, and was described by one early 20th-century British visitor, with shameless exaggeration, as the 'Niagara of Finland'. Nevertheless, the very fine rapids of **Imatrankoski** were responsible for the presence of the grand old (restored) Imatran Valtionhotelli, built to cater to the sightseers who flocked here, including many distinguished, wealthy and high-born guests.

It was the eventual taming of the surging waters which triggered the industrial boom. Today the town is leafy and laconic. From late June to August, the waters are unleashed at 6pm daily, dramatised by Sibelius's music and lighting effects. Construction work at the local power plant can disrupt shows so check first with the local tourist office (tel: 020-617 7777 or 05 667 788; www.gosaimaa.fi).

About 50km (30 miles) on from Imatra, Road 6 comes its closest to Russia. A no-go border zone – up to 3km (2 miles) wide on the Finnish side and 7km (4 miles) on the Russian side – is patrolled by border guards from both countries, and marked by multilingual frontier-zone notices and watchtowers. Soon after, around Parikkala, the road turns north away from the border. Switching to Road 14, you soon come to one of Finland's best-loved beauty spots.

PUNKAHARJU

The last Ice Age bequeathed countless eskers to Finland, but **Punkaharju** ❹ is considered the loveliest of them

Wooden church in Kerimäki.

Lusto, a museum on forestry.

all. In places it is just wide enough to carry the road; elsewhere it widens to carry magnificent pine and birch woods framing the ever-changing permutations of lake and sky, island and skerry, bedrock granite and the 'green gold' forests. The light is ever-changing too, to combine all the main elements of essential Finnish scenery.

In addition to the narrow ridge, the Punkaharju Islands include a large research forest (Tutkimuspuisto) and a protected nature reserve, associated with the superb Forestry Museum, **Lusto** (tel: 015-345 100; www.lusto.fi; June–Aug daily 10am–6pm, May and Sept daily 10am–5pm, Oct–Apr Tue– Sun 10am–5pm). An architectural achievement in its own right, Lusto has a complete exhibition on Finland's forests and anything associated with them – design, wilderness trekking, forestry industry and research. Guided tours are also available for groups of up to 25 people.

Tucked away among Punkaharju's ridges are well-equipped holiday centres and the **Waterpark Kesämaa**

Olavinlinna is the dramatic setting for the Savonlinna Opera Festival.

(Kesämaa; tel: 044 765-2020; www. punkaharjuresort.fi; early June–late-Aug daily, hours vary) for family fun.

In summer, a regular lake steamer sails between Punkaharju and Savonlinna: the trip is a delightful miniodyssey through the islands, taking more than two hours compared with a 20-minute spin along the highway. Road travellers, however, should make a short detour on Road 71 to **Kerimäki** ❺, a typically scattered Finnish rural community harbouring the world's largest wooden church, built in 1848 with a congregation capacity of 3,500 people – larger than the town's population – and a 25-metre (82ft) cupola (tel: 015-576 800; June–Aug daily 9am–1pm; free). Classical music concerts are staged here in summer.

SAVONLINNA

Savonlinna ❻ – the name means 'Savo fortress' – sprawls over a series of interlinked islands. It is the most charming of Finland's main lakeland towns and makes the best base for a stay in the Saimaa region. It has the

spectacular medieval castle of Olavinlinna, as well as spa facilities, excellent lake sports amenities, varied sightseeing and a great deal of culture. Castle and culture combine particularly successfully in the annual International Opera Festival, one of Finland's leading events, which takes place throughout July (see box). The Savonlinna Tourist Information office (Riihisaari; tel: 044 417-4466, daily 10am–7pm) offers free wifi, information and brochures to help with accommodation, sights to see and travel arrangements.

The main venue for this operatic extravaganza, **Olavinlinna** (tel: 295-336 942; www.kansallismuseo.fi/en/olavinlinna; June–mid-Aug daily 11am–6pm, rest of year Mon–Fri 10am–4pm, Sat–Sun 11am–4pm) occupies an islet a short walk from the town centre. With its massive granite walls, ramparts and shooting galleries topped by three great round towers (surviving from the original five), its Knights Hall and grim dungeon, it has everything you'd ever want in a medieval castle. Originally built by the Danish-born nobleman Erik Axelsson Tott in 1475, it was intended to be a main defence against the Russians, but so frequently did the eastern border shift that Olavinlinna often lay too far from the battlefield.

The town of Savonlinna itself grew out of a small trading centre by the castle, its growth greatly hampered by wars and fires. The arrival of steam and the opening of the Saimaa canal provided the necessary stimulus, because the town's situation made it a natural junction for lake traffic.

The days have long gone when the venerable Saimaa fleet was powered by wood-burning engines, but a number of the attractive double-decked wooden vessels, now converted to diesel, continue to ply Saimaa's waters. One impressive sight in Savonlinna is the departure and return of these romantic vessels to the passenger harbour, right by the open-air market on Kauppatori in the centre of town. Another, near the castle, is the museum ship *Salama*, a steam schooner built in 1874, shipwrecked in 1898 and raised from the lake in 1971.

Opera performance at Olavinlinna.

⊘ FINNISH WINE

The week-long Kuopio Wine Festival (tel: 050-402 4519; www.kuopiowinefestival.fi), held each year in June, is a jolly event that showcases European wines at the harbourside Wine Village. For something a little more Finnish, Vaajasalo Island, just east of Kuopio, is the home of Alahovi Berry Farm (tel: 017-362 1129; www.alahovi.com; restaurant open in summer only, times vary; wine shop daily 9am–4pm), the first countryside winery to open in Finland. The farm uses blackcurrants, white currants, apples, strawberries, gooseberries, arctic bramble and cranberries to produce its unique juices, wines, liqueurs and bubbly. In summer, Kuopio Roll Cruises (tel: 0440 266 330; www.roll.fi) will sail you across the water from Kuopio for an afternoon of wine tasting.

The *Salama* is one of three converted old ships that form the inland navigation section (generally mid-June–mid-Sept) of the **Savonlinna Provincial Museum** (Savonlinnan maakuntamuseo; Riihisaari 1; tel: 044-417 4466; daily 10am–5pm, May daily 9am–5pm).

THE NORTHERN ROUTE

Travelling from Savonlinna to Kuopio by lake steamer is a full day's journey, as opposed to a few hours by road. It's a great way to immerse yourself in the region's scenery – from forest and meadow through reed bed or granite shore, timber-built farms and summer cottages huddled along the lakefronts, to islands emerging suddenly from headlands – and watch the reflections tossed from huge sky to broad lake and back again in endlessly varying light and colour tones.

Road travellers have a choice of continuing west from Savonlinna to Mikkeli and thence further west still into the Päijänne lake system (see page 235), or staying with Saimaa to its northern limits beyond Kuopio.

Lakeland house in the mist.

Mikkeli ⑦, a provincial capital, is a pleasant market community and also a historic army town. Mannerheim's headquarters during World War II are now a museum, the **Päämajamuseo** (Päämajankuja 1–3; tel: 015-366 428; May–Aug daily 10am–5pm, Sept–Apr Fri–Sun 10am–5pm). Exhibits include a copy of London's *Daily Telegraph* from 18 December 1939, with the headline: 'Finns smash two Soviet Divisions.'

Also open in Mikkeli is a wartime **Communications Centre** (Viestikeskus Lokki), located inside Naisvuori Hill (tel: 015-366 461; May–Aug daily 10am–5pm).

Those interested in archaeology might like to make an expedition 40km (25 miles) south of Mikkeli to the **Astuvansalmi rock paintings** ⑧. These enigmatic examples of Stone Age art, in a lovely setting by Lake Yövesi, are one of the largest collections discovered in the Nordic countries. The red-ochre designs of running elk, boats and human figures are not easily spotted – pick up a map from Mikkeli or Riistina tourist office to assist. Head south to Riistina, then take road 4323 east.

If you are travelling directly from Savonlinna to Kuopio, the recommended route is to leave Road 14 about 35km (20 miles) west of the former and follow Road 464 via Rantasalmi, a particularly attractive and watery route. This joins Road 5 a little south of Varkaus. Varkaus itself is industrial, although it's worth a trip to the offbeat **Museum of Mechanical Music** (Mekaanisen Musiikin museo; Pelimanninkatu 8; tel: 010-2390 380; July daily 11am–6pm, June Tue–Sun 11am–6pm, Apr–May and Aug–mid-Dec Tue–Sat 11am–6pm, Sun 11am–5pm). Its music boxes, mechanical pianos, hurdy-gurdies and barrel organs are beautifully displayed, and the cacophonic tours are something else entirely. The little town of **Joroinen** ⑨, 15km (10 miles) to the south, is very typical of a smaller Finnish community.

In contrast with its own modernity are the fine old farms and manor houses dotted about these fertile landscapes, some used as settings for the summer music festival. It is also well-known for its annual summer Finntriathlon.

SIGNIFICANT MONASTERY

Road 5 is the direct way to Kuopio, 75km (45 miles) north of Varkaus, while to the west Road 23 leads to the pleasant rural community of Pieksämäki on Saimaa's western fringes. Northeastwards from Varkaus, the same road leads to Joensuu in North Karelia (see page 243), passing close by two major religious houses: the Orthodox monastery **Valamon luostari ⑩** and the **Convent of Lintula**. On all three counts of history, culture and scenery these merit a visit, a recommended possibility being the monastery cruises that depart from Kuopio in the summer months.

The clue to the monastery's history lies in its name. Valamo is the large island on Lake Ladoga on which an Orthodox religious foundation was established in the Middle Ages, attracting a growing number of pilgrims over the centuries, though its fortunes eventually declined. During the Winter War of 1939–40, the surviving handful of elderly monks were forced to leave and were eventually granted the present site of Uusi ('New') Valamo (tel: 017-570 111, 017 570 1810 for accommodation requests; www.valamo. fi), originally an old manor house and outbuildings. One of these outbuildings was adapted as the monks' first place of worship, embellished by the precious 18th-century icons and other sacred objects which they had brought with them.

Valamon luostari has since experienced something of a renaissance. An injection of younger blood ensures its continuance; there is a church, cafeteria, wine shop, souvenir shop and a modern hotel to cater for visitors and pilgrims. The **Convent of Lintula**

(Lintulan luostari; tel: 040-485 7603), a few kilometres away, has a similar but shorter history. The pious inhabitants of both contribute to their upkeep by working the land, although you may find the humbler features of Lintula more conducive to spiritual reflection.

KUOPIO

Kuopio ⑪ is a thoroughly pleasant town and one of Finland's liveliest, with a crowded summer calendar that includes the International Dance Festival in June, which celebrated its 50th anniversary in 2019. Its daily market is one of the most varied outside Helsinki. Here you can try freshly baked *kalakukko* (fish and pork in a rye crust), traditional local fare that is definitely an acquired taste; in season you may be tempted by the varied edible fungi or succulent mounds of berries straight from the forests. There is a smaller market on summer evenings at the passenger harbour (east side of the town).

Like many Finnish country towns that developed in the 18th and 19th

The market hall at Kuopio.

Boats in Kuopio's harbour.

Puijo tower in Kuopio.

The daunting ski jump in Lahti.

centuries, central Kuopio follows a gridiron pattern of parallel streets more familiar to Americans than Europeans. This was designed to provide plenty of firebreaks between the then predominantly wooden buildings, though, alas, it failed in its purpose all too often. Most of the structures that survived the regular conflagrations have been replaced by modern buildings, but the **Old Kuopio Museum** (Kuopion kortellimuseo; Kirkkokatu 22; tel: 017-182 625; https://kuopionkort telimuseo.fi; Tue–Sun 10am–5pm, Wed until 7pm), a few blocks south of the market place, preserves a number of original dwellings complete with authentic furniture, warehouses and even gardens dating from the 18th century to the 1930s – a quiet oasis showing how much of small-town Finland used to look.

A little to the east of the marketplace, the **Kuopion museo** at Kauppakatu 23 (tel: 017-182 603; Tue–Sat 10am–5pm, closed until 2021 for renovation) houses excellent regional collections of a cultural and natural

history order in a castle-like building that is a typical example of Finnish early 20th-century National Romantic style.

Kuopio is the headquarters of the Finnish Orthodox church: on the edge of the town centre, the recently renovated **Ortodoksinen kirkkomuseo** (Karjalankatu 1; tel: 0206-100 266; www.ortodoksinenkirkkomuseo.fi; Tue–Sat noon–4pm) is unique in Western Europe, housing collections of icons (many from the 18th century, some from the 10th century) and sacred objects brought here from Valamo and Konevitsa in Karelia and a few from Petsamo in the far north, all territories ceded to the Soviet Union.

A little further on is Puijo hill, topped by **Puijon torni** (tel: 017-255 5255; Mon–Thu 11am–4pm, Fri–Sat 11am–7pm, Sun 11am–4pm), over 75 metres (250ft) high. The vistas from the tower's viewing platforms and revolving restaurant (open throughout the year) are beautiful, with lakes and forests merging into purple distances. Try to time your visit for an

hour or two before sundown – in good weather the colours are out of this world.

Jätkänkämppä Lumberjack Lodge, 5km (3 miles) out of Kuopio, offers a Lumberjack Evening (600m/yards from Spa Hotel Rauhalahti, Katis-kaniementie 8; tel: 030-608 30; www.rauhalahti.fi; Tue year-round, also Thu in summer), with a buffet, accordion music, singsongs and dancing. This is also your chance to experience the world's biggest **smoke sauna**, which holds 70 people: wash off the sweat and soot by leaping into the cool waters of Lake Kallavesi.

IISALMI

By the time you reach **Iisalmi** ⑫, 80km (50 miles) north of Kuopio on Road 5, you are almost exactly halfway between Helsinki and the Arctic Circle, and you are still – just – in the Saimaa region. Should you launch a canoe from Iisalmi's lakeshore, it would be either level paddling or heading gently downhill all the way to the Gulf of Finland – which is over 400km (250 miles) away.

Iisalmi is a pleasant small provincial town, birthplace of writer Juhani Aho in 1861 (the family home is a museum on the outskirts of town), and site of one of Finland's innumerable battles against the Russians (1808; the Finns won this one, even though they were reputedly outnumbered seven to one). It's also the site of the Olvi brewery, with attached museum, and of Kua-ppi (at the harbour; June–Aug daily), 'the smallest restaurant in the world', which fits two customers. If it's full, the nearby beer hall Olutmestari has an attractive summer terrace.

THE PÄIJÄNNE SYSTEM

In the southwest of the lake region, Päijänne is Finland's longest and deepest lake – extending for 119km (74 miles) as the crow flies, though many times that if you follow its wondrously intricate shoreline. At opposite ends of the lake system are two of Finland's more substantial towns, Lahti and Jyväskylä. The watery topography between the two defeated the railway engineers, but they are linked to the

> ◉ **Tip**
>
> In summer, old-fashioned steamboats cruise from Lahti harbour to lake Päijänne via the Vääksy Canal – companies include Päijänne Risteilyt (www.paijanne-risteilythilden.fi) and Lahden Järvimatkailu (www.lahdenjarvimatkailu.fi).

Lake Kallavesi, Kuopio.

⊘ Tip

Alvar Aalto's last church, built in 1978, is the highly individualistic **Church of the Cross** (Ristinkirkko; Kirkkokatu 4; daily 10am–3pm). Powerful in its simplicity, it makes a fine main venue for the Lahti Organ Festival in early August.

west of Päijänne via Route 24, and to the east of it by a network of slower, more attractive routes. Alternatively, in summer there is the leisurely 10.5-hour waterborne route.

Lahti ⑬ lies 103km (64 miles) north of Helsinki on Road 4. It straddles part of one of Finland's more distinctive topographical features, the extensive ridge system called Salpausselkä, which is regularly the setting for major world skiing championships. Here, too, is the **Lahden Urheilukeskus**, the town's sports centre, with some of Finland's best winter sports facilities, including three ski jumps (with hill sizes HS 70, HS 95 and HS 130). It is the venue for the annual Finlandia Ski Race and the Ski Games.

The sports centre is also home to a recently renovated **skiing museum** (Hiihtomuseo; tel: 050-398 5523; www.lahdenmuseot.fi; Mon–Fri 9am–5pm, Sat–Sun 11am–4pm). Its ski-jump, biathlon and downhill-skiing simulators are great fun, and there are interesting exhibits on Finnish Olympic medallists and a collection of ski

outfits from the past century. In summer, the ski-museum ticket allows access to the top of the sickeningly high **ski jump** (June–mid-Aug Mon–Fri 9am–5pm, Sat–Sun 11am–4pm).

From the viewing platform, the town spreads at your feet. Beyond, the gleaming sheets of Vesijärvi (lake) are linked, by the Vääksy Canal a few miles to the north, to the much more extensive waters of Päijänne. Lahti is a modern place, one of its few older buildings being the Kaupungintalo (Town Hall, 1912), designed, as were so many Finnish public buildings of the period, by Eliel Saarinen. Three blocks to the north is the market, a lively morning spot.

One of the town's most striking pieces of architecture is **Sibelius Hall** (Sibeliustalo; Ankkurikatu 7; box office tel: 0600-39 3949; www.sibeliustalo.fi), a concert-and-conference centre completed in 2000 from birch, spruce, alder, pine and glass. The main auditorium has fantastic acoustics – which is a piece of luck for the Lahti Symphony Orchestra (www.sinfonialahti.fi), who call the building home; and for visitors to the highly respected Sibelius Festival, held here in early September.

The **Lahden Historiallinen museo** (Lahdenkatu 4; tel: 040-482 6044) in Lahti Manor, an exotic late 19th-century building, has good regional ethnographical and cultural history sections, as well as art and furniture collections. It is undergoing renovation until 2021, when it will reopen with a new permanent exhibition.

A short distance northwest is the area known as **Tiirismaa**, home to south Finland's highest hill (reaching a very modest 223 metres/730ft), some of the country's oldest rocks and the snow centre **Messilä** (Messiläntie 308; tel: 03-860 423 in peak season, 03-86011 off-season; www.messila.fi), combining a beautiful manor house, restaurants, hotel, log cabins and a camping site. Downhill

Lakeland scenery.

skiing, snowboarding, cross-country skiing or snowshoe safaris are your winter options, whereas during the summer you can choose from golf or horse riding. Ten kilometres (six miles) further on, the 15th-century grey-stone **Hollola Church** (tel: 03 524 6600 for information on services and opening hours) has some good wooden sculptures and is among the largest and finest of about 80 churches surviving from that period in Finland. Close by is the **Hollola Homestead Museum** (June–Aug Tue–Sun noon–6pm) and some excellent coffee houses.

HEINOLA

From Lahti it's only 35km (21 miles) northeast on Road 75 to the pleasant little town of **Heinola** ⑭, on the way passing Suomen urheiluopisto, the top Finnish Sports Institute at Vierumäki. Taking the popular summer lake route, it is an astonishing – and lovely – 4.5 hours by steamer, 3.5 hours by hydrofoil. A glance at the map reveals the contortions needed for lake traffic plying this route, first negotiating the Vääksy canal north into Päijänne, and later squeezing southeast through narrow straits into the wider waters that lead to Heinola.

There are more narrow straits at Heinola, where the scurrying waters of **Jyrängönkoski** (rapids) provide good sport for local canoeists and for fishermen casting for lake and rainbow trout. You can also try for the latter, with rather more likelihood of success, from the teeming tanks of Siltasaari Fishing Centre by the rapids, where, for a few euros, you can rent a rod and have your catch smoked to eat on the spot or take away.

Heinola blossomed into yet another spa town in tsarist times. There are a number of wooden buildings dating from the turn of the 20th century, including a Chinese pavilion on the ridge-top park, now a restaurant, redolent of a more leisurely age. Not far away, the pond of Kirkkolampi is a focal point of the well-arranged **bird sanctuary and hospital** *(lintutarha)*, with four aviaries (May–July Mon–Fri

Steamships on the lake.

Cotton grass grows abundantly in the lake region.

Jyväskylä.

10am–6pm, Sat–Sun 10am–4pm, Aug–Apr Mon–Thu 7am–4pm, Fri–Sun 7am–4pm; free). The town's main church, an octagonal wooden building from the early 19th century, has a separate bell tower designed by the prolific architect C.L. Engel.

PÄIJÄNNE'S EASTERN SHORE

From Heinola, Road 5 continues northeast to Mikkeli in western Saimaa. From here you could branch north onto Road 13 for Jyväskylä, but there is a slower and more attractive way. For this, leave Lahti north on Road 24 and after 25km (15 miles), soon after crossing the Vääksy canal at Asikkala, branch right onto minor Road 314. This carries you along the several miles of Pulkkilanharju (ridge), another relic from the last Ice Age, which vies with that of Punkaharju for narrowness and magnificence of lake and forest views.

Continue on a series of asphalted but lesser roads via Sysmä and Luhanka, twisting along or across the complex succession of headlands, bays, capes and interlinked islands that make up Päijänne's contorted eastern shore. At **Luhanka** ⑮, the renovated **Peltola Cotters Museum** (Mäkitupalaismuseo; tel: 040-718 6747; early June–mid-Aug daily 11am–5pm) throws light on the unenviable lot of the 19th-century 'cotters' – smallholders who effectively mortgaged their working lives to wealthy landowners in return for a scrap of land whose lease could be revoked at the owner's will.

To rejoin Road 9 (E63) at Korpilahti for the final leg to Jyväskylä you can now use an enormous bridge across Kärkistensalmi, one of Päijänne's many narrow straits. Road 24 provides a more direct main road link all the way from Lahti to Jyväskylä in 174km (107 miles). A particular beauty spot inside a national park, a little way off this route, is the long, slender island of **Kelvenne** ⑯, about 60km (37 miles) north of Lahti, with its lakes, lagoons and curious geological formations. You can reach it from Kullasvuori camping area at Padasjoki. Road 24 also bypasses Jämsä

and joins Road 9 to the south of the town, thereby avoiding the industrial district of Jämsänkoski.

JYVÄSKYLÄ

Jyväskylä ⑰ (pop. 140,188) has contributed much, as an educational centre, to the country's cultural development. At a time when the Finnish language was still regarded by the Swedish-speaking ruling classes as the 'peasants' language', the first Finnish-language secondary school opened here in 1858, and a teachers' training college followed a few years later. It now also has a lively university, whose campus is the work of Alvar Aalto. Indeed, it was in Jyväskylä that this renowned architect embarked on his career, and there are no fewer than 30 major buildings by him around the area, as well as the **Alvar Aalto museo** (Alvar Aallon katu 7; tel: 040-135 6210; www.alvaraalto.fi; Jan–June Tue–Sun 11am–6pm, July–Aug Tue–Sun 10am–6pm, Sept–Dec Tue–Sun 11am–6pm), which has exhibits on his architecture and furniture designs.

As one of the fastest-growing cities in Finland, Jyväskylä is predominantly modern, with a large student population that lends it a young and vibrant air. From the observation platform of the water tower on the ridge running through the town you can gaze across to the lakes. There are sports facilities on the same ridge and at Laajavuori, a winter and summer sports centre on the northwest outskirts of town. Jyväskylä caters for most sports, but is best known as the venue for the Neste Oil Rally Finland (held late July/early August), the fastest event in the World Rally Championship series: 400,000 spectators come here to watch the high-octane proceedings. In late June–early July, the Jyväskylä Arts Festival (www. jyvaskylankesa.fi) chooses a different theme each year, examining its every aspect in seminars, exhibitions, concerts and theatre performances.

For a glimpse into the region's past, go to the excellent **Keski-Suomen museo** (tel: 014-266 4346; Tue–Sun 11am–6pm), the region's

⊙ Tip

A daily bus route links Imatra and St Petersburg, calling at Joutseno, Lappeenranta and Vyborg on the way.

main history museum, next to the Alvar Aalto Museum. Also worth a visit is the **Craft Museum of Finland** (Suomen kasityon museo; tel: 014-266 4370; www.craftmuseum.fi; Tue–Sun 11am–6pm), with excellent displays on traditional handicrafts – it even provides craft materials so you can make your own souvenir.

BEYOND JYVÄSKYLÄ

If you have a little more time, head 32km (20 miles) west on Road 23 to **Petäjävesi**. Built of logs in 1765, the Petäjävesi Lutheran church (tel: 040-582 2461; mid-May–mid-Sept daily 11am–4pm, June–Aug daily 10am–6pm, rest of the year by appointment) here is listed by Unesco as a World Heritage site. It is a stunning example of an architectural tradition unique to eastern Scandinavia, combining Renaissance structure and Gothic vaulting.

Another attractive 18th-century wooden church is at **Keuruu** (June–mid-Aug daily 11am–4pm; charge), a further 28km (17 miles) away. Road 23 continues west to Virrat at the northern end of the Poet's Way route (see page 192).

North of Jyväskylä, Road 4 (E4/75) continues through yet more forested, lake-strewn landscapes harbouring a growing scattering of holiday and leisure centres. After 35km (21 miles) Road 13 forks left to Saarijärvi, focal point of a pleasant holiday area. Just before this, turn south on Road 6304, then shortly east to **Summassaari ⓲** (tel: 030-608 5100; www.summassaari. fi), for spa treatments, a bite to eat or any number of outdoor activities including a Stone Age hiking path, Frisbee-golf, paddling in a dugout canoe, fishing or cross-country skiing. A short distance beyond Saarijärvi in **Kolkanlahti ⓳** is the elegant 19th-century house, now a museum, **Säätyläiskotimuseo** (tel: 014-459 8208; mid-June–mid-Aug Wed–Sun noon–6pm), where Finland's national poet, J.L. Runeberg, worked as a tutor in the 1820s. Back on Road 4 (E4/75), the highway leads ever northwards towards the Arctic Circle.

Canoeing on the lakes.

CANOEING AND KAYAKING

Thousands of lakes, rivers and streams mean that canoeing and kayaking are the ideal way to see the Finnish countryside.

One of the main events in the Finnish sports calendar is the Finlandia Canoe Relay (SuomiMeloo; www. suomimeloo.fi) each June. This unique six-day event – the longest canoe/kayak relay in the world – usually heads through the Saimaa system, and is divided into approximately 25 stages, each stage varying from 10 to 50km (6 to 30 miles). With 187,888 lakes (at the last count) and innumerable rivers to choose from, it is surprising that canoeing only really caught on in Finland in the 1990s. There is now, however, a growing range of packages which allow you to canoe well-paddled routes of varying lengths.

A particularly popular series of waterways forms an overall 350km (217-mile) circuit, beginning and ending at Heinola. This needs 10 to 15 days but can also be fragmented into more manageable two- to five-day sections. Another, along 320km (200 miles) of the Ounasjoki River in Lapland from Enontekiö to Rovaniemi, features sections of true Arctic wilderness; the rapids are mainly Grade I, but it's possible to portage round the most daunting of these. Yet another follows a 285km (177-mile) lake-and-river route taken by the old tar boats from Kuhmo to Oulu.

PADDLING ROUND THE LAKE REGION

If you're attracted to the idea of pioneering across the lakes, the possibilities are legion. Any road map which covers the country on a scale of 1:200,000 will be sufficient for general planning, but absolutely essential for more detail are the special inland waters charts, for example the 1:40,000/1:50,000-scale Saimaa map.

It's not until you are actually in your canoe, however, that the logistical problems of navigation become clear. From a low-riding canoe, one island of rock and pinewood looks very like another. Across wide expanses of water there are few helpful landmarks, so be sure to pack two essentials: a compass and a pair of binoculars.

Other than getting lost, the greatest inconvenience you are likely to encounter is wind squalls. As these can blow up quickly and whip water up into turbulence, head for shelter at the first sign.

Camping may prove more difficult than you might expect in seemingly empty landscapes. Most of the lake shorelines are either rocky or fringed by reed beds. Finding enough space between trees can be a problem even for the smallest tent, and any clearings you come across may belong to a cottage or farm. The national right to pitch your tent anywhere (ihmisoikeus) has become a contentious issue these days due to abuse by some campers, so you should make sure you ask for permission to camp whenever possible (but, of course, this being the Finnish countryside, there is often no one around to ask). It is one of the joys of canoeing in Finland that you may travel for days without any sign of humanity other than a tugboat hauling its train of timber, or a fisherman.

The best way to explore the lakes.

Koli Hills in winter.

KARELIA AND KUUSAMO

The ancient rural communities of eastern Finland are considered the cultural heartland of the country: the region of myths and legends immortalised in the epic poem the *Kalevala*.

Main attractions

Joensuu
Ilomantsi
Lieksa
Nurmes
Kuhmo
Kajaani
Kuusamo

Eastern Finland, which stretches broadly to the country's eastern frontier, is an expansive region where the landscape shifts from the great Finnish Lakelands area to Lappi, or Lapland. Few people live in this wild territory, but the character of Karelia and its distinctive Orthodox churches have charm, tradition and colour.

Finland's most famous and perhaps most photographed scenery stretches below the lofty summit of the Koli Heights above Lake Pielinen; this area offers very good winter skiing, snowshoeing and sledging, as well as whitewater rafting, hiking and fishing in the summer months. The 900km (559-mile) Via Karelia route, running from the border crossing at Vaalimaa right up into Lapland, takes the traveller to the frontier sights, including battlegrounds from World War II.

JOENSUU

Joensuu ❶, at the mouth of the River Pielisjoki, is the 'capital' of North Karelia. It has a relaxed and welcoming air, for the majority of the inhabitants are Karelians, people who have a well-earned reputation for good humour and ready wit, traits particularly in evidence at the town's busy markets.

The **Pohjois-Karjalan museo** (Museum of North Karelia; tel: 050-520 2762; Mon–Fri 10am–5pm,

Sat–Sun 10am–3pm) has excellent exhibits from prehistory, history and the folk culture of this part of Karelia, and is particularly moving on the region's never-ending border struggles and the refugees that they created. The museum is housed in the Carelicum centre, opposite the market square at Koskikatu 5, which also has a Joensuu tourist information office (www.visitkarelia.fi; Mon–Fri 10am–4.30pm, Sat–Sun 10am–3pm), a café and other cultural venues. There is also the **Taidemuseo** (Art Museum;

Map on page 244

Main square of Joensuu.

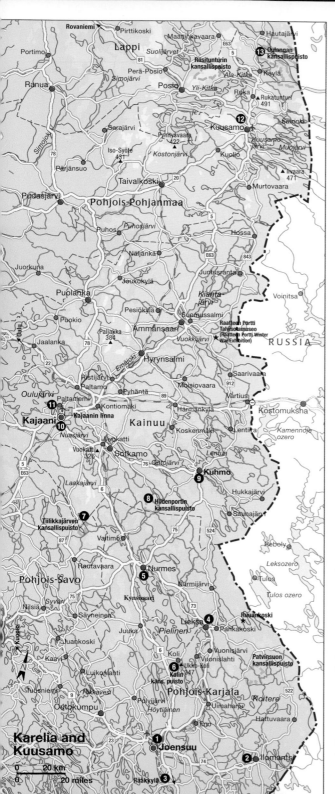

Kirkkokatu 23; tel: 013-337 5388; Tue–Sun 11am–4pm, Wed until 8pm), with an icon collection and Finnish paintings from the 19th and 20th centuries. The **Botania** (botanical gardens; Heinäpurontie 70; https://botania.fi; tel: 050-562 9482; Sun 10am–6pm, Mon–Thu 10am–8pm, Fri–Sat 10am–11pm) feature a range of plant species and the world's most northerly butterfly house. It's possible to try Karelian specialities here: modernised at the gourmet restaurant Kielo (Suvantokatu 12; tel: 013-227 874; Tue–Sat 4–10pm) or in more traditional form at the market, where you can pick up a *karjalanpiirakka* (Karelian pasty).

ILOMANTSI AND RÄÄKKYLÄ

Before turning north, take Road 6 south, then Road 74 east for the 70km (50-mile) drive to **Ilomantsi ➋**. This small town was the scene of heavy fighting in World War II: the outdoor museum **Parppeinvaara** (www.parppeinvaara.fi; daily June and Aug 11am–5pm, Jul 10am–6pm) has the usual historic wooden buildings containing exhibitions on rural life, but also the Border General's Cabin, packed with guns, troop maps and home-made explosives.

The village of Hattuvaara is the most easterly settlement in Finland. This quiet spot contains the **Warrior's House** (Taistelijan talo; tel: 040-017-3607; www.taistelijantalo.fi; daily June–Aug Mon–Fri 10am–6pm, Sat–Sun 10am–4pm), which commemorates Finland's war dead.

On a more peaceful note, this region has been a stronghold of the Orthodox Church since the 14th century: 17 percent of Ilomantsi's residents belong to the Orthodox church – the highest proportion in Finland. Easter is the most impressive festival, but the area is full of old rites, rituals and buildings: Ilomantsi contains the largest wooden Orthodox church in Finland, while Hattuvaara has the oldest.

For more light-hearted music and colour, it would be hard to beat the village of **Rääkkylä** ❸, about 50km (30 miles) south of Joensuu on a secondary road along the southern end of Lake Pyhäselkä. Two local sisters founded the renowned Finnish folk group Värttinä in 1983, which has achieved international acclaim. Koistinen Kantele is also based here: this award-winning company is manufacturer of the most Karelian of instruments, the *kantele*, a stringed contraption similar to a zither.

THE LIEKSA REGION

From Joensuu, take Route 6 north out of the town. Where the road divides, take the right fork eastward (Route 73), which leads along the eastern shore of Lake Pielinen to **Lieksa** ❹. The roads through these backwoods are tarred and well maintained but narrow and sometimes differ little from the minor roads and lanes that lead off into the forest. But usually driving is quiet and simple, with the main routes numbered and villages signposted. In Lieksa, the extensive **Pielinen Outdoor Museum** (Pielisen museo; tel: 040 104-4151; mid-May–mid-Sept daily 10am–6pm, mid-Sept–mid-May Tue–Fri 10am–3pm) is the main attraction, showcasing numerous buildings from different ages which document the settlement of the surrounding area – the oldest is from the 17th century. The outdoor open-air museum closes in winter, but the (less interesting) indoor exhibition remains open.

Lieksa may not be the most prepossessing of towns, but it is an important centre for visitors to this part of Finland's wilderness, which stretches as far as the Russian border. Several large supermarkets have all the food you'll need for camping, and local shops sell equipment. On the main street, the tourist office **Karelia Expert** (Pielisentie 19; tel: 0400-175 323; www.visitkarelia.fi) can arrange fishing guides, bear-watching excursions and trips to shoot the rapids at Ruunna. They can also put you in touch with walking guides: 'Never go hiking on your own' is the oft-repeated warning

Autumn in the Koli Hills lakeland.

KARELIANS

When Finns have gone to war, it has almost always concerned Karelia; this region is said to be the soul of Finland.

The Karelians were one of the earliest communities in Finland, evident in Bronze and Iron Age discoveries, though their true origins are lost in myth and legend. The *Kalevala,* that great epic saga of ancient life in the far north, is really about the Karelians. This long poem, which in the 19th century became the cornerstone of the struggle for national culture, tells how, with magic and sword, the northern heroes fought for survival against the powers of evil. It recounts weddings, funerals, rituals, bear hunts, journeys into the mysterious Otherworld, and finally the heroes' joy as they celebrate in song the salvation of the land of Kalevala from its enemies.

This is a vivid and romantic part of the country, one that has long been an inspiration for Finnish artists, writers and musicians. A Karelian theme

Sibelius was influenced by Karelian music.

runs through a great deal of the music of Jean Sibelius: his *Karelian Suite* reaches sublime heights of elegy and patriotism. In his earlier years, Sibelius was deeply inspired by Karelian folk music, and later on he returned to spend his honeymoon here.

The Karelians emerge into recorded history as a people living in the area of forest and lakes stretching from the present-day south-eastern Finnish-Russian border to the White Sea. Slash and burn was their way of converting the impenetrable woodland into productive fields, and they used the ash as a fertiliser. With these techniques came the production of grain and the need to dry it through steam heat, adapted first for grain-drying and then for relaxation. Thus, the sauna was born.

From the Middle Ages the Karelians began to be affected by Russian influences, although in no sense did they become 'Russified'. The most obvious aspect, the Orthodox religion, is a feature of the Karelian people, although it is accorded the title Greek Orthodox rather than Russian. There are 60,000 adherents and many churches in southeast Finland today.

The terrible Winter War of 1939–40 was fought to save Karelian land and has become the Finns' great *cause célèbre,* but it was only one war out of some 200 which were fought for Finnish Karelia. After the war, the Karelian Isthmus was lost, along with all of East Karelia, now settled by Russians. Many of these areas have since been all but abandoned by the Russian state, with many former Karelian villages dilapidated. Some 400,000 Karelians were resettled to many other parts of Finland, where they continue to live today: few have moved back.

It is a fact that Karelia today exists only as a fragment of its former self. The fractioned border has all but cut it out of the Finnish body politic and its people have dispersed. A line roughly parallel to the border from Lieksa down to the Isthmus now delineates modern Finnish Karelia. Yet even in this small region something distinctive remains. It may be the grandeur of the forest, it may be the distinctive taste of their cuisine, or the lively and talkative nature of the people (in contrast to the more taciturn nature of most other Finns). The Karelian dialect, as distinct from Finnish, however, has declined – although less so on the Russian side of the border.

of this region, and inexperienced walkers in particular should take guided tours, which can be arranged for individuals or groups. Capercaillie, elk, bear, reindeer, lynx, wolverine, and even wolves roam the dense pine forests around Lieksa. Trout, landlocked salmon (a relic of the Ice Age) and coarse fish such as bream all swim in the unpolluted waters of Lake Pielinen and the Pudaskoski River. Join a guided fishing expedition if you would like to try your hand at catching them. A package will include the services of a guide, transport, accommodation and licences. Otherwise, you can buy a fishing licence online through the Federation of Finnish Fisheries Association: www.ahven.net.

The **Ruunaankoski rapids** are a sight not to be missed if you're near Lieksa. For some 16km (10 miles) the Lieksanjoki River plunges through seven sets of foaming rapids and drops around 15 metres (50ft) on the way. Equipped with lifejacket and waterproofs, shooting the rapids is a hoot under the supervision of a proficient guide. The **Ruunaa hiking area** looks right onto the Russian border and is inhabited by wild forest reindeer. Within the area, Ruunaa Visitor Centre (tel: 020 564 5757; May–Sept daily 10am–6pm), near the Naarajoki bridge, can advise on hiking, whitewater rafting and canoeing, and sells maps and fishing permits.

At Vuonisjärvi, 29km (18 miles) to the south of Lieksa, **Paateri** (tel: 040-104 4055; mid-May–mid-Sep daily 10am–6pm) was the studio home of wood sculptor Eva Ryynänen (1915–2001). Every bench and table has a carved design, and tactile-looking sculptures pack the workshop; but her greatest work of art is the spectacular wooden wilderness church that stands below the swaying pine trees on this quiet peninsula.

AROUND LAKE PIELINEN

From Lieksa, Road 73 leads towards **Nurmes ❺**, taking about an hour, and keeping close to the shores of Lake Pielinen. First mentioned in documents in 1556, Nurmes only became a city as recently as 1974. Nicknamed 'the town of the birch', it sits on a ridge between two lakes at the northern end of the Pielinen lake system; it is a pleasant town, with wooden houses built in authentic early Karelian style.

There aren't many sights, but the area is good for activities such as cycling and boating in summer, and ice fishing, cross-country skiing and snowmobiling in winter. The biggest tourist attraction here is actually a 1970s reconstruction of a 19th-century Karelian home. The massive wooden **Bomba House** (tel: 010-783 0450; www.sokoshotels.fi), surrounded by a recently built 'Karelian village', is now the restaurant of the Break Sokos Hotel. It is well known for its Karelian buffet, which includes an assortment of local pies, warm smoked lamb, hearty meat casseroles, cold smoked whitefish, fried wild mushrooms and baked cheese with Arctic bramble jam – all designed to get the taste buds working overtime.

Decorated window at Bomba House.

⊘ Tip

One fascinating experience in Kuusamo is winter rally driving at Juha Kankkunen Race Tracks, where you get to experience the thrill of steering a world-class race car around a snow-powdered track.

At the other end of Lake Pielinen from Nurmes is one of Finland's most treasured pieces of terrain, **Koli National Park** (www.nationalparks.fi/en). The best way to arrive is by a leisurely ferry ride on the MF Pielinen (mid-June to early August) from Lieksa, taking in the wonderful lake scenery, dotted with islands and numerous other boats. The Koli Hills rise halfway down the western side of the lake, the highest, **Old Man Koli** ❻ (Ukko-Koli), reaching 347 metres (1,100ft). Scramble up to the top (there are steps), and spread out below you is a view that has inspired some of the greatest artists, including Albert Edelfelt and Eero Järnefelt, whose paintings immortalised Koli around the turn of the 20th century and did much to stimulate the national awakening of the time (see page 75). Sibelius, too, wove the Koli Hills into his symphonies and, looking down, it is not hard to understand why this countryside is always called Finland's 'national landscape'. The legend goes that Sibelius loved the area so much that he had a grand piano carried to the top of this hill to celebrate his marriage.

THE WILDERNESS WAY NORTH

Finland's wilderness way north has three of the country's glories – sauna, salmon and scenery, the last embodied in its national parks although certainly not confined to them. You will meet these three great assets at almost every turn in Finland, but never so frequently or in such abundance as in the region that starts north of Nurmes, roughly along the line of the Oulu waterway – lake and river – that almost bisects Finland, and stretches north to Rovaniemi (see page 257) and Lapland proper.

For many, however, the biggest attractions in this area are the traditional **saunas**. There is purportedly more than one sauna for every two people in Finland, and visitors will find them everywhere – in hotels, private homes, on board ships, at motels, holiday villages and forest camps. Finns are terribly proud of the sauna, the one word which the Finnish language has

The lynx is one of the wild animals that dwell in the Karelian forests.

offered to the rest of the world, and nothing better complements the end of a long northern day in the open air to refresh and revitalise body and soul (see page 166).

On the stove or in the stream there is only one really classic fish in this area and that is the Atlantic salmon. Though Finland has no sea border with the Atlantic, thanks to the Ice Age, this region retains an Atlantic legacy in the salmon that swim in the large natural landlocked lakes and in the smaller waters well stocked with the species.

NATIONAL PARKS

Northern Karelia is known for its national parks, where nature is left as untouched as possible but some amenities are provided for visitors; marked trails, campsites and cabins are set in the larger parks, with hotel accommodation just outside the parks proper. With so much unspoilt territory, it may hardly seem necessary for Finland to designate national parks, but it has 40, and some of the best of them are found along this wilderness way north.

From the east of the country, the natural route into the area is from Nurmes on Road 75 to Kuhmo, or via Road 6 north, either turning right onto Road 76 just before Sotkamo to reach Kuhmo or continuing left on Road 6 for Kajaani on Oulujärvi (lake) to the west. From the west coast, the natural route would be from Oulu (see page 220) along the waterway connecting the Oulu River, Lake, Kajaani and Kuhmo.

Heading north from Nurmes on Road 6, turn left onto Road 5850 towards Rautavaara, and after some 50km (32 miles) you come to the remote **Tiilik-kajärvi National Park** ❼ (Tiilikkajärven kansallispuisto), near Rautavaara. It was established to conserve the uninhabited area of Lake Tiilikka and the surrounding bogs.

Hiidenportti National Park ❽ (Hiidenportin kansallispuisto) is southeast of Sotkamo and also best reached from Road 6. Turn right onto Road 5824, and some 25km (16 miles) on you come to the park on the left. This is a rugged area, with the narrow Hiidenportti Gorge, a large rift valley

The Kuhmo region is famous for its herds of rare forest reindeer.

Brown bears in Kuhmo.

While trekking might not be the first thing that comes to mind when thinking about Finland, the country holds thousands of miles of trails, walkways and manicured paths perfect for hiking.

Camping by the Kitkajoki river near Kuusamo.

with rock sides dropping some 20 metres (70ft) to the floor of the gorge. Both the park and the neighbouring Peurajärvi hiking and fishing area have designated trails, marked with orange paint, and campsites. At Peurajärvi, a three-hour or one-day permit allows anglers to catch one/three salmon respectively. Although you could wriggle through a complicated series of minor roads on the Sotkamo route from here, unless you are feeling very adventurous, it is probably a lot easier to go back to Road 18.

Both in and outside the parks, the further north you go, the more likely you are to find reindeer. These semi-domesticated animals are the main source of income for many people living in these parts, and it is very important to take special care on roads – reindeer may be around at any time of the year.

THE FINNISH FRONTIER

Kuhmo is a frontier town surrounded by dense forests in the wilderness area of Kainuu. The largest municipal area in Finland, Kainuu covers 5,458 sq km (2,100 sq miles). Close to the Russian border and remote and empty though the area is, Kuhmo has established an international reputation through the annual Kuhmo Chamber Music Festival, which celebrated its 50th anniversary in 2019 (see page 88). The festival is held in the Kuhmo Arts Centre (Kuhmo-talo; Koulukatu 1; tel: 08-6155 5451), another of those architecturally astonishing wooden concert halls at which the Finns excel. Around 50km (30 miles) southeast in Saunajärvi is the Winter War Memorial marking Finland's desperate 100-day struggle in 1940 against overwhelming odds. Travel agents in Kuhmo arrange trips across the border to Russian Karelian villages, but visas are required and can take up to a week to arrange.

At one time this entire area was devoted to making tar, by a lengthy process of felling, splitting and then burning (primarily pine) trees to extract the sticky liquid that formed the basic ingredient. Once it was in barrels, peasants loaded their small boats for the slow journey down through lake and river to the port of Oulu where, in a rare symbiosis, shipbuilders bought it for their own craft and entrepreneurs shipped it abroad. In the 19th century Finland was the biggest exporter of tar in the world.

In Kuhmo, **Juminkeko** (Kontionkatu 25; tel: 08-6530 670; www.juminkeko.fi) is a cultural centre that stages exhibitions and events designed to promote the traditions of the Kalevala.

The wilderness around Kuhmo is one of the best places in Finland for **wildlife watching**. Two local companies, Taiga Spirit (tel: 040-7468 243; www.taigaspirit.com) and Wild Brown Bear (tel: 040-546 9008; open Apr–Oct; www.wbb.fi), can arrange for you to overnight in an animal hide, with the possibility of seeing white-tailed eagles, wolverine, wolves and brown bears.

North of Kuhmo, near the village of Lentiira, is Lentiiran Lomakylä, one of the most welcoming and comfortable holiday village chalet complexes by the lake. With a wood-fired sauna and cold beer included, this must surely be Finnish tourist hospitality at its very best (tel: 0440-297 214; www.lentiira.com).

Some 50km (32 miles) north of Lentiira, at the eastern end of Raate road (Raatteentie) is the **Raatteen Portti Winter War Exhibition** (Raatteen Portti Talvisotamuseo; Raatteentie 2; tel: 0400-892 192; www.raatteenportti.fi; late June–mid-Aug daily 10am–7pm, early May–late June and mid-Aug–mid Oct daily 10am–5pm, end Oct noon–4pm, mid-Feb–early-Mar noon–4pm) is a rich collection of artefacts, models, maps and photographs dating from the Battle of Raate Road, a battle fought – and won – by the Finns during the Winter War of 1939–40. The Winter War Monument is also here. At the time of writing the museum is undergoing renovation and being expanded.

KAJAANI AND PALTANIEMI

A long straight road through some of Finland's darkest forests leads west out of Kuhmo to Sotkamo and then onwards to **Kajaani** ⑩, the area's principal town, on the eastern edge of Oulujärvi (lake) and once the collecting point for barrels of tar ready for their journey to the coast.

Kajaani was founded in 1651 by the Swedish governor general Count Per Brahe in the shelter of an existing fortress designed as a bastion against Russia. In 1716, the fortress fell and the whole town was razed during the disastrous war between Sweden and Russia. The town still has the ruins of the 1604 castle. The Town Hall is yet another structure designed by the well-travelled German architect C.L. Engel, who was responsible for so much of early Helsinki's architecture (see page 149).

The old tar boat canal and the lock keeper's house by the Kajaani River are still visible. Famous residents have included Elias Lönnrot, who at one time lived in Kajaani, and the town is also known as the home of Finland's longest-serving president (nearly 26 years), Urho Kekkonen.

The Tsar's Stable in nearby **Paltaniemi** ⑪ (tel: 08 6155 2555; www.kajaani.fi/en/services/paltaniemi) is a relic of a visit by Tsar Alexander I. Also in Paltaniemi is the birthplace of the poet Eino Leino, and the city has a Cultural and Congress Centre. Heading some 20km (12 miles) from the centre, you reach Ruuhijarvi Wilderness Village, which offers peaceful fishing grounds and old hunting lodges which are open all year.

The road from Kajaani to the coast at Oulu hugs the shores of Lake Oulu, plunging first into thickly wooded hill country. Before entering Oulu (see page 220), the route passes through Muhos, which has the second-oldest church in Finland, dating from 1634. Oulu continues the tradition of

see page 220

see page 149

Dense birch forest.

tar-making, and the lakeland town still lights tar pits on Midsummer's Eve.

Distances are long in this scantily populated area. Road 20 travels 360km (225 miles) across the whole breadth of the country, from Oulu and **Kuusamo**, with little in between.

FURTHER NORTH

Kuusamo ⓬, a regional hub close to the Russian border, lies in the midst of marvellous wilderness country. Tundra stretches as far as the eye can see in any direction, and areas of forest are filled with raging rivers where water foams through gorges and canyons, some bare, others a dense dark green. The main sound in these parts is a mixture of rushing water and wind high up in the pines. There are dozens of rapids, some suitable for canoeing, others for fishing. The Oulankajoki and Iijoki (rivers) are excellent for family canoeing trips, but the Kitkajoki calls for experienced canoeists only.

There are literally thousands of excellent fishing spots in both rivers and lakes. The 'Russian' brown trout rise in the rivers from Lake Paanajärvi in greater numbers each year thanks to efficient tending of the fishing grounds. This is also berry country, with blueberries, raspberries, lingonberries and cloudberries filling the landscape of the Arctic tundra with colour. The only snag is the number of mosquitoes: they multiply rapidly in the northern summer, so take plenty of protection.

In both summer and winter, this vast unspoilt area is given over to recreation. In the middle, Karhuntassu Tourist Centre (tel: 040-860 8365; www.ruka.fi) has been specially built to provide information on every kind of activity, plus accommodation and most other aspects of the region. In winter, the area is excellent for skiing, and the skidoo or snowmobile comes into its own. Snowmobiling is both an exhilarating and a practical way to get around this snowbound landscape, though many consider this modern convenience outweighed by its noise and fumes.

There are two national parks near here. The largest, **Oulanka** ⓭ (Oulangan kansallispuisto), to the north, stretches over a largely untouched region of 270 sq km (105 sq miles), bordering the Oulanka River. It is a landscape of ravines and rushing torrents, sandbanks and flowering meadows. Karhunkierros (The Bear's Trail), the most famous walking route in Finland, stretches some 80km (50 miles) through the pine forests and quiet river banks of Oulanka canyon, over the county border into Lapland. A few kilometres will give the flavour of the trail, but to cover the whole route, staying at campsites or forest cabins en route, takes several days. In winter the area is given over to winter sports, with some 28 ski pistes.

Almost imperceptibly on the way north, the landscape and culture have changed from the traditions of Karelia to the traditional lifestyles of the Sami people. From here on, it is all clear: the land is Lappi.

Photographers near Kuusamo.

ELK AND WOLF HUNTING

The large numbers of elk and wolf – the 'big game' of the Finnish forests and tundra – continue to attract skilled hunters.

Lurking in the northern forests and tundra of Finland are two of the largest European mammals, the elk and the wolf. The fact that both survive in large numbers has meant a great deal of sport for local hunters, in season.

The great bull elk of Finland, standing 1.8 metres (6ft) high at the shoulder, gazes through the northern forest. Crowned by massive horns, this impressive animal (which is the same species, Alces alces, as the North American moose) is not the sluggish, lumbering giant it appears to be. Silent as night, wary, elusive, fast and with highly developed senses, this titan of the tundra and one-time co-habitant with the mammoth tests the limits of hunting skills to the utmost.

The justification for shooting elk is the paramount need to protect both food and the young timber that is so important to Finland's economy. The elk breeds so well in modern Finland that around 37,000 elk-hunting licences are granted each year, each one permitting the killing of one adult elk and two calves. Hunters, however, have no place in pest control. It is the thrill of the chase that brings the elk hunter with his .300 calibre rifle and his pack of dogs to the forest on the last Saturday in September – the start of the short elk-hunting season.

The challenging conditions of the sub-Arctic tundra make the pursuit of the elk arduous and competitive. With dense trees and thick brush, trained dogs are needed to aid the hunter in his quest. A dog can hold an elk at bay simply because it is disinclined to move.

If the quarry moves, the dogs will hunt it by following its scent. The signal for the hunter is the renewed barking of the dog, because this means the elk is standing still and the approach can begin. Now comes the most critical time of the hunt, for if an elk is tolerant of a dog, it is most decidedly intolerant of man. The ground is covered in material which, to quote an old advertising slogan, 'snaps, crackles and pops'. The hunter must proceed with light footsteps, and may have to crawl on his belly for the final approach. It is sudden movement that attracts attention, and a day's effort may be ruined by one false move.

Wolf-hunting is a much-debated topic in Finland. It is estimated that only 140 to 165 wolves exist in Finland; but they prey on domestic reindeer, the livelihood of the Sami people, and so hunting licences are granted each year to safeguard the reindeer stock. In 2013, the Finnish Nature League criticised the government's culling policy and called for a hunting ban on wolves, which are classed as Vulnerable on the IUCN Red List of Threatened Species. In 2016, the government agreed to the culling of all, but 68 wolves. This debate rages on as the positions of each side become evermore polarised.

Hunting wolves is a difficult affair, but the Finns use an ingenious method of encirclement. From large spools strapped to their backs, the men lay a line of string with red flashes through the woods. It can take up to two days to set the lines but instinct tells a wolf not to cross them. The helpers then drive the wolves to where the hunters are waiting. The guns now have some advantage, though the cunning and speed of wolves often saves them from the bullet – only a small number of wolves are successfully shot each year.

You can venture out on elk-hunting tours with guides in several areas of Finland, with three- or four-day trips being the most popular. Hunting usually means living in a hut or cabin. After many hours in the open, nothing is more welcome than the ritual of the sauna to replenish body and soul.

Wolves are common in northern Finland.

The Sampo icebreaker at Kemi.

LAPLAND

Usually associated with Christmas and bleak Arctic landscapes, Lapland is also a thriving region of quaint farming and fishing communities.

Deep in the Finnish Arctic, Lapland is one of the most magical parts of the world, filled with juxtaposition and wonder – gorgeous coniferous forests fronting barren tundra wastelands, fast-flowing rivers and rapids alongside tranquil campsites, man-made glass-roof igloo hotels for viewing the outstanding Northern Lights, and Sami nomads proudly melding their traditional lives with mobile phones and snowmobiles. It is without a doubt the one place in Finland that most captures the imagination and inspires the senses.

Two main roads wend their way northwards through the province of Lapland (Lappi). Road 4, sometimes called the Arctic Road, links Kemi with Rovaniemi before continuing through ever more sparsely inhabited landscapes to empty into Norway at Utsjoki. The other is Road 21 (E8), which follows the Tornio Valley upstream from Tornio on the coast, continuing beside various tributaries that form the border with Sweden, eventually to cross into Norway near Kilpisjärvi. This is the river route of the Arctic Canoe Race, and the road that accompanies it is also sometimes known as the 'Way of the Four Winds', after the four points of the Sami traditional male headgear. Bridges and ferries provide links with Sweden.

The Northern Lights.

ARCTIC LANDSCAPE

These two routes extend across Finnish Lapland for 540km (330 miles) and 457km (284 miles) respectively. Both cover a great deal of Arctic countryside, but from neither will you glean anything but the faintest hint of what Lapland is all about. For that, you must depart from the main routes – preferably from the minor ones too – and set out on foot or in a canoe or, in winter, on a pair of skis. Yet you don't need to venture very far, for there are silent spaces within a few hundred

Main attractions

Rovaniemi
Sodankylä
Tankavaara
Ivalo
Inari
Utsjoki
Kemi
Tornio
Enontekiö
Kilpisjärvi

Map on page 256

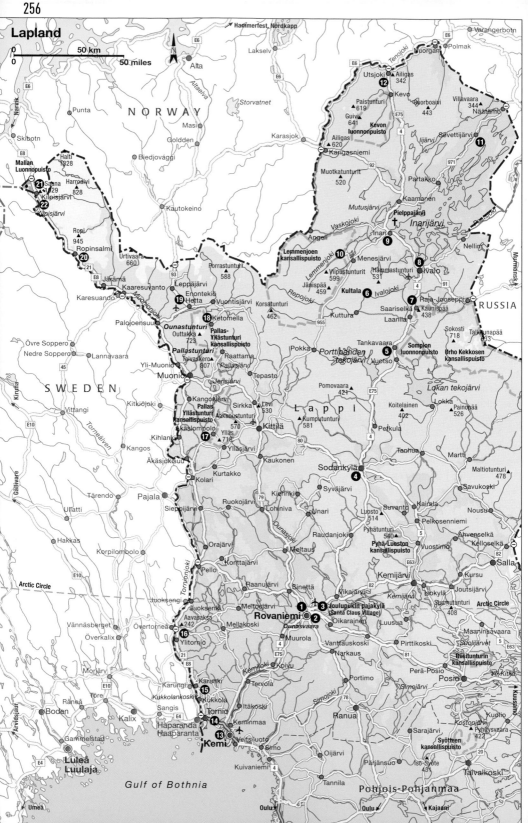

Lapland

0 ——— 50 km

0 ——— 50 miles

N

metres of the most modern hotel that feel caught in another epoch entirely. The vital need for proper clothing and equipment, however, cannot be over-stressed: climatic changes occur with ferocious suddenness and, for all its magnificence, the Arctic wilderness can be a ruthless place where Mother Nature reigns supreme.

As you progress northwards the trees become more spindly, the forests more sparse, the settlements fewer, the hills more numerous – until you reach the sweeping undulations of the bare-topped fells of northern and northwestern Lapland. Up above the ever-descending tree line, vegetation begins to creep and crawl – dwarf juniper and willow and miniature birch cling to the fellsides among the mosses and the lichens, the minuscule campions and tiny saxifrages. In summer it is vital to bring along plenty of mosquito repellent.

In 1944 the German army followed a scorched-earth policy as it retreated northward into Norway. As a result, any old buildings that survive are largely away from the main roads. But despite the monumental changes wrought on the province by the second half of the 20th century (see page 103), at least some elements of an age-old way of life endure.

ROVANIEMI

From the coast at Kemi, Road 4 follows the Kemijoki Valley, where a rash of timber-based industries has spawned a succession of communities. You reach **Rovaniemi ❶** within 115km (70 miles). This, the administrative capital of Lapland, all but nudges the Arctic Circle and is the launching point for most trips into the province. The town, well placed at the confluence of the Ounasjoki and Kemijoki rivers, has been completely rebuilt since World War II, nearly quadrupling its population (now about 63,000) in the process. In early summer, timber is still floated down the Ounasjoki from the forests

of central Lapland for processing into paper and other commercial products.

The reconstruction plan for Rovaniemi was devised by Alvar Aalto , with a street plan shaped like a rein-deer's head and antlers. Aalto also designed the fine Lappia Hall complex on Hallituskatu, containing a theatre and congress facilities and, next to it, the Library. Not far from Lappia Hall, the main Lutheran church features a modern altar fresco, *The Source of Life*, by Lennart Segerstråle.

The beautiful **Arctic Centre** (Arkti-kum), half-buried underground and thus offering a sensation of midnight sun through the glass ceiling, has exhibits illustrating Arctic history and culture (tel: 016-322 3260; www.arktikum.fi; June–Aug daily 9am–6pm, Dec, except Christmas Eve, daily 10am–6pm, rest of year Tue–Sun 10am–6pm). Also in the Arktikum building, the **Lapland Provincial Museum** gives visitors a good introduction to Lapland's flora and fauna, Sami traditions and Rovaniemi's history. You can also get a feel for life in a bygone age from

⊙ Tip
A magical experience for the tots is **Joulukka** (tel: 0600-301 203; www.joulukka.com). Elves take you to their cabin in the snowy woods for storytelling, biscuit-baking and an audience with 'the proper Father Christmas'.

The Arktikum provides a fascinating insight into the Arctic.

the 19th-century farm buildings at the **Rovaniemi Local History Museum** (Pöykkölä 4; tel: 050-325 2017; www.totto.fiö; June–Aug Tue–Sun 11am–5pm), 3km (2 miles) south on Road 78.

A joint ticket is available that allows admission to Arktikum and the nearby **Pilke Science Centre** (Tiedekeskus Pilkkeeseen; tel: 020 639 7820; www.sciencecentre-pilke.fi; Tue–Fri 9am–6pm, Sat–Sun 10am–4pm), an interactive exhibition about tree-felling and the Finnish forest that is most rewarding with kids in tow.

Korundi House of Culture (Lapinkävijäntie 4; www.korundi.fi; tel: 016-322 2822; Tue–Sun 11am–6pm, Thu until 8pm) was once the town's bus depot, and one of only a handful of buildings that escaped the all-consuming flames in 1944. There is a minimalist concert hall for the Chamber Orchestra of Lapland; and the town's modern Finnish art museum is also based here. The city is also home to a number of interesting events: the Arctic Lapland Rally in late January, the Reindeer Race in late March and the Snowmobile Races in early April. Rising up from the confluence of the Ounasjoki and Kemijoki to the southeast of town are the wooded slopes of **Ounasvaara ❷**, now a well-developed skiing area and site of annual international winter games. It is also a favourite gathering place on Midsummer Night.

LAND OF SANTA CLAUS

Around 8km (5 miles) from Rovaniemi on Road 4, soon after the turn-off for the airport, the **Santa Claus Workshop Village ❸** (Joulupukin Pajakylä; www.santaclausvillage.info; daily, hours vary) straddles the Arctic Circle (Napapiiri). It's a heavily commercial spot, but the wide eyes of its small (and not-so-small) visitors make it hard to humbug. Santa Claus's post office handles more than half a million letters a year from children from almost 200 countries, and there is a collection of souvenir shops, a puppet theatre, art exhibitions, a few reindeer and, of course, Santa Claus (see page 123).

A second Santa hangs out at **Santa Park** (tel: 0600-301 203; www.santapark.

The colours of summer in Lapland.

com; mid-Nov–end Nov daily 10am–5pm, Dec–early Jan until 6pm), a man-made cave inside the Syväsenvaara Hill some 2km (1 mile) south of the Arctic Circle, with ice sculptures and a mini-train ride. A number of fell areas east of Road 4 in southern Lapland have been developed for winter and summer tourism. One of the best is centred on Pyhätunturi, about 135km (84 miles) northeast of Rovaniemi. Another, just north of it, is Luostotunturi, south of Sodankylä. There are popular hiking and skiing routes between these two centres.

By this point you will have noticed the landscapes – predominantly forested – becoming progressively emptier. However, there are reindeer aplenty and the occasional elk, so do drive slowly; keep your eyes open and your camera handy – legend has it that white reindeer bring good luck.

Sodankylä ❹, on Road 4 some 130km (80 miles) from Rovaniemi, is the first substantial settlement along this route, a long-established community reputed to be the coldest in Finland. It is the home of the five-day Midnight Sun Film Festival

(www.msfilmfestival.fi) held each June. Next to its 19th-century stone church, its wooden predecessor is Lapland's oldest church, dating from 1689. Road 5 comes into Sodankylä from the southeast and minor byways wander off east and west to link tiny scattered communities.

GOLD COUNTRY

Northwards, there's little to detain you for the next 100km (60 miles) or so until, a few miles beyond Vuotso, you reach **Tankavaara ❺**. Gold panning has been practised in various parts of Lapland for well over a century, and at Tankavaara there is an entertaining **Gold Village** (Kultakylä; tel: 016-626 158; www.tankavaara.fi). Its Gold Prospectors' Museum (Kultamuseo; www.kultamuseo.fi; June–Sept daily 9am–6pm, Oct–May Mon–Fri 10am–4pm) not only chronicles man's historical endeavours to discover gold, but for a modest fee provides tuition and allows you to pan for gold yourself for an hour, a day, or several days, in an authentic wilderness setting. The village also offers cabin and camping

You can have a go at gold panning in Gold Village, Lapland.

Santa Claus is Lapland's most famous export.

⊙ **Fact**

Mosquitoes, midges, blackflies, horseflies, and other biting insects are the curse of any visit to Finland's northern regions for around eight weeks, starting in mid-June. Four species (Culiseta, Aedis communis, A. punctor and A. pionips) cause the most irritation. It is only the females that bite. Most people are surprised to learn that malaria only disappeared from Finland in the 1950s.

Husky safari.

accommodation. At nearby **Kultala** ⑥ (*kulta* is the Finnish word for gold), in trackless wilderness to the northwest, on the banks of the Ivalojoki you can also observe a gold-washing station dating from 1870.

About 40km (25 miles) further north there is a great deal more self-catering accommodation, together with modern hotels, spas and sports facilities, centred on Laanila and **Saariselkä** ⑦. The latter is an immensely popular winter sports centre, with skiing, snowshoeing, husky and reindeer rides and ice fishing; but there are plenty of summer activities too. Saariselkä tourist office (Kelotie 1; tel: 020-639 7200; www.saariselka.fi; Mon–Fri 9am–5pm, also at peak times Sat 10am–4pm) has more information. To the east of Saariselkä are the forests and slopes of a huge area of primeval fell extending to the Russian border, an excellent area for skiing with plenty of wilderness huts. Much of this region is designated as a national park named after Urho Kekkonen, Finland's longest-serving president.

IVALO AND INARI

In another 23km (14 miles), you pass the turn-off for Ivalo airport, Finland's northernmost. **Ivalo** ⑧ itself straggles along the east bank of the Ivalojoki. It's the largest community in northern Lapland, with all the usual facilities, though Sami culture is much less in evidence here than in Inari. There is, however, an attractive little wooden Orthodox church tucked away in the woods, serving the Skolt Sami, a branch of the Sami people who formerly lived in territory ceded to the Soviet Union in 1944. They have different costumes, language and traditions to Finnish Sami, and some now breed sheep in addition to (or occasionally instead of) reindeer. A number of Skolt Sami families live in Nellim, about 45km (29 miles) northeast of Ivalo near the Russian border.

Ivalo's Lutheran church stands near the bridge which carries Road 4 over the Ivalojoki; then it's a further 39km (27 miles) to **Inari** ⑨ – much of it a delightful route along the contorted shores of Lake Inari. Inari village makes an excellent base for wilderness

⊙ SLEDGING

The easiest way to traverse Lapland's vast and largely flat (or gently undulating) landscape has always been on skis or sledges; the latter less exhausting for longer distances. There are many different types of sledging, but the most popular and readily associated with northern Finland is the dog sledge. Four or six husky dogs, hardy creatures naturally acclimatised to snow and ice, are harnessed to the front of a sledge, with passengers standing on the back runners. Unlike horses, however, the huskies are not readily controllable, so keeping the sledge stationary – or bringing it to a halt – is achieved by means of a hook wedged deep in the snow. Once the hook is withdrawn, the dogs immediately lurch forward.

Reindeer sledging, as epitomised by images of Santa and his sleigh each Christmas, is another method of getting around, with the advantage that these animals can cover longer distances (and are better at coping with deep snow cover), although they are slower than the dogs. Many centres in Lapland now offer sledging excursions for tourists – contact tourist information offices in main towns for more details. It is essential that the right equipment is worn: thermals, waterproofs, hats, balaclavas, and goggles combat the dampness and icy bitterness of the snow, and a pair of good gloves is absolutely vital.

exploration; you can lodge at the lovely boutique rooms in Villa Lanca (tel: 040-748 0984; www.villalanca.com).

Though smaller and rather more scattered than Ivalo, Inari is nevertheless the administrative centre for a vast area, and a traditional meeting place for colourfully costumed Sami people during weddings and other festivities, especially the Church festivals of Lady Day and Easter. Other interesting shops in town include a silversmith's workshop and knife-maker Petteri Laiti's studio.

The focus of many Sami festivities is the simple modern church by the lake's shoreline. **Lake Inari** is Finland's third-largest, covering 1,300 sq km (808 sq miles) and is dotted with about 3,000 islands, some of them considered sacred according to Sami tradition. It is a wild, lonely, beautiful lake, the theme of numerous haunting songs and many legends. Boat trips and sightseeing flights are available during the summer to holy Ukko Island (particularly revered by the local Sami).

Inari's excellent **SIIDA** (tel: 0400-898 212; www.siida.fi; June–Sept daily 9am–7pm, Oct–May Tue–Sun 10am–5pm) chronicles how the life of the Sami has changed (and how it hasn't) over the years. There is also an open-air museum, as well as exhibits on early Skolt Sami culture and modern Sami life. The SIIDA building also houses Metsähallitus's Northern Lapland nature centre (Ylä-Lapin luontokeskus; tel: 0206-39 7740), which sells fishing permits and assists in hiking plans for those wishing to explore the wilderness. From the museum a marked trail covering a return journey of some 15km (9 miles) leads to a remote 18th-century wooden church at Pielppajärvi, one of Lapland's oldest surviving buildings. It's a beautiful spot that is also accessible by boat.

For further exploration, check what's on at the **Sámi Cultural Centre Sajos** (www.samediggi.fi), down by the river: this endeavour has frequent events, including concerts of indigenous music

and foodie evenings. If you are in the market for traditional handicrafts, pay a visit to **Sami Duodji** (Mon–Fri 10am–5pm), located within the centre.

TOWARDS NORWAY

The minor Road 955 from Inari leads 40km (25 miles) southwest to **Menesjärvi**, a Sami settlement from which you can continue by road then by river boat or on foot up the wild and beautiful **Lemmenjoki Valley**  ('warm river') to a remote gold prospectors' camp. It is best to see this isolated and extensive national park area of canyon and forest with a hired guide. From Menesjärvi, Road 955 continues across Lapland to join Road 79 north of Kittilä.

Around Inari and north of it, the road passes a number of attractive holiday centres, mostly of the self-catering variety. After 26km (16 miles) you come to Kaamanen, from which a minor road branches northeast 100km (60 miles) to **Sevettijärvi** , the modern main settlement for the Skolt Sami. An interesting time to visit is during the Easter Orthodox festival. While there, visit the Sami

Hiking in Lapland.

Women in traditional Sami costume.

⏱ Fact

The world's northernmost zoo, Ranua Wildlife Park (tel: 040-517 7436; www. ranuazoo.com), is at **Ranua**. Its 50 species include polar bears (the only ones in Finland), brown bears, lynx, wolves and the wolverine – one of the most endangered animals in the Nordic countries.

Fun in the snow.

graveyard, with its unusual turf-covered graves.

Just a couple of kilometres north of Kaamanen you have a choice of routes to the Norwegian border: to go north on Route 4 to the town of Utsjoki, 94km (58 miles) away, or bear northwest along Road 92 to the border 66km (41 miles) away at Karigasniemi.

Whichever direction you head, the landscapes get hillier, wilder and even emptier as you progress. You will also pass the coniferous tree line, beyond which only the hardier dwarf birch survive on the lower fell slopes, their gnarled and weathered forms looking curiously biblical in this barren Arctic countryside.

The route to Utsjoki is more beautiful, passing a series of lakes close to the eastern fringes of the Kevo Nature Park, where Turku University runs a sub-Arctic research station. **Utsjoki** ⓬ itself is an important Sami community – good for fishing and hiking – close to Finland's northernmost point. Its church (1860) is one of the few pre-World War II churches still standing in Lapland. The village and road follow the Utsjoki downstream to join with the Tenojoki, a famed salmon river.

Both Utsjoki and Karigasniemi are dominated by 'holy' fells known as *Ailigas*, the one dominating Karigasniemi reaching over 620 metres (2,000ft). From these border points you can join the Norwegian road system for a variety of routes, eventually returning into western Lapland at Kilpisjärvi or Enontekiö.

WESTERN LAPLAND

Your route through western Lapland is likely to begin at Kemi on the Gulf of Bothnia about 80km (50 miles) south of the Arctic Circle. The earlier stretches of the Way of the Four Winds or Road 21 (E8) follow the Tornionjoki River and the Swedish border, and present a very different face of Lapland from the Arctic Road. The countryside here is much more populated than you'd imagine, and served by Finland's northernmost railway branch as far as Kolari.

Kemi ⓭ called the seaport of Lapland or, rather optimistically, the 'Pearl of the Gulf of Bothnia'. Largely destroyed in

World War II, the town is now a port and industrial centre. The **Kemin Jalokivigalleria** (tel: 016-258 878; www.experience365.fi/gemstone-gallery; Mon–Fri 10am–4pm) has a collection of 3,000 gemstones and copies of some of Europe's most famous crown jewels, including the crown of the king of Finland – who never in fact reigned. If you are this far north in winter, you can take an icebreaker excursion (see page 263), or visit **Lumilinna** (tel: 016-258 878; www.experience365.fi/snowcastle), a remarkable Snow Castle built afresh from new blocks of snow each year, which also contains a chapel, a restaurant with tables made of ice, and even a few chilly hotel rooms.

TORNIO AND BEYOND

Kemi lies at the mouth of the Kemijoki River and just on the border a little way north is **Tornio** ⑭ near the mouth of the Tornionjoki. As Tornio (pop. 22,000) ends, the Swedish town of Haparanda begins, and, since its founding in 1621, this border position has made Tornio the scene of much bitter fighting, the last time during World War II.

Fortunately, the town's three major churches have survived – and **Tornio Church**, with its separate bell tower, is one of the most beautiful in Finland. Completed in 1686, it is dedicated to the Swedish Queen Eleonora. Alatornio Church, on the outskirts, is a vast edifice, the largest in northern Finland, and able to hold a congregation of 1,400. It is a splendid example of Jaakko Rijf's neo-classical style. Tsar Alexander I ordered the building of an Orthodox church in 1825. After Finnish independence in 1917, the building lay empty until 1987, when it was restored, reconsecrated and reopened to serve the 150 Orthodox Christians who live locally.

The fine **Aine Art Museum** (Aineen taidemuseo; Torikatu 4; tel: 050-594 6868; www.tornio.fi/aine; Tue–Thu 11am–6pm, Fri–Sun 11am–3pm) houses the Aine Kuvataide Foundation art collection and a historical museum of western Lapland. On a clear day, the best place to get a view of the town is from the observation platform on top of the water tower.

Tornio Golf Club on the Finnish-Swedish border is perhaps the oddest

◉ Tip

One of the most fascinating experiences in Finland is a trip out on an 1961 icebreaker, *Sampo* (tel: 016-258 878; www.experience365.fi/icebreaker sampo; sales@visitkemi.fi; late Dec–early Apr), which displays its remarkable power to force its way through ice up to 2 metres (6ft) thick. This invigorating trip may be pricey, but it is well worth the memory of casting yourself off an icebreaker into freezing cold Arctic waters wearing a bright red survival suit. The boat departs from Ajos port, 11km (7 miles) south of Kemi.

The Sampo icebreaker tour.

in Europe, geographically speaking. During a round of 18 holes, you play 11 in Sweden and seven in Finland – and there's a one-hour time difference between the two. It opens in June when conditions allow and the season lasts until October, or when the snow arrives. It is a rare delight to play a night round in summer, thanks to the midnight sun. After the sixth hole in Finland – just after midnight – you will cross the border and continue in Sweden – yesterday.

In its southern stages, Road 21 passes through a string of small communities mainly based, in these marginally milder and more fertile conditions, on agriculture and dairy farming. Around 15km (9 miles) north of Tornio off Road E78, you will come to **Kukkolankoski** , the longest (3,500 metres/yds) free-flowing rapids in Finland. At the highest point the fall is 18.8 metres (45ft). The rapids have been famous for fish since the Middle Ages. Today, fishermen balance precariously on a crude boardwalk over the fast-flowing river, and still use the old technique of a long-handled

Lapland's fell country.

net. At the nearby Café Myllypirtti (daily June–Sept 10am–6pm), freshly grilled and skewered white fish is the main item on the menu.

About 70km (43 miles) north of Tornio, beyond Ylitornio, is the 242-metre (794ft) **Aavasaksa Hill** , the most southerly point from which the midnight sun can be seen, attracting considerable throngs for Midsummer Eve festivities. A few miles nearer Juoksenki, you cross the Arctic Circle. The scenery now gets wilder as you pass between Pello and Kolari. A little south of the latter Tornionjoki is replaced by a tributary, the Muonionjoki, at the Finnish–Swedish border.

FELL COUNTRY

About 10km (7 miles) north of Kolari, a worthwhile detour by minor Road 940 to the right leads to **Akäslompolo** . The village, set along the shores of a small lake amid magnificent forested hills and bare-topped fells, is well-equipped for winter tourists coming to **Ylläs**, (www.yllas.fi), Finland's biggest ski resort with 63 downhill runs and ample

opportunities for cross-country skiing, snowshoeing, dog-sledging and more.

A marked trail follows the chain of fells stretching northwards from here, eventually leading, in about 150km (90 miles), to the beginning of the Pallas-Yllästunturi National Park. The park contains a number of glorious trails, and there is overnight shelter available in untended wilderness huts – these are even marked on the 1:200,000 road maps.

From Akäslompolo you can continue north along minor roads and in 31km (19 miles) turn left onto Road 79. This is the main road from Rovaniemi, providing an alternative approach to western Lapland. After a further 10km (7 miles), Road 957 to the right is highly recommended as the best approach to Enontekiö. A further branch left off this route leads from Road 79 to the lonely hotel complex of Pallastunturi, magnificently cradled in the lap of five of the 14 fells which make up the Pallastunturi group (the highest being Taivaskero at 807 metres/2,647ft).

From here the choice of fell walks includes the long-distance 60km (37-mile) trail north from Yllästunturi across the fells to Enontekiö. Road 957 brings you to the upper Ounasjoki Valley via the small community of Raattama to **Ketomella 18**, where there's a car ferry across the river, offering a view of a number of venerable old farm buildings. Along the entire route you get lovely views of first the Pallas, then the Ounas fells. At the junction at Peltovuoma you turn west for Enontekiö and, eventually, Palojoensuu, back on Road 21.

ENONTEKIÖ

Enontekiö 19, also known as Hetta, is the attractively situated administrative centre of this extensive, sparsely populated area. The village sprawls along the northern shore of Ounasjärvi (lake), looking across to the great rounded shoulders of the Ounastunturi fells – the highest of which is Outtakka at 723 metres (2,372ft). Once completely isolated, it's now accessible by air and road from all directions, with a road link north into Norway.

Most of Enontekiö's buildings are modern, including the pretty wooden

⊙ **Tip**

For a guided hike around Kilpisjärvi, contact Harriniva, Käsivarrentie 14703 (tel: 0400-155 100; www.harriniva.fi) or Kilpissafarit, Tsahkalluoktantie 14 (tel: 040-5455 123; https://kilpissafarit.fi).

church whose altar mosaic depicts Sami people and reindeer. There's a good range of accommodation available, from campsites to top-class hotels, all set up for the avid fishermen, hikers and canoeists for whom this makes an excellent holiday centre. It is also a main centre for the Sami of western Lapland, most of whom live in lone farmsteads or tiny communities in and around the area. Here, too, the Sami festival of Marianpäivä (www.marianpaivat.fi) is held in mid to late March – these Mary's Day celebrations are the largest of their kind in the Nordic countries, with music, dancing, reindeer races and lassoing competitions.

From Palojoensuu, Road 21 continues northwest along the Swedish border following the Muonionjoki and Könkämäeno valleys. The scenery becomes ever wilder and more barren, especially once you cross the tree line.

At **Järämä**, 10km (6 miles) further from the tiny settlement of Markkina, German soldiers built fortifications during the Lapland War of 1944. Many of these bunkers have been restored and are now open to the public.

THE FAR NORTHWEST

A little south and north of **Ropinsalmi** ⑳ there are good views respectively of Pättikkäkoski and Saukkokoski, two of the more testing rapids on the Muonionjoki River. The mountains reach ever greater heights; Finland's highest, Halti, soars up to 1,365 metres (4,478ft) on the Norwegian border (the highest point is actually on the Norwegian side).

More accessible and distinctive is **Saana** ㉑, 1,029 metres (3,376ft) above the village and the resort of Kilpisjärvi. **Kilpisjärvi** ㉒ is an excellent launching pad for wilderness enthusiasts. There is a lake of the same name whose western shore forms the border with Sweden, and a marked trail which takes about a day leads to the boundary stone marking the triple junction of Finland-Sweden-Norway. The Mallan luonnonpuisto, a nature reserve to the north of the lake, requires a permit for entry, but once you are within it there is a pleasant 15km (9-mile) trek.

Ready for action.

Birch trees.

FINLAND

TRAVEL TIPS

GETTING THERE

By Air

Finnair is the national carrier of Finland and operates international and national routes. Both Finnair (www.finnair.com) and British Airways (www.britishairways.com) connect London and Helsinki with daily flights. Finnair (and many other airlines, including Lufthansa, SAS and KLM) fly direct between Helsinki and most European capitals. Finnair also links with several North American cities, including New York. You may be able to find value-for-money package fares and charter flights from New York or London, but they are rare; try the internet sites of the airlines for offers.

Several budget airlines fly to Finland. Norwegian Air Shuttle (www.norwegian.com) flies year-round from Helsinki to numerous European countries, including Denmark, France, Germany, Ireland, the UK and other parts of Scandinavia. It even has some flights to the United States and some international routes from Kittila, Oulu and Rovaniemi.

From Helsinki, Finnair, Norwegian and SAS (www.flysas.com) fly numerous domestic routes to a number of Finnish towns and cities, including several to north Finland airports, and have cross-country flights between some of them.

By Sea

You can travel to Finland by boat from Sweden, Germany and Estonia. **Viking Line** (www.vikingline.com) and **Tallink-Silja Line** (www.tallinksilja.com) run daily routes between Stockholm and Helsinki. These ferries are luxurious with restaurants, saunas, swimming pools, tax-free shops and children's playrooms. The all-night discos on these ships are legendary, often opening at 8pm and continuing to play loud dance music (but not necessarily serve alcohol all night) until the ship arrives at its eventual destination. There are several links from Germany to Finland: Finnlines (www.finnlines.com) sails daily from Helsinki to Travemünde, and from Malmö to Travemünde.

There are plenty of services to choose from for a trip between Helsinki and Tallinn. Tallink-Silja Line makes the trip several times daily in two hours. Viking Line has a slightly slower service (2.5 hours) three times a day and Eckerö Linjen (www.eckerolinjen.se) offers 1–2 connections daily in 2.5 hours.

It's generally less expensive to travel by ferry from Stockholm to Turku or from Kapellskär in Sweden to Naantali in western Finland and then overland to Helsinki rather than by direct ship to Helsinki. Viking provides very cheap bus tickets for the overland trip; the ferry ticket is also cheaper as the voyage is shorter. You can also travel to Finland's Åland Islands by boat from Stockholm, Grisslehamn (with Eckerö Linjen) and Kapellskär in Sweden; or from Turku – Viking and Tallink-Silja Line have daily services to Mariehamn. Also, Wasaline operates boats between Vaasa and Umeå.

Eckerö Linjen
Tel: 018-28 000
www.eckerolinjen.se
Finnlines
Tel: 09 2314 3100
www.finnlines.com
Tallink-Silja Line
Tel: 040-547 541 222
www.tallinksilja.com
Wasaline
Tel: 0207-716 810
www.wasaline.com
Viking Line
Tel: 0600-41577
www.vikingline.fi

By Rail

It's a long haul to Finland from just about any other country by rail, because you inevitably finish the long rail trip north with a long ferry journey from either Germany or Sweden to Helsinki. From Britain, the fastest route is to take the Eurostar to Brussels; then the high-speed train to Cologne; then the sleeper train to Copenhagen; then the train to Stockholm; then the boat or boat and train to Helsinki. Total travel time is about 48 hours. Rail travel to the far north of Finland requires completion by bus as Finnish rail lines only run as far as Kemi, Oulu, Rovaniemi, Kemijärvi and Kolari.

GETTING AROUND

On Arrival

Finland's main international airport, Helsinki-Vantaa, is connected by Finnair City Bus (€6.90) and local bus (€5.50) to Helsinki. Travel time is approximately 35 minutes. The Finnair bus stops at many of the major hotels on the way from the airport to the city centre, but picks up only at the central railway station and the Hesperia Park bus stop on the reverse route. There is also a 'shared' taxi stand at the airport. Expect to pay around €50 for a taxi to any destination in the city centre.

Public Transport

By Air

Finnair, SAS and Norwegian Air Shuttle operate domestic flight services. Fares are relatively inexpensive, and in the summertime they can drop tremendously. It is a good idea to fly if, for example, you want to get to Lapland from the south

Finland has a very efficient rail service.

but don't want to spend days driving there, or taking the overnight train.

By Rail

The Finnish state-owned railway company, Valtion Rautatie (VR), operates an excellent network of trains throughout much of the country. Most trains are very comfortable, punctual and speedy; particularly impressive are the 220km/h (137mph) Pendolino trains running from Helsinki to Oulu, Kuopio, Kajaani and Joensuu. The largest selection of train services is in the southern part of the country, with superb ties between Helsinki and Karelia, the lake region and the southern coast. Further north, direct connections are a bit more spartan, sometimes requiring at least one change of trains; if you are travelling to Vaasa from Helsinki, for example, you will need to make a connection in Seinäjoki.

Though few areas of Lapland have been laid with railway tracks – in part to preserve the unspoilt nature of its Arctic wilderness – there is a direct overnight connection between Helsinki and Rovaniemi. Most night trains also have a car-carrying service, so you can take your vehicle with you. Solid bus connections in the far north make up for the lack of trains.

There is also the high-speed direct Allegro train service, linking Helsinki and St Petersburg. The current duration of the journey is approximately 3.5 hours, with four departures per day. Buy tickets from the station or the VR website, or telephone 0600-41 900. You will need your passport and a visa to travel; the latter will take at least a week to arrange. For those looking to travel to Moscow the Tolstoi train offers a single departure from Helsinki on Monday through Friday and again on Sunday. As with the Allegro, you will need a visa and passport to make this journey.

Eurail Passes (for non-European visitors) and InterRail Passes (for European visitors) can be used on the Finnish railway system: seat reservations are recommended for busy times. For information on special offers, group discounts and discounts for rail/ferry journeys, see the VR website.

Finnish Railways (VR)
Vilhonkatu 13, 00101 Helsinki
Tel: 0600-41 900
www.vr.fi

By Boat

If there is one aspect of topography that defines Finland's great outdoors, it is the body of water known as the lake. The country has nearly 188,000 of them, from tiny ponds to massive, sea-sized reservoirs. Throughout the year, the lake is a focal point for transport for Finns – by ski or skidoo when frozen over in wintertime, or by ferry, passenger boat or canoe in the summer. Ferries and passenger boats in Finland also play a large role where international destinations are concerned (see page 270). From June to August there are regular boat services along Finland's waterways and – naturally – the Lake region is the best point of departure for such exploration of the country.

There are several Lakeland ferry routes particularly worth pursuing, including the Silverline (from Tampere to Hämeenlinna) and the Poet's Way (from Tampere to Virrat). Further east are numerous tours along the country's largest lake, Saimaa, with daily departures from Lappeenranta, Kuopio, Savonlinna, and Punkaharju; especially nostalgic are the elegant old steamships, still powered by burning birch logs.

☉ Sailing around the Baltic

Visas are usually required for travel to Russia – most Finnish travel agents can organise these for non-Finns, but be sure to allow at least one week for processing. Visa-free visits are possible if passengers arrive by ship, stay in Russia for less than 72 hours, and take the ship's organised excursion bus into the city. Always check visa requirements with your travel agent and book at least several weeks in advance.

Most Western nationalities may enter Estonia, Latvia, and Lithuania without a visa, and day trips to Tallinn (Estonia) are extremely popular and recommended. There may be more than 20 departures on an average summer day, and discounts are not unusual. Look especially at the front page of the main Finnish newspaper *Helsingin Sanomat*, which frequently advertises such discounts, especially in the warmer months.

Tickets are available at the ferry terminals in Helsinki, but you will usually find better rates and discounts online.

Russian Tours/Lähialuematkat
Tel: 09-6689 5751
www.russiantours.fi
Offers two to four-day trips to St Petersburg, with lodging on board and in St Petersburg. Travel to some Russian ports including St Petersburg is now visa-free if the stay in the port does not exceed 72 hours and the tour has been booked through an authorised tour operator.

St Peter Line
Tel: 09-6187 2000
http://stpeterline.com
The Princess Anastasia and the Princess Maria sail between Helsinki and St Petersburg, the former sailing a longer route via Stockholm and Tallinn.

Canoeing is another, slightly more leisurely way, to explore Finnish waters, especially in the Lake Päijänne region. There are great canoeing experiences to be had around Nurmes, while trips along the Saramojoki River from the village of Saramo are good for beginner and intermediate-level canoeists. Lieksa is another ideal departure point for canoe trips, with routes beginning either at Jonkeri or Aittokoski. Otherwise, in Nurmijärvi, try the fairly leisurely paddling route that follows the Lieksajoki to Pankasaari. Many other operators run trips on the lakes; for more information, contact the central or regional tourist boards (see page 280).

In the harbour capital of Helsinki, boats are generally an important mode of transportation for leisure-time activities only – especially exploring the islands around the perimeter of the city. Helsinki's only real commuter island is Suomenlinna, with ferries travelling back and forth one to four times every hour (schedule depends on season). Most of these ferries are part of the public transport network of Helsinki. Other Helsinki islands closer to the coast are connected by road.

Päijänne Cruises Hildén
Tel: 010-320 8820
www.paijanne-risteilythilden.fi
Lakeland Lines
Tel: 04 4026 6330
https://lakelandlines.fi
Saimaan Laivamatkat
Tel: 015-250 250
www.saimaacruises.fi
Silverline and Poet's Way
Tel: 010-422 5600
www.hopealinja.fi

Traffic congestion is not usually a problem in Finland.

By Bus and Coach

Finland is greatly dependent on buses for transporting the bulk of its passenger traffic. There are coach services on 90 percent of Finland's public roads (40,000 long-distance departures a day), and these also cover the areas that trains don't, particularly in the north and in smaller areas throughout the country where rail coverage is erratic. The head office for long-distance bus traffic is **Matkahuolto**, Lauttasaarentie 8, 00200 Helsinki, tel: 020-710 5000. Timetable enquires can be made at the **National Timetable Service**, tel: 020-04000 (€1.99 per minute plus local telephone charges) or online at www.matkahuolto.fi.

There is no penalty for buying a ticket on the coach, but you cannot get group discounts (for three adults or more on trips over 80km/50 miles) from the coach ticket-seller. Accompanied children under four travel free; those aged between four and 12 receive a 50 percent discount; those aged between 12 and 16 receive a 30 percent discount (proof of age required).

Visitors can reserve long-distance coach seats (for a small fee) by calling Matkahuolto or visiting the main bus station in the Kamppi shopping centre at the top of Simonkatu in Helsinki.

Driving

Finland's roads are not too clogged with traffic, although they do get very busy between the capital and the countryside on Fridays and Sundays during the summer. There are few multi-lane motorways. Most are two-lane only.

Pay close attention to road signs showing elk and reindeer zones. These animals really do wander onto the roads in Finland and collisions with them can be very serious. Use caution at all hours, but especially at dusk when elk are most active. Snow tyres are legally required from December to February.

Foreign cars entering Finland should have a sticker on the back demarcating the country in which they are registered. In most cases, your own insurance with a green card will suffice in Finland, but check ahead to be sure. If you are driving a foreign car and are involved in an accident, contact the **Finnish Motor Insurers' Centre**.

For more information about driving in Finland contact:

Finnish Motor Insurers' Centre
Itämerenkatu 11-13, 00180 Helsinki
Tel: 040-450 4520
http://lvk.fi
Finnish Transport Agency
PO Box 33, 00521 Helsinki
Tel: 0295-343 000
www.liikennevirasto.fi

Rules of the Road

Driving rules, regulations and norms in Finland are relatively straightforward. Drive on the right, overtake on the left. Use of headlights is compulsory, even during the daytime (UK cars must sweep their lights right). Wearing of seat belts is also compulsory.

Traffic approaching from the right has right of way. Exceptions are on roads marked by a triangle sign; if this is facing you, you must give right of way; similarly, if you are on a very major thoroughfare it is likely that the feed-in streets will have triangles, giving you the right of way. On roundabouts (rotaries), the first vehicle to reach the roundabout has right of way.

Speed limits are signposted. Generally the limit in built-up areas is 30km/h (18mph); outside built-up areas, it is usually 80km/h (50mph) unless a road sign indicates otherwise; and on motorways 100km/h (62mph) to 120km/h (75mph). In winter, motorway speeds are generally 20km/h (13 mph) lower. Never ever risk drink-driving in Finland. The limit is very low (0.5 percent blood alcohol) and the fines very steep; imprisonment of up to six months is also not unheard of. Taxis are available throughout the country, even in the backwaters; be safe, do as the Finns do and use them if you've been drinking. In, and around, Helsinki, Uber drivers are becoming more ubiquitous so there are any number of options to get home after a night out.

It is illegal to use a mobile phone while driving unless a hands-free device is used. A driving ban can be instituted for those that repeatedly violate this statute.

Taxis

Taxis operate throughout the country, with a 10km (6-mile) trip costing around €20. In Helsinki, taxi stands are located throughout the city centre, including outside the Central Railway Station, around Senate Square, along Esplanade Park and at the ferry terminals.

You'll find taxi stands in the centres of other large cities, as well as at most major airports, bus and railway stations. Otherwise local telephone books list the number of the nearest company (under *Taksi* in the *White Pages*). In Helsinki, the phone number to pre-book a taxi is 0100-0600 (there is a charge for this). Otherwise, call 0100-0700 if you want one immediately (i.e. within 5 or 10 minutes). The cost of an advance order is €6.90; this will be added to the fare shown on the meter. It is cheaper to hail a cab on the street (the yellow light on the roof will be illuminated if it's available for hire), though this isn't always as easy as it sounds. If you are heading to the airport, the yellow Airport Taxi operates taxi runs on a shared basis, which brings the price down: tel: 0600-555 555.

For information on stands and phone numbers for ordering in other Finnish cities, contact:

Finnish Taxi Association (Suomen Taksiliitto)
Nuijamiestentie 7, 00400 Helsinki
Tel: 020-775 6800
www.taksiliitto.fi

Bicycles

Finland is one of the best places in Europe to cycle, with thousands of well-engineered and well-indicated cycle paths and a gently rolling landscape with few real hills. Similarly, the number of outfits renting cycles has grown over the past decade and cycles are now fairly easily hired in many towns. Your best bet is the local tourist office or YHA youth hostel. Bicycles can be taken on many Finnish trains for a fee of €5 (not on Pendolinos; bike spaces on InterCity trains must be reserved ahead); in some areas they can also be carried on buses – this is most commonly done on the buses in Åland.

Be aware that the roads tend to be worse in the more remote regions of the far north, so make sure you have a bike repair kit with you. In the capital, one major summer hire point is Greenbike (Bulevardi 32; tel: 050-550 1020; www.greenbike.fi, Tue–Fri noon–6pm, Sat 10am–2pm); phone for bicycle hire out of season. In the Åland archipelago, a very popular summer cycling destination, there is a Ro-No rental outlet (www.rono.ax/en) on both harbours of Mariehamn.

VisitFinland has a good website on cycling (www.visitfinland.com/tags/ cycling), with information on national cycle routes, recommended tours and cycling-related events.

Hitchhiking

Hitching a ride is less common than it used to be as a means of getting about in Finland. This means you may have to wait a long time to get picked up, particularly at weekends and in the furthest reaches of Lapland, where traffic can be pretty thin. Hitchhiking is prohibited on Finland's motorways; the smaller secondary routes are a better option, anyway. As with anywhere in the world, however, safety can never be guaranteed on the road, and this mode of transport is on the whole not to be recommended.

⊘ Getting around Helsinki

Helsinki is so small and efficient that there is no better way to get around than your own two feet. Still, if you want to travel by public transport, trams are by far the best way of getting around. Purchase a **Helsinki Card** at the Tourist Office at the Central Railway Station (also available from hotels or you can choose to download it instantly to your smartphone) for 1, 2 or 3 days; with this you get free entry to museums and unlimited transport by bus, tram, metro, commuter trains and the Suomenlinna ferry in Helsinki, as well as assorted discounts at restaurants and concerts.

The 2, 4 and 6 trams double as a sightseeing route, covering a figure-eight around most of Helsinki. Catch either of them from in front of the railway station.

Alternatively, you can get a Helsinki Regional Transport Authority (HSL) ticket lasting from one to seven days. This also entitles you to unlimited use of public transport and can be purchased from a number of outlets: from HSL customer service points below ground at the railway station, vending machines at metro stations, and from the tourist office.

Bus drivers and conductors on commuter trains will only sell single-ride tickets and one-day tourist tickets. Tram drivers do not sell any tickets – you must buy one from a machine before boarding.

Route maps are available in the tourist office and are posted at nearly every stop. Note that there is an extra fare charged on regional journeys (to Espoo and Vantaa) and a night fare applies from 2–4.30am on all the buses. Most buses and trams run from 6am until 1am, but ask the tourist office about night buses in Helsinki and to Espoo and Vantaa.

Helsinki's public transport system is well integrated, so tickets generally allow you to make any number of changes within one hour of purchase, using other modes of public transport if necessary (buses, trams, the metro, commuter trains and the ferry to Suomenlinna). Tram tickets are an exception – these are valid only on trams.

Helsinki operates two metro lines: the first runs east from the city, serving local commuters in and out of town; a second line opened in 2017 running west from Helsinki with an extension expected in 2022. The metro is fast and clean, with trains running at 5- to 10-minute intervals, but the service shuts down shortly around 11.30pm so is not suitable for late-night travel. Still, the city is so easy to navigate on foot and by tram, there will probably be little reason for you to use this mode of transport. When travelling on the metro, purchase single tickets from the vending machine before entering the platform.

Snowmobiles

The snowmobile has evolved as a defining aspect of Sami society in the north of Finland. For Samis, snowmobiles are most definitely a core means of transportation for plying the fells, valleys, mountains, plateaus, iced-over lakes, tundra and permafrost of Lapland. The vehicle is now as integrated as the ski or the snow-shoe for Arctic Finns.

For visitors, however, it is largely a means of recreation and thrill-seeking, with hundreds of skidoo-able trails. Numerous tour companies organise snowmobile/ skidoo trips around all areas of Lapland.

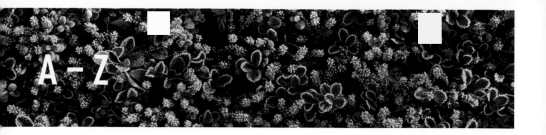

A – Z

A

Accommodation

You can depend on Finnish accommodation being clean and in good shape, but prices remain high. If you have patience, however, there are bargains to be hunted out. Big discounts (up to 60 percent) are available in some hotels at weekends, and in summer when they lose their business and conference trade.

Budget accommodation includes youth and family hostels, *guesthouse* accommodation, family villages, farmhouses, camping and various forms of self-catering. During the summer holidays – usually beginning 1 June – some student residences become summer hostels. The local tourist boards and booking centres will provide up-to-date prices, including details of weekend and summer discounts.

General information is available from **VisitFinland** (www.visitfinland.

Taking a break in Helsinki.

com) which also has a good hotel search engine.

Chain Hotels

In addition to foreign chain hotels, Finland has many large hotel chains of its own. The cheapest chain, Omena, keeps costs low by not having reception staff: book and pay for rooms online and check in using a keycode. Standard mid-range hotel chains include Sokos Hotels and Cumulus, which on the whole offer fairly comfortable services in most big towns, though many of their rooms often lack character. Some other chains, such as Scandic and Radisson Blu, offer more upmarket services. On the whole, such hotels will provide extremely clean rooms with most modern amenities, as well as standard (chain) restaurants – with identical menus – all around the country.

Best Western Finland
Katajanokanlaituri 5, 00160 Helsinki
Tel: 0800-12010
www.bestwestern.fi
Omena Hotels
Tel: 0600-555 222
www.omenahotels.com
Scandic Hotels
Revontulenkuja 1, Espoo, 02100
Tel: 08-517 517 00
www.scandichotels.fi
Sokos Hotels (SOK)
Tel: 020-123 4600
www.sokoshotels.fi

Camping, Farmstays, Bed and Breakfast

Farmstays are not terribly common in Finland but they do exist in certain parts of the country. Bed and breakfasts and rural inns are much more common, and are usually run as small family entities. Often you will find tiny huts and cabins in the middle of national parks that are rented out by their owners. Campsites in Finland are

plentiful, and you can almost always be guaranteed that they will have a sauna somewhere on their grounds – possibly near a lake or riverbank. Additionally, many campsites offer inexpensive accommodation in wooden cabins, which may or may not have kitchens.

Hostels

Finland has a widespread network of over a hundred youth and family hostels, which vary from small farmhouses to manors, camping and special centres. They usually have family rooms (2–4 guests) or dormitories (5–10 guests). About half of these hostels are open year-round, the remainder in summer only.

Details of hostels and the Finnish Youth Hostel cheque system are available from **Hostelling International Finland (Suomen Retkeilymajajärjestö – SRM)**, Yrjönkatu 38B 15, 00100 Helsinki, tel: 045-7733 2944, www.hostellit.fi.

Admission Charges

Few bars charge admission fees per se, but many places in Finland have a 'wardrobe' charge of around €2.50, which you'll have to pay whether or not you have a coat or jacket on. Clubs may charge anywhere between €5 and €12 for entry, while tickets for music concerts can cost upwards of €15, depending on the fame of the band.

Discounts are usually available at museums and attractions for children, students and senior citizens.

Age Restrictions

The legal age for drinking beer and wine is 18, and spirits is 20. Most bars will not admit anyone under the age of 18, while some have a minimum age of 21. The age restriction for clubs is generally 21, though sometimes this may be 20, 22, or even 24 – if you look younger, take ID. While most hostels do not impose an age restriction, this may not be the case when the establishment has a bar on the premises. The Viking Line and Tallink-Silja Line ferries have restrictions regarding unaccompanied youths – you have to be 18 or over, or 21 or over, to board certain boats on certain days – check the websites for the specifics.

Helsinki-Vantaa airport is well connected to the capital.

B

Budgeting for your Trip

Compared to other countries in Europe, Finland is expensive. A hotel room in most cities is likely to cost upwards of €100 per night, though cheaper ones can be found. Meals are similarly highly priced, with an average two-course meal for two plus wine at a mid-level restaurant costing upwards of €90. Museums usually cost between €6 and €12. Groceries tend to be around the EU average for items, while very late at night you can get some fairly inexpensive food items at the ubiquitous *grilli* kiosks in larger cities (for example, a €3–4 hamburger).

Business Travellers

Doing business in Finland is comparatively straightforward compared to other countries in Europe. For one, nearly every Finn speaks superb, near-native English – and many are rather eager to speak it to show you this fact. But Finns also tend to be quite easy to get along with when it comes to business issues, and rather straightforward when it comes to contract negotiation and deal signing. Otherwise, you probably won't notice too much difference from business practices in other Western European countries – with the exception that you'll probably be spending more time in the sauna talking about the finer points of your business, somewhat more so than in other countries, anyway.
Business Hours: Everything is done earlier. Lunch is earlier (as early as 11am, with 1pm generally being the

outside limit), and many offices operate 8am–4pm as opposed to 9am–5pm; in summer offices often close as early as 3pm, even 2pm on Fridays.
Business Style: There is a marked lack of bombast. Finns tend not to dress anything up, but rather present things as they are, warts and all. In other words, they are terribly honest, and do not go in much for exaggeration of any kind, whether it relates to a person or a business deal. Hence, their way of selling things might seem a bit subdued compared to other countries. But Finns are also more likely to be sympathetic and reserved than aggressive and braggart – especially in business matters. As Bertolt Brecht famously once put it, 'Finns are silent in two languages.'
Business Entertaining: You are as likely to be invited on a ski outing or sailboat ride as on a night out on the town. These days, Finns tend not to drink at lunch, but after-hours drinking is still de rigueur – people on business accounts are about the only ones who can afford long spells of drinking. If you are invited to visit a sauna with a Finn, by all means accept the invitation, as it is likely to work in your favour in business dealings.
Business Etiquette: It is ill-advised to be late for business meetings – Finns tend to be very punctual and courteous, though quite formal. Handshakes are used for meeting business as well as casual acquaintances; most people have business cards (hand the card to the other person so that they receive it facing in their direction).

Holidays: Finally, try to avoid business in July and early August. The Finnish summer is short and sacred, and you'll find some offices nearly deserted of staff at these times. (Conversely, this is a good time for tourists, who can often benefit from the many hotel discounts offered to compensate for the lost business trade.) Other blackout periods are the spring skiing break in late February (southern Finland) or early March (northern Finland), plus two weeks at Christmas and a week at Easter.

C

Children

Overall, Finland is a family- and child-orientated society, and hence one that is generally safe for children. Public conveniences usually include baby-changing areas and most restaurants can provide highchairs. Children are almost always accepted in all hotels. In Helsinki, the Tourist Board can provide a list of qualified childminders. In the cities, public transport is geared for use by those with prams, as well as wheelchairs, and getting around with children is easier than in almost any other country.

Climate

What to Bring

The best advice on packing for Finland is to bring layers of clothes, regardless of the season. While it is famous

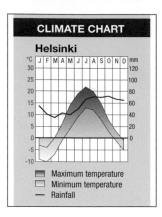

CLIMATE CHART

Helsinki

- Maximum temperature
- Minimum temperature
- Rainfall

for frigid winters – when gloves, long underwear, hats, woollen tights and socks, and several layers of cotton topped by wool and something water-proof are recommended – Finland also has very sunny and temperate summers. As a result, sun block and a sun hat are as essential at these times as warm clothes are in the winter.

In winter, bring heavy-duty foot-wear, not only to keep out the damp but also to avoid damage to good shoes ruined by salt and gravel put down to melt ice on the pavements. Spring and autumn are rainy, and summers are usually pleasantly dry and sunny, but occasionally wet. A good insect repellent is a must if you're travelling in the far north or central Finland in summer, to ward off the ubiquitous mosquitoes.

Crime and Safety

Finland is one of the safest countries in Europe. You may find in the larger cities a number of very drunk people wandering around after hours, but they will mostly be harmless to others. Vandalism is the only real notice-able sign of crime – often perpetrated by young teenagers trying to act cool. Occasional pickpocketing has been known on the Helsinki metro and at the main railway station: take com-mon-sense precautions with valu-ables and you should be fine.

Customs Regulations

Goods from EU countries destined for personal use can be taken freely in and out of Finland by EU citizens, although tobacco products are supposed to sport health warnings in Swedish and Finnish. Note that a person has to be 20 years or over

in order to possess or transport strong alcohol (drinks containing more than 22 percent by volume of ethyl alcohol) and at least 18 years to possess or transport mild alcohols and tobacco products. For enquiries about goods or changes in regulations contact the Customs Information Service, tel: 0295-5201; www.tulli.fi/en. The following items are permitted to be brought into Finland from non-EU countries.

Cigarettes/Tobacco

Any visitor over 18 years of age may bring in 200 cigarettes or 250g (half a lb) of tobacco products duty free.

Alcohol

Any visitor aged 20 or over can bring in 1 litre of strong alcohol (over 22 percent) or 2 litres with a maximum alcohol content of 22 percent; in addition to that, 4 litres of wine and 16 litres of beer. For visitors 18–19 years of age, the quantity limit is the same, but must not include strong alcohol.

Animal Quarantine

Pets vaccinated against rabies are in most cases allowed into Finland. Pets must be microchipped, and have a 'pet passport' showing that they have been vaccinated at least 21 days before entry. Double-checking these requirements is crucial because rules change from year to year.

Electricity

Finland uses electricity at 220 volts AC (two-pin plug).

Embassies and Consulates

Helsinki has embassies for most large European nations. The following is a list of English-speaking embassies in the capital. Canada, Pohjoisesplanadi 25B (tel: 09-228 530; www.canadainterna tional.gc.ca/finland-finlande); Ireland, Erottajankatu 7 (tel: 09-682 4240; www.irishembassy.fi); UK, Itäinen Puistotie 17 (tel: 09-2286 5100; www.gov.uk/government/world/ finland); US, Itäinen Puistotie 14B (tel: 09-616 250; https://fi.usembassy.gov).

Australia has a consular office at Museokatu 25B (tel: 010-420 4492), but its nearest embassy is in Sweden.

Etiquette

In general, Finns are courteous, particularly to foreign guests. However, they do not squeak 'Sorry!' any time they brush past you on the street, not even if they tread on your toes; they do not use the Finnish term for 'Sorry' or 'Excuse Me' (Anteeksi) in such situations. Rather, this term is used for graver offences or extreme polite-ness. For minor offences, a simple 'Oops' is usually enough. If you spend time in a Finnish sauna with locals, be aware that nearly every Finn will attend a sauna session naked. There is no sexual associa-tion with the sauna ritual whatso-ever – it is much more about being close to nature and feeling free and uninhibited. If you are going to a Finn's house for dinner, bring a plant or flowers for the host or hostess and, if you plan to drink, a bottle of wine. However, if you are out with Finns at a bar, be aware that buying rounds is not an aspect of Finnish culture. If you offer to buy rounds for a group of Finns, your generosity will be looked at with some bemusement. More importantly, however, your new Finnish friends will not buy you a round in return – it just isn't done.

Festivals

Though Finland is well known for its quirky and off-the-wall yearly festivals (e.g. wife-carrying and air guitar), the summer months also see hundreds of arts, music and cultural festivals as well. Thousands flock to the tango

☉ Emergencies

National emergency number (police, fire, ambulance): 112
Helsinki 24hr medical helpline: 116 117
Helsinki 24hr pharmacy: Mannerheimintie 96, tel: 0300-20 200

festival in Seinäjoki (www.tangomark kinat.fi), east of Vaasa; to the river-side concert park and intimate club venues of the 50 year old Pori Jazz Festival (Hallituskatu 8, 28100 Pori; tel: 010-391 6000, 010-522 3200; www.porijazz.fi); and to Joensuu's loud and lively Ilosaarirock. From a weekend bluegrass festival in diminutive Loviisa (see page 176) to a grandiose, month-long opera festival held in Savonlinna's medieval castle, there is plenty to occupy your time. For more on festivals in Finland, see page 88.

Helsinki Events

Come late summer, the capital hosts the Helsinki *Juhlaviikot* (festival weeks), a broad-ranging two-week-long arts festival featuring everything from classical music to circus acts. Artists are enlisted from Finland and abroad, and venues all over the city participate. Information from:

Helsinki Festival Office
Kalevankatu 6, FI-00100 Helsinki
Tel: 09-6126 5100
www.helsinginjuhlaviikot.fi

Also in August, the Flow Festival (www.flowfestival.com) is centred on indie/rock music, with arts events taking place around the edges. In late June/early July, the three-day Tuska Open-Air Metal Festival (www.tuska-festival.fi) brings 30,000 metalheads to the city. For a complete change of pace and noise level, the unique Rock Church (Temppelinaukion kirkko) in Töölö, Helsinki (see page 157) hosts a springtime chamber-music festival. During the rest of the year, the main classical events are at the Helsinki Music Centre, Finlandia Hall, and the Finnish National Opera House (see page 155).

Turku Events

Turku is another lively musical city, with its own jazz and tango festivals, two rock festivals and one all-encompassing music festival.

The two biggest shindigs are the three-day Ruisrock (Urho Kekkosenkatu 4-6 B; tel: 044-966 1384; www.ruisrock.fi), the oldest and biggest of Finland's rock festivals, held in early July; and the Turku Musical Festival (Sibeliuksenkatu 2, 20100 Turku; tel: 02-262 0812; www.turkumusicfestival.fi), a two-week carousel of classical and contemporary music concerts.

Buying tickets for public transport is easy.

Held in mid-August, it attracts visiting composers and international musicians.

Tampere Events

Tampere has always had its share of theatrical happenings and Finnish music, with numerous concerts in its cathedral, churches and halls. Its three main musical events, run by Tampere Music Festivals, are the Tampere Biennale, a festival of new Finnish music held in April; the Tampereen Sävel vocal music festival in June; and the Jazz Happening, in November. For information on all three, contact:

Tampere Music Festivals
Tullikamarinaukio 2, 33100 Tampere; tel: 040 647 5760; www.tamperemu sicfestivals.fi

Since the grand opening of the Tampere Hall, the largest concert and conference venue in the Nordic countries, interest in all types of musical forms has soared. The main auditorium is one of the great concert halls of the world. More information at:

Tampere Hall
Yliopistonkatu 55, 33100 Tampere
Tel: 03-243 4111
www.tamperehall.com

H

Health and Medical Care

You'll have little to worry about health-wise in Finland. However, you may have an uncomfortable time if you coincide with the mosquito season, which descends on the northern and central parts of the country in July and into August. Enquire in Finland about the most effective mosquito repellents from chemists, who know their own brand of insect best.

Visitors from the EEA are covered for emergency medical treatment on presentation of a European Health Insurance Card (EHIC); take your passport along as well as ID. Health and travel insurance is still recommended, however. There is usually a nominal charge for treatment: a visit to a public health centre will cost between €12 and €40, while an overnight hospital stay will cost around €50. Almost any *terveysasema* (public health centre) or *sairaala* (hospital) will treat you; you can also schedule regular appointments at a *terveysasema* (listed as such in telephone directories). The Emergency section is generally called *Ensiapu*.

Post Brexit, British citizens should check the new regulations in place. Non-EEA visitors should arrange health insurance before travelling.

In Helsinki, **Haartman Hospital** (Haartmaninkatu 4, Helsinki; tel: 09-4711) has 24-hour emergency-duty doctors. Visit www.hus.fi for more information on other hospitals and specialist departments in the Helsinki region.

Pharmacies (Apteekki) charge for prescriptions, but not outrageously. There is usually at least one pharmacy open in larger towns on a late-night basis. In Helsinki, the Apteekki at Mannerheimintie 96 is open 24 hours (tel: 300 20 200). You can also get around-the-clock health-service information and medical advice by phoning 09-10023.

I

Internet

There is excellent internet connectivity all around the country. In 2010, Finland became the first country in the world to make broadband access a legal right. Finland's hotel internet services are the most developed of anywhere in the world, with nearly every hotel offering Wi-fi. Many cities, the capital included, even offer password-free networks that anyone can connect to any time. Helsinki's NextMesh Wi-fi network currently covers popular tourist areas (such as Kluuvi and Kampli shopping centres, the railway station and Esplanadi) and is growing.

L

LGBTQ Travellers

Finland has progressed in leaps and bounds since homosexuality was legalised in 1971. LGBTQ lifestyles are readily accepted in the country's larger cities and towns, though somewhat less so in smaller communities. Helsinki has a number of gay nightlife venues, as do several other Finnish cities. A good resource for gay-friendly bars, clubs, hotels, saunas, etc. is the GayMap section of the Swedish lifestyle magazine QX (www.qx.se/gay-map). The week-long Helsinki Pride (http://helsinkipride.fi) is Finland's largest LGBT event. It takes place

at the end of June and in 2018 attracted 100,000 visitors making it one of Finland's largest ever public events. Seta (Pasilanraitio 5, 2nd floor, Helsinki; tel: 050-572 3259; www.seta.fi) is an organisation that campaigns for LGBTQ equality.

M

Maps

Maps of Finland and its cities and towns are readily available in most tourist offices. More detailed maps – for example, hiking or kayaking maps – are published by Karttakeskus (www.karttakeskus.fi); you can buy their maps online, or from Finnish bookshops such as the Suomalainen Kirjakauppa chain.

Media

Newspapers and Books

No one has yet been able to come up with a good explanation as to why papers published in Europe cannot arrive in Finland on their day of publication. But, with the exception of the *International Herald Tribune,* which arrives on the afternoon of its publication date, you'll have to wait a day and a half for British newspapers to get to Helsinki. The papers are sold at the Helsinki railway station, in at least two bookstores (Suomalainen Kirjakauppa at Aleksanterinkatu 17, and Akateeminen Kirjakauppa at Pohjoisesplanadi 39, where you can also get books in English), and at the

The Rock Church, Helsinki

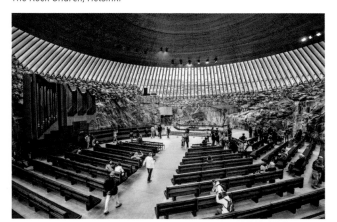

larger hotels in other cities, as well as at main airports.

Radio and Television

The Finnish national broadcasting service Yle operates four television channels, 13 radio channels and services along with 25 regional radio stations. Yle Mondo (www.yle.fi/ylemondo) is a 24-hour world radio station that broadcasts through digital TV throughout the country, and also in the Helsinki area on 97.5 FM: you can hear the news in English at 3.30pm (Mon to Fri) and 3.29pm (Sat and Sun). The news in English is also broadcast daily on Yle Radio 1 (87.9 FM in the Helsinki region) at 3.55pm. For up-to-date schedules, visit Yle at www.yle.fi. The BBC's World Service and other English-language television channels are usually available in hotels.

Money

Since early 2002, Finland has used euro (€) notes and coins. There are 100 cents (Finnish: *sentti*) to the euro. Euro coins come in denominations of 1, 2, 5, 10, 20 and 50 cents, and 1 and 2 euros. Controversially, however, Finnish shops and businesses usually won't accept 1- or 2-cent coins, and prices are rounded off to the nearest factor of 5. Notes come in denominations of 5, 10, 20, 50, 100, 200 and 500 euros; the lowest amount you can withdraw from a cash machine is €20.

Credit Cards

MasterCard/Access, Visa, Diner's Club and American Express credit cards are widely accepted in Finland.

Common currencies can be exchanged easily in banks.

Most cash machines (ATMs) marked OTTO will give euros if you have a bank card with an international PIN number (Visa, Cirrus, Plus, MasterCard, Maestro and so on).

O

Opening Hours

Shop opening hours are fairly straightforward in Finland. Generally shops are open from Monday to Saturday, except small food stores, which are allowed to stay open on

Åland Islands postage stamps.

Sunday also. Shops usually open between 9am and 5pm Monday to Friday, and between 9am and 3pm on Saturday. Helsinki tends to have longer business hours: many larger stores and supermarkets are open until 9pm on weekdays and until 6pm on Saturday. The only really late-opening places are in the tunnel under the Helsinki railway station, open Monday to Saturday 7am to 10pm and Sunday 10am to 10pm. Larger shopping outlets, such as Stockmann's department store and the shops in the Forum shopping mall diagonally across from it on Mannerheimintie in Helsinki are open weekdays 9am to 9pm, Saturday 9am to 7pm and Sunday noon to 6pm.

Banking hours are generally Monday to Friday from either 9 or 10am to 4–6pm. Some exchange bureaux open later, particularly at travel points such as airports and major harbours, as well as on international ferries.

Postal Services

Post offices are generally open 9am to 5pm. Services include stamps, registered mail and poste restante. The main post office in Helsinki is by the central railway station (Elielinaukio 2F, 00100 Helsinki; Mon–Fri 8am–8pm, Sat–Sun 10am–2pm). When post offices are closed, there are stamp machines outside and in the railway station. The machines are orange and mounted on the walls, as are the post boxes. You can also buy stamps from R-Kioski shops, bookshops and hotels.

Religious Services

The Lutheran Church is the state Church of Finland, with 70 percent of Finns counted as Lutherans. There is a small Greek Orthodox population, and just eight Catholic parishes in Finland.

In Helsinki, services in English are held at the Rock Church (Temppelinaukion kirkko; see page 157); there are both Lutheran and ecumenical services here. There is also one synagogue and just a few mosques in Helsinki, for those of Jewish or Muslim faith.

Smoking

Health-conscious Finland has jumped on the growing global bandwagon of anti-smoking. Smoking is not permitted indoors in public buildings and other places open to the public, except in designated smoking zones. Such areas do not exist in facilities expressly made for children or other persons under 18. You must be 18 years or older to buy cigarettes or other tobacco products in Finland. Tobacco advertising is banned, and the government has announced its intention to phase out smoking completely over the next 30 years.

Telephones

Callers from outside Finland should dial the international code (00 in Europe; 011 in the US), then the country code (358) followed by the local area code and phone number, omitting the initial zero (0). Due to the proliferation of mobile phones, coin-operated public phone boxes have all vanished. Hotels usually add surcharges for telephone calls made from your room. A cheaper way to make calls while in Finland is to buy a prepaid Finnish SIM card and use that in your own mobile (see the following section).

To call abroad from Finland, dial 00, then the country code and number (for example, 00-44 for the UK; 00-1 for the US). For UK numbers, omit the initial 0 of the area code.

Dial 02 02 02 or 118 for Finnish directory enquiries.

The front of the *White Pages* telephone directory also has directions for foreigners.

Mobile Phones

Finland is a nation of mobile-phone users, and the easiest way to make calls while in Finland is by using a mobile phone. The country is covered by the 900/1800 Mhz GSM network – most European phones are compatible, although your phone may need to be unlocked in order

☉ Public Holidays

1 Jan New Year's Day
6 Jan Epiphany
Mar/Apr Good Friday, Easter Sunday, Easter Monday
1 May May Day
May Ascension (40 days after Easter)
May Whitsun (50 days after Easter)
A Fri/Sat between 20–26 June Midsummer Eve/Day
Early November All Saints' Day
6 Dec Independence Day
24 Dec Christmas Eve
25 Dec Christmas Day
26 Dec Boxing Day

to link up with the network. US phones work on a slightly different frequency, so US visitors should check with their phone company first regarding usability.

For the cheapest calls, buy a Finnish SIM card and use that in your own phone. For around €10 you can get a SIM card with a Finnish number and €7 of talk time. The cards (and their refills) can be picked up at any R-Kioski shop. Consult the person behind the counter regarding the best card for you: different Finnish mobile providers offer different deals at different times. You can now also buy prepaid microSIM cards that can be used in devices such as iPads.

International Dialling Code
358.

Toilets

In Helsinki there are public toilets in various locations throughout the city. Several central places include beside the Old Market Hall, in Esplanade Park and in Sibelius Park. There is an entry charge. Otherwise, you could visit the public toilet on Sofiankatu, which is suitable for wheelchairs. The fee here should be paid to the attendant.

Tourist Information

Finland has over 50 main tourist information offices, marked with an 'i' for information. Summer tourist offices spring up along harbours and lakes where need dictates.

Information on travel for the entirety of Finland is available from **VisitFinland**, but as they no longer

Snowmobiling is a fun way to get around.

have an office in Helsinki, you should either contact them before you leave your home country or try to go through the very helpful Helsinki Tourist Information. A full listing of all tourist offices can be obtained at the Helsinki offices.

Main Tourist Offices
VisitFinland (Finnish Tourist Board)
www.visitfinland.com (no public office)
Helsinki Tourist Information
Kaivokatu 1, 00100 Helsinki
Tel: 09-3101 3300
www.visithelsinki.fi
VisitRovaniemi
Maakuntakatu 29–31, 96200 Rovaniemi
Tel: 040-829 0676
www.visitrovaniemi.fi
VisitTampere
Kelloportinkatu 1 B, 33100 Tampere
Tel: 03-5656 6800
www.visittampere.fi
Turku Touring
Aurakatu 4, 20100 Turku
Tel: 02-262 7444
www.visitturku.fi
Visit Åland
Storagatan 8, 22100 Mariehamn
Tel: 018-24000
www.visitaland.com

Tourist Publications
Useful publications in Helsinki include the *Helsinki Times* (www.helsinkitimes.fi), a weekly English-language newspaper that lists cultural and tourist events, available in bookshops and kiosks; *City* (www.city.fi), a weekly newspaper in Finnish but featuring a calendar of cultural events and restaurant listings; *Helsinki This Week* (www.helsinkithisweek.com), a free listings magazine distributed around the

☉ Time Zone
Greenwich Mean Time (GMT) + 2 hours;
Eastern Standard Time (EST) + 7 hours.

city; and brochures put out by the Tourist Board.

Travellers with Disabilities

Finland has strong accessibility plans in place. New buildings are legally required to have access for disabled people, in terms of ramps, lifts, toilets, etc. With careful planning, transport should also go smoothly; when ordering a taxi, specify your needs (wheelchair is *'pyörätuoli'*). Helsinki metro is accessible for wheelchair-users, but other forms of public transport may be a bit more problematic, although some city buses 'kneel', making it easier to board, and many tram stops are raised. The state railway VR has induction loops and Braille numbering on newer trains. Assistance is available for wheelchair users by contacting VR customer services (tel: 0600-41 900; www.vr.fi) or individual station offices. Wheelchair spaces are limited, so it's best to reserve one ahead of time.

V

Visas and Passports

Generally, citizens of most Western countries do not need visas to travel to Finland (but always check before you travel); a valid passport will suffice. Finland is also a member of the Schengen countries. The Nordic countries only stamp you in once for a three-month tourist stay, so if you arrive via, say, Sweden, you won't need to be stamped at the Finnish border.

It is difficult for non-EU citizens to work in Finland; if you want to work, contact a Finnish Embassy or Consulate outside Finland well before you go. An employer's letter is usually needed in advance of the work permit being granted.

Regulations can change, so always check the latest situation before you travel. Post Brexit, British citizens should check for any new entry regulations.

LANGUAGE

GETTING BY

Hello *Päivää or terve*
How do you do? *Kuinka voit?*
Good morning *Hyvää huomenta*
Good day *Hyvää päivää*
Good evening *Hyvää iltaa*
Goodbye *Näkemiin or hei hei*
Yes *Kyllä or Joo*
No *Ei*
Thank you *Kiitos*
How do I get to...? *Miten pääsen...?*
aircraft *lentokone*
bus/coach *bussi/linja-auto*
train *juna*
Where is...? *Missä on...?*
right *oikealla*
left *vasemmalla*
straight on *suoraan or eteenpäin*
What time is it? *Paljonko kello on?*
It is (the time is)... *Kello on...*
Could I have your name? *Saisinko nimesi?*
My name is... *Nimeni on...*
Do you speak English? *Puhutko englantia?*
I only speak English *Puhun vain englantia*
Can I help you? *Voinko auttaa sinua?*
I do not understand *En ymmärrä*
I do not know *En tiedä*

EATING OUT

breakfast *aamiainen*
lunch *lounas*
dinner *illallinen*
to eat *syödä*
to drink *juoda*
I would like to order... *Haluaisin tilata...*
Could I have the bill? *Saisko laskun?*
Cheers *Kippis (Swedish: skål)*
toilet *vessa*
gentlemen *miehet (Swedish: herrar)*

ladies *naiset (Swedish: damer)*
vacant *vapaa*
engaged *varattu*

SHOPPING

to buy *ostaa*
money *raha*
How much does this cost? *Paljonko tämä maksaa?*
It costs... *Se maksaa...*
Free, no charge *Ilmainen or Ilmaiseksi*
clothes *vaatteet*
blouse *pusero*
jacket *takki*
jersey *neulepusero or villapusero*
shoes *kengät*
skirt *hame*
suit *puku*
shop *kauppa*
food *ruoka*
grocers *ruokakauppa*
handicraft *käsityö*
off-licence *alko*
launderette *pesula*
dirty/clean *likainen/puhdas*
entrance *sisäänkäynti*
exit *uloskäynti*
no entry *pääsy kielletty*
open *avoinna, auki*
closed *suljettu, kiinni*
push *työnnä*
pull *vedä*

DAYS OF THE WEEK

Monday *Maanantai*
Tuesday *Tiistai*
Wednesday *Keskiviikko*
Thursday *Torstai*
Friday *Perjantai*
Saturday *Launantai*
Sunday *Sunnuntai*
today *tänään*
tomorrow *huomenna*

yesterday *eilen*

NUMBERS

1 *yksi*
2 *kaksi*
3 *kolme*
4 *neljä*
5 *viisi*
6 *kuusi*
7 *seitsemän*
8 *kahdeksan*
9 *yhdeksän*
10 *kymmenen*
11 *yksitoista*
12 *kaksitoista*
13 *kolmetoista*
14 *neljätoista*
15 *viisitoista*
16 *kuusitoista*
17 *seitsemäntoista*
18 *kahdeksantoista*
19 *yhdeksäntoista*
20 *kaksikymmentä*
30 *kolmekymmentä*
40 *neljäkymmentä*
50 *viisikymmentä*
60 *kuusikymmentä*
70 *seitsemänkymmentä*
80 *kahdeksankymmentä*
90 *yhdeksänkymmentä*
100 *sata*
1000 *tuhat*

USEFUL WORDS

doctor *lääkäri*
hospital *sairaala*
chemist *apteekki*
police station *poliisilaitos*
parking *paikoitus*
phrase book *turistin sanakirja*
dictionary *sanakirja*
to rent *vuokrata*
room to rent *vuokrattavana huone*
Could I have the key? *Saisko avaimen?*

HISTORY

Finland in Europe by Matti Klinge. A well-illustrated book with emphasis on Finnish history under Russian rule and after independence.

The Sami People: Traditions in Transition by Veli-Pekka Lehtola. An excellent illustrated history of the Sami people that details the lives of these traditional herdsmen, increasingly caught between their nomadic past and their settled present.

A Short History of Finland by Singleton & Upton. As the name suggests, this book covers Finland's history in brief, and is perhaps the best-written account of the past two millennia.

ART AND ARCHITECTURE

Alvar Aalto by Richard Weston. A very well-informed introduction to the life and work of Finnish architect Aalto, with excellent photographs.

Golden Age: Finnish Art 1850–1907 by Markku Valkonen. Includes works by Edelfelt, Gallén-Kallela and Schjerfbeck.

A Guide to Finnish Architecture by Kaipia & Putkonen. A fascinating town-by-town guide to individual buildings, with plenty of photos and illustrations.

Helsinki: An Architectural Guide by Arvi Ilonen. Features the capital's most important architectural landmarks and details on individual buildings.

FICTION

The Egyptian by Mika Waltari. The novel that made Finnish writer Waltari's name – a great epic of Sinuhe, the Egyptian.

Harjunpää and the Stone Murders by Matti Joensuu. Set in modern-day, war-ridden Helsinki, this detective novel is by one of Scandinavia's

⊘ Send us your thoughts

We do our best to ensure the information in our books is as accurate and up-to-date as possible. The books are updated on a regular basis using local contacts, who painstakingly add, amend and correct as required. However, some details (such as telephone numbers and opening times) are liable to change, and we are ultimately reliant on our readers to put us in the picture.

We welcome your feedback, especially your experience of using the book "on the road". Maybe you came across a great bar or new attraction we missed.

We will acknowledge all contributions, and we'll offer an Insight Guide to the best letters received.

Please write to us at:
Insight Guides
PO Box 7910
London SE1 1WE

Or email us at:
hello@insightguides.com

most esteemed and popular crime writers.

Seven Brothers by Aleksis Kivi. The cornerstone of Finnish literature and the first novel ever written in Finnish.

Finn Family Moomintroll by Tove Jansson. The first of Jansson's bestselling children's books following the lives of the beloved Moomins.

Troll: A Love Story by Johanna Sinisalo. This heralded debut novel concerns a photographer who finds a troll outside his apartment block (also published under the title *Not Before Sundown*).

Under the North Star by Väinö Linna. A quintessential Finnish novel by one of the country's most outstanding writers, this is volume one in a trilogy that depicts the development of Finnish society from the late 19th century to the years just following World War II.

The Year of the Bull by Oscar Parland. This engrossing story follows the life of a young boy during the post-war society of Finland c.1918.

The Year of the Hare by Arto Paasilinna. A great example of a contemporary Finnish novel, with Finnish satire throughout.

Purge by Sofi Oksanen. While set in Estonia this award-winning novel by the Finnish author and playwright focuses on two generations of women during and following the Soviet occupation.

SPECIALIST

Finnish Sauna, Design, Construction and Maintenance (the Finnish Building Centre). Among the many books on Finnish sauna, this one is the most practical, and is popular among home-builders.

Under the Midnight Sun by Liisa Rasimus (Ajatus). An excellent guide to Finnish food and the Finnish way of life.

OTHER INSIGHT GUIDES

Other Insight Guides which highlight destinations in this region include Scandinavia, Russia, Norway and Sweden.

CREDITS

INSIGHT GUIDE CREDITS

Distribution
UK, Ireland and Europe
Apa Publications (UK) Ltd;
sales@insightguides.com
United States and Canada
Ingram Publisher Services;
ips@ingramcontent.com
Australia and New Zealand
Woodslane; info@woodslane.com.au
Southeast Asia
Apa Publications (SN) Pte;
singaporeoffice@insightguides.com
Worldwide
Apa Publications (UK) Ltd;
sales@insightguides.com
Special Sales, Content Licensing and CoPublishing
Insight Guides can be purchased in bulk quantities at discounted prices. We can create special editions, personalised jackets and corporate imprints tailored to your needs.
sales@insightguides.com
www.insightguides.biz

Printed in China by RRD

All Rights Reserved
© 2019 Apa Digital (CH) AG and
Apa Publications (UK) Ltd

First Edition 1992
Seventh Edition 2019

Every effort has been made to provide accurate information in this publication, but changes are inevitable. The publisher cannot be responsible for any resulting loss, inconvenience or injury. We would appreciate it if readers would call our attention to any errors or outdated information. We also welcome your suggestions; please contact us at:
hello@insightguides.com

www.insightguides.com

Managing Editor: Carine Tracanelli
Author: Fran Parnell
Updater: Matthew Mello
Head of DTP and Pre-Press: Rebeka Davies
Layout: Aga Bylica
Picture Editor: Tom Smyth
Cartography: original cartography Geodata, updated by Carte

CONTRIBUTORS

This fully revised edition was managed by Insight's Managing Editor **Carine Tracanelli** and updated by **Matthew Mello**.

It builds on the excellent foundations created by the writers of previous editions, notably **Fran Parnell**, whose passion for Scandinavia began while studying Anglo-Saxon, Norse and Celtic at Cambridge University. Since then, she has travelled regularly in the region,

writing travel guides to Finland, Iceland, Sweden and Denmark, between climbing glaciers and cross-country skiing.

Past contributors also include **Doreen Taylor-Wilkie, Kristina Woolnough, James Lewis, Anne Roston, Sylvie Nickels** and **Robert Spark**.

Many of the superb images in this book were taken by Insight favourite **Gregory Wrona**.

ABOUT INSIGHT GUIDES

Insight Guides have more than 45 years' experience of publishing high-quality, visual travel guides. We produce 400 full-colour titles, in both print and digital form, covering more than 200 destinations across the globe, in a variety of formats to meet your different needs.

Insight Guides are written by local authors, whose expertise is evident in the extensive historical and cultural

background features. Each destination is carefully researched by regional experts to ensure our guides provide the very latest information. All the reviews in **Insight Guides** are independent; we strive to maintain an impartial view. Our reviews are carefully selected to guide you to the best places to eat, go out and shop, so you can be confident that when we say a place is special, we really mean it.

Legend

City maps

	Freeway/Highway/Motorway
	Divided Highway
	Main Roads
	Minor Roads
	Pedestrian Roads
	Steps
	Footpath
	Railway
	Funicular Railway
	Cable Car
	Tunnel
	City Wall
	Important Building
	Built Up Area
	Other Land
	Transport Hub
	Park
	Pedestrian Area
	Bus Station
	Tourist Information
	Main Post Office
	Cathedral/Church
	Mosque
	Synagogue
	Statue/Monument
	Beach
	Airport

Regional maps

	Freeway/Highway/Motorway (with junction)
	Freeway/Highway/Motorway (under construction)
	Divided Highway
	Main Road
	Secondary Road
	Minor Road
	Track
	Footpath
	International Boundary
	State/Province Boundary
	National Park/Reserve
	Marine Park
	Ferry Route
	Marshland/Swamp
	Glacier / Salt Lake
	Airport/Airfield
	Ancient Site
	Border Control
	Cable Car
	Castle/Castle Ruins
	Cave
	Chateau/Stately Home
	Church/Church Ruins
	Crater
	Lighthouse
	Mountain Peak
	Place of Interest
	Viewpoint

INDEX

INSIGHT ⊙ GUIDES

OFF THE SHELF

Since 1970, **INSIGHT GUIDES** has provided a unique perspective on the world's best travel destinations by using specially commissioned photography and illuminating text written by local authors.

Whether you're planning a city break, a walking tour or the journey of a lifetime, our superb range of guidebooks and phrasebooks will inspire you to discover more about your chosen destination.

INSIGHT GUIDES

offer a unique combination of stunning photos, absorbing narrative and detailed maps, providing all the inspiration and information you need.

PHRASEBOOKS & DICTIONARIES

help users to feel at home, when away. Pocket-sized with a free app to download, they go where you do.

CITY GUIDES

pack hundreds of great photos into a smaller format with detailed practical information, so you can navigate the world's top cities with confidence.

EXPLORE GUIDES

feature easy-to-follow walks and itineraries in the world's most exciting destinations, with our choice of the best places to eat and drink along the way.

POCKET GUIDES

combine concise information on where to go and what to do in a handy compact format, ideal on the ground. Includes a full-colour, fold-out map.

EXPERIENCE GUIDES

feature offbeat perspectives and secret gems for experienced travellers, with a collection of over 100 ideas for a memorable stay in a city.

www.insightguides.com